BRAVE Theory

Tony Carlton

BRAVE Theory

Military Transition, Trauma, and Reintegration

Springer

Tony Carlton
The Department of Exercise, Health,
and Sport Sciences
PennWest Global Online
California, PA, USA

ISBN 978-3-032-13694-7 ISBN 978-3-032-13695-4 (eBook)
https://doi.org/10.1007/978-3-032-13695-4

This Springer imprint is published by the registered company Springer Nature Switzerland AG
The registered company address is: Gewerbestrasse 11, 6330 Cham, Switzerland

To the heroes who returned home but never received the reintegration they deserved, losing their lives silently. To the heroes who never made it back, giving the ultimate sacrifice abroad.

This book is for you!

Foreword by Dr. Tyton Brunner

I felt honored when Tony invited me to read early drafts of what would become Battlefield to BRAVE and BRAVE Theory—Military Transition, Trauma, and Reintegration. I knew writing a foreword for a friend, especially one with such a layered history, demanded more than praise. It required depth, honesty, and assurance to the reader that this work is worth their time. I met Tony in our DHSc program, where we walked parallel paths through our doctoral studies. In countless late-night discussions and shared frustration over methodology, I became his "battle buddy," who witnessed his intellectual growth and the internal transformations he quietly endured. I saw, firsthand, how he navigated survivor's guilt, the weight of military experience, and the pull toward purpose beyond service. His journey was never abstract to me because I lived parts of it alongside him. This vantage point allows me to speak confidently about the significance of Battlefield to BRAVE. I did not merely see Tony emerge as a scholar; he emerged as a synthesizer, bridging memoir, theory, and practice in ways few do.

Tony's experience as a Navy Corpsman and later immersion in academic rigor uniquely situate him to write this book. He does not simply talk about trauma, resilience, or reintegration; he embodies them. Over years of listening to veteran narratives, teaching, and consulting, Tony developed BRAVE Theory (Building Resilience and Advancing Veteran Empowerment), a multidimensional framework engaging psychological, physical, social, and economic domains. His theory does not rehash popular self-help tropes; it's rooted in empirical insight and tempered by real-world grit.

What Tony Offers in BRAVE Theory Is Twofold:

1. This is a roadmap for veterans (and those who serve them). Whether one is coming home or walking beside someone who is, Tony offers guidance grounded in compassion and structure.

2. A scholarly contribution to trauma and reintegration discourse. For readers accustomed to high theory, Tony's voice respects rigor; for those more comfortable in stories, his narrative bridges the heart and head.

As you hold this book in your hands, it's clear that Tony isn't speaking from an ivory tower. He warmly invites you into his journey: his struggles, recovery, and hope. You'll discover parts of his story that might surprise you but also find helpful frameworks you can use immediately. Whether you're a veteran, clinician, educator, policymaker, or just a curious reader, Tony's work can deepen your understanding of reintegration to survive and truly thrive. I encourage you to begin BRAVE Theory with openness. Tony's voice is vulnerable, his learning is hard-won, and his vision is expansive. May his story resonate, his theory guide, and your journey, wherever you start, be made braver by what you find between these pages.

California, PA, USA Dr. Tyton Brunner, DHSc

Foreword by Thomas J. "TJ" Eldridge

Some people enter your life for a reason, while others completely change its course. For me, that person is Dr. Tony Carlton, a Navy/Marine Doctor, scholar, mentor, and friend who gave my life renewed purpose and direction. When I first met Tony, I was like many veterans; I carried the discipline and scars of service but lacked the structure and mission that had once defined my every decision. Tony saw through that immediately. He did not just mentor me; he pushed me to rebuild myself with the same precision, purpose, and pride that the military instilled in us both.

Tony's story is about consistent personal growth. From his days attached the Marine Corps to earning his Doctor of Health Science at PennWest University, he has always kept learning, mentoring, and serving. What stands out is not just his achievements but how he turns challenges into motivation, inspiring those around him. He shares his wisdom with honesty, always guiding rather than preaching.

Tony encouraged me to pursue my degree and keep going toward my graduate studies. He saw potential where I saw uncertainty and reminded me that leadership evolves beyond the uniform. His words reignited a sense of honor and duty within me that I hadn't felt in years.

Reading his book is like sitting across from Tony after a tough workout, when you feel clear-headed and re-energized. His words come from real experience, not from lectures or textbooks, but from combat deployments, late-night missions, setbacks, and successes. He doesn't just tell his story; he opens a window into the mindset behind it. I learned that impact is measured in the lives you influence and the character you help shape in others. That truth is woven into everyday life and on every page of this book. It is more than a reflection of his life; it is a roadmap for perseverance, resilience, discipline, and purpose.

As you read, you will walk beside a man who embodies grit and humility, a man who has led through hardship, learned through adversity, and continues to serve through leadership and passing on knowledge. Tony Carlton does not just talk about leadership; he lives it. His story reminds us all that even when our mission changes, the drive to lead and support others never fades.

Tony, you did not just change my life. You gave it renewed purpose, meaning, and direction. Just as I began this journey searching for direction, your influence allowed me to find it. For that, I will always be grateful.

May the Journey Never End...

Thomas J. "TJ" Eldridge
PennWest University Graduate Student
Exercise Science & Sport Psychology,
Spring Lake NC. USA

Preface

The story of this book begins before I was a scholar. Some of the struggles that show up after service start long before the uniform, such as family instability, trauma, or loss. The military covers it up with structure and discipline, but the cracks remain. It also begins in dusty compounds and triage under fire. As a Fleet Marine Force (FMF) Navy Corpsman with the Marines, resilience meant to keep pushing forward. It was something I lived. Years later, after coming home, I learned resilience can fade when the mission ends and the structure is gone.

This book is my attempt to build a framework out of that reality. The Building Resilience and Advancing Veteran Empowerment (BRAVE) Theory came from my doctoral work and my time with fellow veterans and tactical athletes. It is built on research and, more importantly, on veterans' voices. Too many programs break veterans into pieces: therapy without a career path, job training without addressing trauma, and financial advice without belonging. BRAVE puts the pieces back together.

I wrote this now because timing matters. Two decades of war are behind us, and new generations of veterans are still moving through broken networks of support. Science has advanced simultaneously; mindfulness, epigenetics, and the social identity model all prove resilience isn't fixed. It can be inherited, trained, and measured. This book moves in that direction. Becoming a scholar wasn't easy as I was still carrying wounds from war and the weight of trying to fit in as a veteran in academic settings. The Doctor of Health Science (DHSc) program became part of my healing process. As I built evidence, I was also rebuilding myself. BRAVE came from hundreds of studies, the lived experience of veterans, and my own hard lessons about identity and transition. This book is for scholars, practitioners, policymakers, veterans, and families. My story runs through it, but it is not the focus. It gives context.

I did not do this alone. Mentors in the DHSc program pushed me to anchor practice in evidence. Dr. Tyton Brunner's work on resilience and foster youth strengthened my own. Veterans like TJ, the first case in the WELL Program, showed what BRAVE looks like in real life. My wife, Megan, kept me steady, and my stepdaughter, Taylor, reminds me daily why this work matters. If you are a veteran, practitioner, or student,

I hope BRAVE is useful. It is a way to see reintegration as a whole while treating each veteran as an individual. Test it. Use it. Change it.

California, USA Dr. Tony Carlton, DHSc

Competing Interests The author has no competing interests to declare that are relevant to the content of this manuscript.

Disclaimer

This book is intended for educational and informational purposes only. It does not constitute medical, psychological, or legal advice and should not be used as a substitute for professional diagnosis, treatment, or consultation with qualified professionals. The experiences, reflections, and interpretations presented in this book are those of the author and do not -necessarily represent the official policies or positions of the Department of Defense, Department of Veterans Affairs, or Pennsylvania Western University.

About This Book

BRAVE Theory: Building Resilience and Advancing Veteran Empowerment brings together lived experience, evidence, and applied practice to address the challenges of the military-to-civilian transition. It draws from psychology, physiology, social identity, and economics research. BRAVE frames reintegration as a multidimensional process instead of a set of isolated problems. The book shows that resilience is not fixed but is inheritable, trainable, and measurable. Through a mix of narrative, case studies, and evidence, it also illustrates how veterans can rebuild autonomy and purpose in civilian life. This book is written for scholars, practitioners, policymakers, and veterans themselves. It bridges research and practice and offers a framework that can be used, tested, and adapted to improve programs and policies while staying grounded in the reality of veteran experience.

Permissions Statement

The author confirms that all material contained within this publication is original and created by the author. No third-party copyrighted material, figures, or data requiring permissions are included.

Contents

About the Author

Dr. Tony "Doc" Carlton, DHSc, is a Fleet Marine Force (FMF) Navy Corpsman veteran, rehabilitation coach, and scholar. He earned his Doctor of Health Science (DHSc) from PennWest University, where he developed the Building Resilience and Advancing Veteran Empowerment (BRAVE) Theory as part of his veteran transition and resilience research. He founded the Mindfully Tactical Foundation, which delivers programs such as the WELL Program (Warrior Empowerment, Lifestyle, and Leadership) and the PATH Initiative (Preparing, Advancing, Transitioning Heroes) to support veterans in higher education and civilian life.

Beyond academia and nonprofit work, Carlton is a director of rehabilitation and performance science in professional hockey and continues to mentor veterans navigating education, career, and identity after service. His work bridges evidence-based research with lived experience, bringing forward practical, adaptable, and grounded frameworks for the reality of transition.

He lives in North Carolina with his wife, stepdaughter, and their animals.

Chapter 1
A Life before Theory

1.1 Introduction—A Life before Uniform

The challenges veterans face after service doesn't start at discharge. For many of us, the foundation is built long before enlistment. Death, instability, and broken systems were already part of our lives. These early life experiences shape who we are and influence how we handle trauma later. Research confirms what many veterans with difficult upbringings already know: adverse childhood experiences (ACEs) are common among veterans and are strongly associated with long-term mental health conditions such as PTSD, depression, substance use, and suicidality (Aronson et al., 2020; Blosnich et al., 2021; Carroll et al., 2017).

These outcomes are part of ongoing patterns that start in childhood and persist across various systems, including the military (Slavin et al., 2024). ACEs not only increase the risk of mental health issues but also influence stress responses, attachment formation, and perceptions of oneself within systems of authority (Laird & Alexander, 2019). For many veterans, trauma is an ongoing process rather than a one-time event. See Table 1.1 *for construct definitions, mechanisms, indicators, and BRAVE domain mapping.*

As I would later learn through my doctoral research, resilience begins taking shape long before we can name it. Part of it is inherited, influenced by genetic and neurobiological factors that impact stress regulation and adaptability (van IJzendoorn & Bakermans-Kranenburg, 2015; Domschke et al., 2025). Much of it is molded in our earliest years, through the relationships, environments, and challenges that form our "resilience blueprint." This blueprint can be strengthened or eroded over time depending on later experiences, a process supported by evidence showing that environmental inputs can (epigenetically) modify stress response systems (van Assche et al., 2023). At the time, I didn't know the language or science behind it, but I understood the reality: early conditions had already forged in me the capacity to endure and adapt. Those early lessons in survival would be tested repeatedly, from my first significant life challenges to the crucible of combat service.

T. Carlton, *BRAVE Theory*, https://doi.org/10.1007/978-3-032-13695-4_1

Table 1.1 Core constructs and mechanisms shaping pre-service foundations of reintegration

Construct	Concise definition	Primary mechanisms (biopsychosocial)	Typical indicators/ measures	Chapter 1 application	BRAVE domain (s)
Adverse childhood Experiences (ACEs)	Cumulative exposure to abuse, neglect, and household dysfunction before age 18.	HPA-axis dysregulation; heightened allostatic load; insecure attachment; altered threat appraisal	ACEs questionnaire; perceived stress; health comorbidity screens	Father loss; housing instability; early anger and distrust of authority	Psychological, physical, social
Protective adult/ moral role model	Stable, values-consistent caregiver who provides modeling, structure, and co-regulation.	Buffering of stress reactivity; attachment security; prosocial norm internalization	Social support scales; attachment measures; moral identity internalization	“Grandfather code” as anchor for effort, service, and integrity	Psychological, social
Identity strain/ disruption	Tension between previous role identity and current self during major transitions	Self-schema conflict; loss of role coherence; cognitive dissonance	Identity distress survey; military-to-civilian questionnaire (M2C-Q); role conflict scales	Shift from aspiring operator to corpsman; later from combat medic to clinic staff	Psychological, social
Posttraumatic Growth (PTG)	Positive change emerging from struggle with highly challenging life events	Meaning-making; accommodative learning; expanded agency	Posttraumatic growth inventory (PTGI)	BUD/S failure reframed as catalyst for purpose and service orientation	Psychological
Stress inoculation/ adaptation	Performance gains after managed exposure to stress with recovery	Autonomic conditioning; improved appraisal; coping repertoire expansion	Heart-rate variability (HRV); perceived stress scale; coping inventories	Training failures and field stressors that later enhanced readiness	Psychological, physical
Dual-role strain (healer–combatant)	Simultaneous obligation to treat and to fight in the same theater	Moral-praxis conflict; role overload; compassion fatigue risk	Role conflict/role overload scales; moral Injury scales; professional quality of life (ProQOL)	FMF Corpsman duties under fire; triage under resource constraints	Psychological, social

(continued)

Table 1.1 (continued)

Construct	Concise definition	Primary mechanisms (biopsychosocial)	Typical indicators/ measures	Chapter 1 application	BRAVE domain (s)
Hypervigilance & emotional blunting	Persistent threat scanning paired with narrowed affect to maintain function	Amygdala hyperactivation; reduced prefrontal regulation; dissociation	PTSD checklist (PCL-5); dissociative experiences scale (DES)	First convoy IED; Musa Qala blast; "numb to feel, present to act"	Psychological, physical
Decompression gap	Abrupt shift from high-threat context to low-threat role without staged down-regulation	Arousal–context mismatch; sleep/ circadian disruption; impaired executive function	Pittsburgh sleep quality index (PSQI); M2C-Q; cognitive screening	Immediate reassignment to pediatrics; chronic insomnia and irritability	Physical, psychological
Institutional betrayal/mistrust	Harm from institutions meant to protect (denial, dismissal, stereotyping)	Invalidated identity; reduced help-seeking; learned non-engagement	Institutional Betrayal questionnaire; healthcare system distrust scales	Dismissive VA encounters; "mindfulness isn't for people like you"	Social, psychological
Cultural competence gap in care	Provider–veteran cultural mismatch that impairs alliance and safety	Threat cue overlap; language and norms misalignment; weak alliance	Working Alliance inventory; cultural competence/ responsiveness indices	Assignment to culturally triggering provider; disengagement from groups	Social, psychological
Moral leadership as protective factor	Internalized ethics that guide behavior under stress and loss	Purpose anchoring; prosocial goal orientation; self-regulation	Moral identity/ internalization scales; purpose in life (PIL)	Grandfather's service ethic shaping responses to failure and war	Psychological, social
Embodied trauma & somatic load	Long-term physical sequelae of chronic stress/trauma exposure	Inflammation; pain interference; metabolic and sleep dysregulation	Pain interference (PROMIS); inflammatory markers; PHQ-15; PSQI	Persistent sleep disturbance; cumulative fatigue post-deployment	Physical

Note This table summarizes key constructs referenced in Chap. 1 and maps them to BRAVE domains. Abbreviations: HPA = hypothalamic–pituitary–adrenal; HRV = heart-rate variability; ACEs = Adverse Childhood Experiences; PTGI = Posttraumatic Growth Inventory; PCL-5 = PTSD Checklist for DSM-5; DES = Dissociative Experiences Scale; PSQI = Pittsburgh Sleep Quality Index; M2C-Q = Military-to-Civilian Questionnaire; ProQOL = Professional Quality of Life

Military service provides structure, identity, and purpose. For some individuals, it represents the first dependable system that requires accountability. However, it also fosters suppression, emotional detachment, and a culture of silence regarding loss. When early trauma intersects with the trauma of war, the consequences are not always immediately apparent, but they are nonetheless measurable. This chapter examines what preceded the uniform early disruptions of identity, the moral grounding imparted by my grandfather, and the institutional failures that influenced my journey into the military. Reintegration begins not only after discharge but significantly earlier.

1.2 Father Loss and the Formation of Trauma

I was ten years old when I lost my father in a coal mine explosion. He suffocated from methane after a blast cut off the oxygen flow underground. That day marked the start of everything changing. People talk about losing someone, but you also lose your foundation. The core of our family was gone, and I had little time to figure things out. My grandmother, who had always been the glue of my mother's side of the family, helped us pick up the pieces for a while and held everyone together through sheer force of will. When she passed shortly after, the second pillar holding my world up collapsed. My father's side of the family had little to do with us, but after his death, they suddenly appeared. Instead of helping, they used my brother and I as leverage in disputes over money. I learned quickly that even family could turn cold when there was something to gain. My mother eventually moved on, and although it was not right away, the man she chose never sat right with me. I was sent to live with my grandfather and uncle. They provided for me, but I did not feel chosen. I felt removed or displaced. That sense of being pushed aside stayed with me. Once you have been displaced like that, it reshapes how you see everything. Family, friendships, and institutions no longer feel safe. It teaches you that people will not put you first.

Childhood trauma is a difficult start that influences how your brain and body respond to stress throughout your life. Research shows that losing a parent early on is associated with long-term mental health issues, including depression, anxiety, and attachment and identity problems (Slavin et al., 2024). I didn't know that back then. I just knew I was angry, confused, and already exhausted. There's also a physical cost. Studies on ACEs show that trauma before age 18 increases the risk for heart disease, substance use, and early death (Felitti et al., 1998). It prepares you to survive, not to thrive. And for many of us who later joined the military, that was already a default setting.

When people ask why veterans struggle after service, they often look at the deployments. But for some of us, the damage started way before that. We were already dealing with loss, chaos, and instability before we put on the uniform. The military just gave it structure.

1.3 The Grandfather Code

After my father died, I lived with my grandfather and uncle. My grandfather was the moral center of everything I learned about how to live. He served in the Korean War in the Army's 23rd Regiment, second Division. He was declared killed in action (KIA) and then spent 28 months as a POW. He was released during Operation Big Switch on August 21, 1953, according to Department of Defense (DOD) records. He carried both the memories and the physical damage. One of his scars was a fist-sized hole in his back from a battlefield injury. He lived in constant pain but never let it stop him.

He became a preacher. During the week, he worked hard: manual labor, farm work, and running a loader at the mine. On Sundays, he stood tall in the pulpit like it mattered. He went back to the same mines that had killed my father, not out of necessity, but because that's what family meant to him. My grandmother's medical needs went far beyond what his military retirement covered, and he did what needed to be done. I watched him give jobs to struggling men, hand out cash quietly when someone couldn't pay their light bill, and never ask for thanks. That was just his way.

He lived according to his values. He allowed me to fail and ensured I learned from it. He believed in doing things right the first time and taught that "character is what you do when no one's watching." This kind of consistent, supportive adult example matters. Research calls these "protective factors" the presence that buffers against the long-term effects of trauma (Laird & Alexander, 2019). Studies show that even a stable, caring adult can significantly reduce psychological harm from early adversity and boost long-term resilience (Laird & Alexander, 2019; Slavin et al., 2024).

In the research, this is called "buffering" (Laird & Alexander, 2019). In real life, it's just who he was. He didn't stop the trauma from happening, but he gave me something to anchor to. When I hit walls or when college went bad, when I failed training, or when I questioned everything, I still heard his voice in my head. That's why I don't say he raised me. He grounded me. And that gave me a way to survive what came next.

1.4 The First Real Failure

When I walked into the Navy recruiter's office in Morristown, Tennessee, I didn't care what came next if it was forward. I passed the ASVAB and the physical tests with ease. I was in shape and focused, and when they told me I could choose any job, I went straight for special forces. I wanted the challenge. I thought I needed it. BUD/S, Basic Underwater Demolition/SEAL training, doesn't reward that ambition though. It tests limits you didn't know existed. It strips away whatever image you had of yourself and pushes you past exhaustion, through pain, and into silence. I started strong. I was fast, durable, and disciplined. But none of that guarantees anything. Eventually, I fell behind, and that was it. I failed. I sat on the sidelines and watched others move forward while I packed my gear. There's no ceremony for those who don't make it. Later, I tried again at SWCC School, the Special Warfare Combatant-craft Crewman (SWCC) program. The course was different, but the outcome was the same. I fell out. Another bag packed and another quiet walk away.

It was the first failure that hit hard. It wasn't because I didn't finish, but because I had based my identity on the idea that I could. That kind of loss can either toughen you or throw you off. In my case, it did both. I was angry at myself, the system, and the notion that effort wasn't enough for a while. But something about that moment made me rethink things. I wanted to prove I belonged and build something bigger than a job title. That failure sparked a fire within me that I didn't know I had.

In elite military pipelines like BUD/S, failure is common. Around 90% of candidates do not complete the program (U.S. Department of Defense, Office of Inspector General [DoD OIG], 2025). Attrition is physical and mental. Research on identity disruption in special forces selection settings shows that candidates often link success or failure to their entire self-concept, especially those with high intrinsic motivation or unresolved trauma (Laird & Alexander, 2019; Slavin et al., 2024). That means when you fail out, it not only doesn't feel like you didn't pass a course but failed as a person.

But it can also become the turning point. Studies on posttraumatic growth (Tedeschi & Calhoun, 2004) and what's called stress inoculation theory (Carroll et al., 2017) show that those who experience failure in high-pressure environments often emerge with stronger adaptive coping skills if the experience is processed constructively. For me, it wasn't immediate. But over time, that loss shifted something inside. I started taking ownership instead of blame.

The Navy redirected me to Corpsman School (HM) in Great Lakes, Illinois. A Corpsman is the Navy's enlisted medic; with Marines, you're often the first and sometimes the only medical professional on scene: sick call, trauma triage, hemorrhage control, airway management, needle decompression, and the 9-line are just a few of the tasks we handle. I learned every system, practiced every procedure, and graduated ready for what came next. I received my orders and headed to Fleet Marine Force (FMF), which was attached to the Marines. This was during the height of Operation Iraqi Freedom (OIF). Everyone knew what that meant and where we were headed. At FMF Training Battalion, things moved quickly. We studied anatomy and bandaging wounds alongside drilling tactics, land navigation, convoy security, and trauma response under fire. They made sure we were combat medics. That's the difference. There's no time to second-guess when you're the first line of care in a firefight. Later, the FMF warfare device wasn't something you wore lightly. It meant you knew how to fight and save; both could happen simultaneously. You became "doc."

That training gave me something I hadn't had before: an identity I could live inside and a title with a purpose. When I deployed, it all clicked. The scenarios weren't in a book anymore. They were real, and they were happening in front of me. There was no time to be scared or reflect; only act purposefully. But it never left me the idea that it all started with failure and maybe that's what made me ready when it counted.

1.5 The First Convoy

When we landed in Iraq, everything we had trained for became real. The heat hit like a wall, and the smell was different: diesel, dust, and something else I couldn't identify. Our first convoy rolled out just days after arrival. There was no easing in. We got on the truck, double-checked our weapons, and rolled out. The first time outside the wire changes you. Every pile of trash looks like an IED. Every rooftop seems to be watching you. I remember gripping the handle inside the HUMV so tightly that my hand went numb. I didn't say much. None of us did. There's a tension in that kind of silence that presses against your chest. Then the blast hit. It only took off a tire, thank God. That was the first explosion I experienced. No one was hurt, but something inside me shifted. That kind of fear doesn't fade but becomes part of my baseline.

Combat exposure is violent and unpredictable. According to Shelef et al. (2024), one of the most harmful aspects of combat is not only the trauma itself, but the persistent psychological strain from being constantly surrounded by threat, especially for medics, who carry the dual burden of treating casualties under fire while being part of the combat unit themselves. That's what alters your nervous system and leaves you always on guard. You learn to scan everything like parked cars and shadows. Your body stays in constant threat detection and doesn't turn off when you come home.

Over time, those early missions became routine, but the anxiety didn't. I started feeling numb and more distant. I could still function, maybe even better, but something was slipping away. That's common in prolonged combat environments. The Shelef et al. (2024) study found that medics in particular exhibited signs of dissociation and emotional distress, often years after exposure, sometimes taking decades to seek help because of stigma or perceived resilience expectations. Emotional blunting becomes a way to cope, but over time, it can chip away at your sense of self.

There was never a shortage of patients. Civilians arrived at the gate with wounds from old mines, fresh IEDs, and stray bullets. We saw children, mothers, and elderly men with burns and missing limbs. Some were innocent. Some weren't. But we treated them all. That's part of the job. The worst were the kids. We treated a boy once who had been playing soccer and stepped on a device buried years earlier. That kind of thing doesn't just make you angry; it makes you hollow. You can't carry that pain and still show up the next day unless you find somewhere to put it.

Finding places to put the pain, the trauma, questions, and the weight of it all became our job. Sometimes, we stuffed it down. Sometimes, we joked through it. But mostly, we kept moving because stopping meant feeling, and that wasn't safe. This was the first time I truly understood what being a healer and witness means. I wasn't only patching wounds, I was watching lives fall apart, and sometimes, I was the last person someone saw before they died. It taught me that medicine in war isn't clean. It's quick, messy, and filled with choices you'll have to live with forever.

That first convoy marked the start of everything, such as operating under fire, watching friends fall apart, and wondering if I was still the same person I'd been before. The military teaches you how to respond under pressure and manage chaos, but it doesn't teach you how to grieve or make sense of it when you return and realize you're not the same. And I wasn't.

1.6 Afghanistan Was Different

During Operation Enduring Freedom (OEF), Afghanistan was a different kind of war. The terrain was different, and the silence wasn't peaceful. In Musa Qala, we set up our casualty collection point (CCP) and forward operating base (FOB) for our third Battalion seventh Marines weapons company. After a few days of operations, I could identify the Marines' voices over the radio well enough to know who was yelling. That wasn't normal. I listened to my guys under fire and couldn't do anything until they reached me at the FOB. That kind of helplessness doesn't just fade.

The blast that changed everything didn't hit me directly; it struck a 7-ton truck parked where we had been sleeping hours earlier. I don't remember the exact moment of the explosion. I remember kneeling, blood on my hands, Marines screaming, and my CO yelling at me for the 9-line. Bird support was more than twenty minutes away. That's a long wait. That was the first time I realized numbness wasn't just a symptom, it was a form of survival.

Repeated trauma exposure leaves marks, and it alters the architecture of how we feel. Lanius et al. (2010) describe this as a process of emotional shutdown, where the brain suppresses emotional processing in response to prolonged, inescapable threat. Their fear conditioning and stress sensitization model shows how repeated trauma leads to hyperactivation of the amygdala and diminished prefrontal control, resulting in emotional overmodulation manifesting as dissociation, numbing, and detachment. In simpler terms, the brain adapts by cutting off feelings it no longer has the bandwidth to process. It doesn't mean the emotion is gone. It just gets buried deeper to keep you moving.

Corpsmen face a unique kind of burden. We're expected to be both medics and fighters, providers of care and instruments of war. That dual role is operational and existential. No amount of training prepares you for the moment those roles collide. I wasn't just there to treat the wounded; I was also expected to defend them. And sometimes, that meant making impossible decisions under fire. Research confirms what many of us have lived: combat medics carry the double weight of exposure to life-threatening chaos and the emotional toll of caregiving in that same space. Shelef et al. (2024) found that medics embedded in frontline units often experience combat-related psychological impacts equal to or greater than their non-medic counterparts. What struck me was how many of us didn't seek help until years later, not because we weren't affected, but because we believed we had to be the strong ones. We're trained to respond, not reflect. But the triage calls you make in those moments, like the ones you couldn't save, don't fade. You carry them. Quietly. Until they don't stay quiet anymore.

The biological effects are real. When you operate in sustained high-stress environments like combat zones, your body responds in the moment and adapts to survive. In a simulated close-quarters combat scenario designed to mirror the intensity of real military operations, researchers found that professional soldiers experienced significant increases in sympathetic nervous system activity, heart rate, muscle strength, and blood lactate, all markers of the body's acute fight-or-flight response. At the same time, cortical arousal decreased, indicating diminished information processing capacity under pressure (Clemente-Suárez et al., 2018).

This physiology is your operating system being rewritten. The limbic system ramps up, threat detection goes into overdrive, and higher-level executive functioning diminishes. Soldiers in the study showed a mismatch between what their bodies were experiencing and what they perceived, underestimating their exertion despite overwhelming physiological stress markers. That tracks. Because in combat, you push through the fog, not realizing the toll until later. It explains why so many of us come home still wired for war, stuck in a body that doesn't know the fight is over.

I didn't talk about any of this when I got back. One day, I was in active operations; the next, I was in a hospital job like someone had flipped a switch. I was expected to act like nothing happened. But everything had. I was good at my job in Afghanistan because I shut everything down, like my emotions, fear, and hope. That's how I kept people alive. But that exact mechanism that made me effective over there is the same one that hollowed me out here. It kept me moving, but it cost me parts of myself I didn't realize were missing until much later.

1.7 Coming Home Wasn't Relief

Coming home didn't feel like peace. One day, I was doing combat triage under fire; the next, I was supposed to run a pediatric clinic. Still in uniform, but nothing around me made sense. There was no decompression or staged transition, just an abrupt shift from life-and-death urgency to paperwork and patient checkups. On paper, I was thriving. I had one of the highest evaluations for my rank, but I was on autopilot. I couldn't write a grocery list, but could still coordinate mass casualty care without hesitation. The mismatch between what my nervous system was prepared for and what my daily environment demanded should have been a warning sign. But it wasn't. No one noticed, and I didn't have the words to explain it.

Research confirms that this kind of post-deployment mismatch is common. When service members transition directly from high-threat environments into administrative or civilian roles without decompression, rates of psychological distress, sleep disruption, and cognitive impairment increase significantly (Carroll et al., 2017; Wood et al., 2018). Wood et al. (2018) studied U.S. Marines returning home either after a 12-day sea voyage or within 24 hours by air following combat in Iraq. While long-term outcomes were ultimately similar for both groups, the study emphasized that decompression, whether formal or informal, can have time-dependent effects on mental health and reintegration. Physically, you may be home, and neurologically, you're still downrange.

Sleep never came easily, and honestly, it still doesn't. My mind refused to quiet down. I was irritable and quick to anger. None of this was unique to me, though it's well-documented. Hypervigilance, irritability, and sleep issues are common responses to trauma, especially in those who have seen combat (Clemente-Suarez et al., 2018). But we don't call it that. We internalize it. Move on. That's what we're trained to do, mission first and others before myself. The system didn't know what to do with me either. When I left the Navy, I felt I had no choice. I was so far gone by then that I can barely remember the details. What I remember feels like watching someone else's life on a screen, seeing myself in the clinic, moving through the motions, but not there. I wasn't living it, just observing it from a distance. I had no plan, just a DD-214 to prove I had served my country honorably. That was it.

When I finally went to the VA, I felt like a suspect instead of a patient. Providers rotated so often I never saw the same face twice, and trust never took root. I couldn't speak freely. And when I finally asked about therapy, I was told mindfulness and yoga "weren't for people like me." Knowing what I know now, that one sentence told me everything about how they saw me and what they thought I was worth.

This is a personal grievance and a structural problem. Studies show that many veterans feel dismissed or stereotyped by providers unfamiliar with combat culture, which leads to disengagement from care (Bloeser et al., 2021; Cheney et al., 2018; McCormick et al., 2019). The Bloeser et al. (2021) study on Gulf War Illness describes these experiences as institutional betrayal, where institutions responsible for health cause harm through denial, neglect, or dismissal. Their findings indicate that betrayal often invalidated conditions, downplayed service-related exposures, or labeled symptoms as psychological when they were not. The impact was frustration that led to a loss of trust.

McCormick et al. (2019) add another dimension: the cultural gap between military and civilian worlds. Their qualitative analysis found that veterans described military culture in terms of shared values like patriotism, discipline, camaraderie, and mission-first commitment, but also described the post-service reality as disparate from civilian culture, marked by interpersonal difficulties, perceived loss of purpose, and reluctance to communicate experiences with non-military people. Those who felt this gap most acutely often reported they would only talk to other veterans or, occasionally, to mental health professionals perceived as culturally competent. My experience mirrored that; civilian providers didn't speak the same language I did, and I didn't have the energy to translate (McCormick et al., 2019; Aronson, 2020).

I was given four medications: one to wake me up, knock me down, force sleep, and numb the hours in between. I wasn't feeling or dreaming; I was floating. Friends drifted away. Family ties frayed. No one noticed. And when I was finally assigned a psychiatrist, they sent me to someone of Afghan descent. It wasn't about hate or racism; it was about timing. My nervous system was still fighting a war where the enemy looked like him. He had done nothing wrong, but the cultural and sensory overlap with my trauma meant I couldn't separate therapy from threat. McCormick et al. (2019) note that this kind of cultural misalignment in provider–veteran relationships can further alienate veterans from care.

Group therapy was no better. Some stories didn't match my reality; some felt performative. I didn't need an audience; I needed help. But help wasn't built for someone like me. Bloeser et al. (2021) found that when veterans sense that care systems were not designed with their realities in mind, they often disengage entirely. I did. When trust is broken early, the damage lasts. Institutional mistrust and perceived stigma are strongly linked to decreased use of mental health services, even in high-distress veterans (Bloeser et al., 2021; McCormick et al., 2019). I wasn't weak or unstable. I was unsupported. And when you go unsupported long enough, you start to believe the problem is you, not the system.

1.7.1 Institutional Betrayal

Institutional betrayal happens when organizations responsible for care, such as health systems, educational institutions, or government agencies, downplay, misattribute, or ignore valid needs. In veteran care, common forms include dismissing diagnoses, changing providers frequently, and offering culturally mismatched interventions, which damage trust. It is important to distinguish betrayal from typical service dissatisfaction; betrayal involves breaching role responsibilities, leading to disengagement and poorer health behaviors. Solutions include ensuring continuity of care, transparent waitlist policies, informed provider choices, and clear acknowledgment of military service culture.

1.8 Recalibrating in Isolation

When a transition fails, it's rarely because someone didn't try. I did everything I was supposed to by following instructions, keeping my appointments, and showing up. But the structure I had in uniform didn't exist on the outside. Without a clear mission, I began to question my place. The loss of identity after service is called "identity strain"—the tension between who you were in the military and who you're expected to be afterward (Aronson, 2020; McCormick et al., 2019). A silent pressure builds daily, especially when an unstructured civilian environment abruptly replaces the military's collective identity and mission-first mindset.

Isolation distorts the sense of time. You lose your routine. There's no more accountability or social structure. Your body may be safe, but your mind isn't. This disconnect is both common and dangerous. Veterans without strong post-service support are at significantly higher risk for depression, substance use, and suicide, particularly in the first year after separation (Carroll et al., 2017; Laird & Alexander, 2019). Carroll et al. (2017) note that social disconnection and lack of purposeful activity are among the most persistent predictors of post-service mental health decline, while Laird & Alexander, (2019) emphasize that sustained social integration is one of the most protective factors against suicidal behavior in veterans.

What finally broke the cycle for me wasn't the therapy or medication. It was a dream, and I don't know what anyone else believes, but it was clarity. It's something that pulled me back from the edge. I don't remember all the details, but I know it wasn't just my subconscious. It felt like something, or someone, was watching over me. Maybe it was luck. Perhaps it was spiritual. But I woke up feeling like I'd been given another shot at life and realizing I was wasting it. I wasn't living for myself and honoring the guys who lost their lives so I could have this one. That dream didn't fix everything, but it stopped the spiral and made me choose to fight again.

1.9 The True Beginning

Most people believe the story begins when the uniform comes off, but it doesn't. The true beginning is when you realize the system has no answers and choose to keep going anyway. Research shows this rupture is common. McCormick et al. (2019) found that many veterans first enter a profound disconnection from civilian life, marked by loss of purpose, mistrust, and reluctance to engage, before rebuilding begins. Bloeser et al. (2021) describe this early stage as institutional betrayal, when trusted systems fail to respond, pushing veterans toward self-reliance or despair. All subsequent efforts, research, advocacy, and the BRAVE theory grew from this place. It was born in collapse, and Tedeschi and Calhoun (2004) call it the shattering of the "assumptive world." Laird & Alexander (2019) emphasize that resilience often emerges in response to breakdown, not in its absence. You can't talk about reintegration without first understanding disintegration. This was my initial phase, and it happened to me. BRAVE began here when I had to choose to disappear or rebuild. This was my origin of trauma and purpose.

Academic Synthesis

Chap. 1 situates the earliest stages of my personal and professional trajectory within the broader empirical literature on trauma, resilience, and veteran reintegration. While often framed as beginning at separation, the successful or otherwise reintegration process can be traced to pre-service life experiences that shape vulnerability and adaptive capacity long before enlistment. My story reflects how ACEs, moral modeling, institutional trust, and formative failures interact to create risk and resilience pathways.

The early loss of my father in a mining accident represents a personal tragedy and aligns with decades of research linking ACEs to long-term health and psychosocial consequences. Foundational work by Felitti et al. (1998) established the graded relationship between cumulative ACE exposure and elevated risks for depression, PTSD, substance misuse, and chronic illness. Subsequent veteran-specific studies confirm this pattern, with high ACE prevalence associated with poorer mental health outcomes and increased suicide risk (Aronson et al., 2020; Blosnich et al., 2021;

Carroll et al., 2017; Laird & Alexander, 2019; Slavin et al., 2024). The prevalence data from these studies illustrate that many veterans carry unresolved developmental trauma into service, where it intersects with combat exposure to compound vulnerability.

Protective factors also emerge in this period. My grandfather, a former POW, embodied moral courage and consistency, attributes that resilience literature identifies as critical for mitigating the long-term effects of early adversity. Laird and Alexander (2019) note that stable, supportive relationships can buffer neurobiological and psychological impacts of ACEs, fostering adaptive coping capacities that may later support recovery and growth.

Not all formative events were protective. My failure at BUD/S training was initially felt as a loss of identity, but over time, it became a turning point. This aligns with the mechanisms described in Posttraumatic Growth (Tedeschi & Calhoun, 2004) and stress inoculation frameworks, where facing high-pressure failure, if processed constructively, can improve adaptive coping and resilience. Instead of being a setback, such moments can serve as catalysts for rebuilding identity, as long as they are integrated rather than avoided.

My service as an FMF Corpsman placed me in a dual-role context as a healer and combatant, consistent with Shelef et al.'s (2024) findings on the psychological toll of medics embedded in frontline units. The blast in Musa Qala and my subsequent emotional numbing mirror the neurobiological pathways described by Lanius et al. (2010), where repeated trauma exposure leads to hyperactivation of the amygdala, diminished prefrontal regulation, and emotional overmodulation manifested as detachment or dissociation. Combat physiology research further supports this account; Clemente-Suárez et al. (2018) found that soldiers in high-intensity combat simulations displayed elevated sympathetic activity and reduced cortical arousal, a mismatch between perceived and actual exertion, like my own experiences under fire.

The post-deployment phase revealed structural and cultural barriers to care. Studies by Bloeser et al. (2021), Cheney et al. (2018), and McCormick et al. (2019) document how veterans encountering institutional betrayal, cultural misalignment, and discontinuity of care often disengage from treatment, even when distress remains high. My own experience of being told that mindfulness was "not for people like me" is emblematic of the subtle, yet damaging, forms of stigma these authors describe. The result was a withdrawal from the belief that available systems neither understood nor valued my experience.

Chap. 1, therefore, frames "A Life Before Theory" as a biography and a case study of the layered origins of reintegration challenges. Early adversity, moral exemplars, formative failures, combat role strain, and systemic care breakdowns are all situated within established empirical research. This synthesis underscores the central premise of the BRAVE Theory: reintegration does not begin when the uniform comes off; it starts with the cumulative interplay of pre-service, in-service, and post-service experiences that shape the veteran's trajectory long before they step back into civilian life.0.

Key Takeaways

- **Reintegration begins long before discharge**. Early life adversity, including Adverse Childhood Experiences (ACEs), shapes vulnerability, coping capacity, and perceptions of authority well before enlistment (Aronson et al., 2020; Blosnich et al., 2021; Carroll et al., 2017; Felitti et al., 1998; Slavin et al., 2024).
- **Protective relationships buffer trauma's impact**. Stable, supportive figures such as consistent caregivers or moral role models can mitigate early adversity's long-term neurobiological and psychological effects (Laird & Alexander, 2019; Slavin et al., 2024).
- **Formative failures can catalyze growth**. When processed constructively, setbacks in high-pressure environments, such as elite military training, can promote adaptive coping, identity reconstruction, and resilience (Tedeschi & Calhoun, 2004; Carroll et al., 2017).
- **Dual roles intensify combat strain**. Serving as a healer and combatant creates unique moral, operational, and emotional pressures that heighten long-term psychological risk (Shelef et al., 2024; Lanius et al., 2010; Clemente-Suárez et al., 2018).
- **Systemic and cultural barriers can derail recovery**. Institutional betrayal, lack of cultural competence, and discontinuity of care contribute to disengagement from treatment, reinforcing isolation and mistrust (Bloeser et al., 2021; Cheney et al., 2018; McCormick et al., 2019).

Applied Learning Prompts

1. Define "identity strain" and name two indicators operationalizing it in the military–civilian transition.
2. Give one mechanism by which a protective adult buffers ACE-related risk and one likely long-term outcome.
3. Describe how decompression gaps manifest physiologically and behaviorally in the first 90 days post-deployment.
4. Distinguish institutional betrayal from routine dissatisfaction in care and list one system-level remedy.

References

Aronson, K. R., Perkins, D. F., Morgan, N. R., Bleser, J. A., Vogt, D., Copeland, L. A., Finley, E. P., & Gilman, C. L. (2020). The impact of adverse childhood experiences (ACEs) and combat exposure on mental health conditions among new post-9/11 veterans. *Psychological Trauma: Theory, Research, Practice, and Policy, 12*(7), 698–706. https://doi.org/10.1037/tra0000614

Bloeser, K., McCarron, K. K., Merker, V. L., Hyde, J., Bolton, R. E., Anastasides, N., Petrakis, B. A., Helmer, D. A., Santos, S., Litke, D., Pigeon, W. R., & McAndrew, L. M. (2021). Because the country, it seems though, has turned their back on me: Experiences of institutional betrayal among veterans living with gulf war illness. *Social Science & Medicine, 284*, 114211. https://doi.org/10.1016/j.socscimed.2021.114211

Blosnich, J. R., Garfin, D. R., Maguen, S., Vogt, D., Dichter, M. E., Hoffmire, C. A., Bernhard, P. A., & Schneiderman, A. (2021). Differences in childhood adversity, suicidal ideation, and suicide attempt among veterans and nonveterans. *American Psychologist, 76*(2), 284–299. https://doi.org/10.1037/amp0000755

Carroll, T. D., Currier, J. M., McCormick, W. H., & Drescher, K. D. (2017). Adverse childhood experiences and risk for suicidal behavior in male Iraq and Afghanistan veterans seeking PTSD treatment. *Psychological Trauma: Theory, Research, Practice, and Policy, 9*(5), 583–586. https://doi.org/10.1037/tra0000250

Cheney, A. M., Koenig, C. J., Miller, C. J., Zamora, K., Wright, P., Stanley, R., Fortney, J., Burgess, J. F., & Pyne, J. M. (2018). Veteran-centered barriers to VA mental healthcare services use. *BMC Health Services Research, 18*(1), 591. https://doi.org/10.1186/s12913-018-3346-9

Clemente-Suárez, V. J., Palomera, P. R., & Robles-Pérez, J. J. (2018). Psychophysiological response to acute-high-stress combat situations in professional soldiers. *Stress & Health, 34*(2), 247–252. https://doi.org/10.1002/smi.2778

Domschke, K., Schiele, M. A., Crespo Salvador, Ó., Zillich, L., Lipovsek, J., Pittig, A., Heinig, I., Ridderbusch, I. C., Straube, B., Richter, J., Hollandt, M., Plag, J., Fydrich, T., Koelkebeck, K., Weber, H., Lueken, U., Dannlowski, U., Margraf, J., Schneider, S., … Deckert, J. (2025). Epigenetic markers of disease risk and psychotherapy response in anxiety disorders–A longitudinal analysis of the DNA methylome. *Molecular Psychiatry*. Advance online publication. doi:https://doi.org/10.1038/s41380-025-03038-5

Felitti, V. J., Anda, R. F., Nordenberg, D., Williamson, D. F., Spitz, A. M., Edwards, V., Koss, M. P., & Marks, J. S. (1998). Relationship of childhood abuse and household dysfunction to many of the leading causes of death in adults: The adverse childhood experiences (ACE) study. *American Journal of Preventive Medicine, 14*(4), 245–258. https://doi.org/10.1016/S0749-3797(98)00017-8

Laird, C. W., & Alexander, P. (2019). Prevalence of adverse childhood experiences among veterans. *Clinical Social Work Journal, 47*(4), 384–393. https://doi.org/10.1007/s10615-019-00703-5

Lanius, R., Frewen, P., Vermetten, E., & Yehuda, R. (2010). Fear conditioning and early life vulnerabilities: Two distinct pathways of emotional dysregulation and brain dysfunction in PTSD. *European Journal of Psychotraumatology, 1*, 5467. https://doi.org/10.3402/ejpt.v1i0.5467

McCormick, W. H., Currier, J. M., Isaak, S. L., Sims, B. M., Slagel, B. A., Carroll, T. D., Hamner, K., & Albright, D. L. (2019). Military culture and post-military transitioning among veterans: A qualitative analysis. *Journal of Veterans Studies, 4*(2), 121. https://doi.org/10.21061/jvs.v4i2.121

Shelef, L., Bechor, U., Ohayon, O., Tatsa-Laur, L., & Antonovsky, A. (2024). The psychological impact of exposure to battle on medics: A cross-sectional study of ex-soldiers who sought help from the IDF combat reaction unit. *Military Medicine, 189*(3–4), e781–e788. https://doi.org/10.1093/milmed/usad368

Slavin, A. Z., Fischer, I. C., & Pietrzak, R. H. (2024). Differential associations of adverse childhood experiences and mental health outcomes in U.S. military veterans. *Journal of Psychiatric Research, 172*, 261–265. https://doi.org/10.1016/j.jpsychires.2024.02.040

Tedeschi, R. G., & Calhoun, L. G. (2004). Posttraumatic growth: Conceptual foundations and empirical evidence. *Psychological Inquiry, 15*(1), 1–18. https://doi.org/10.1207/s15327965pli1501_01

U.S. Department of Defense, Office of Inspector General. (2025, February 7). *Management advisory: Naval Special Warfare Command should relocate, reschedule, or cancel Navy Sea, Air, and Land (SEAL) candidate water training when water bacteria levels exceed state safety standards (Report No. DODIG-2025-067)*. https://media.defense.gov/2025/Feb/10/2003644357/-1/-1/1/DODIG-2025-067_REDACTED%20SECURE.PDF

Van Assche, E., Hohoff, C., Zang, J., Knight, M. J., & Baune, B. T. (2023). Epigenetic modification related to cognitive changes during a cognitive training intervention in depression. *Progress in*

Neuro-Psychopharmacology and Biological Psychiatry, 127, 110835. https://doi.org/10.1016/j.pnpbp.2023.110835

van IJzendoorn, M. H., & Bakermans-Kranenburg, M. J. (2015). Genetic differential susceptibility on trial: Meta-analytic support from randomized controlled experiments. *Development and Psychopathology, 27*(1), 151–162. https://doi.org/10.1017/S0954579414001369

Wood, M. D., Adler, A. B., Bliese, P. D., McGurk, D., Castro, C. A., Hoge, C. W., & Koffman, R. (2018). Psychological adjustment after combat deployment: Decompression at home versus at sea. *Military Behavioral Health, 6*(4), 259–270. https://doi.org/10.1080/21635781.2017.1412842

Chapter 2
Breaking the Silence

This chapter maps how identity strain, cumulative trauma, and cultural mismatch fuel post-service withdrawal and how catalyst events, practical regulation, and peer mentorship reignite purpose. After reading, you'll be able to: (1) explain identity strain and MIS; (2) analyze how "catalyst" moments can trigger posttraumatic growth; (3) evaluate how education/support help or hinder recovery; (4) apply exercise/mindfulness/goal projects to regulate arousal; (5) design peer mentorship for reciprocal gains; (6) spot institutional misalignment and plan around it.

2.1 Introduction—Breaking the Silence

After leaving the military, I felt confused, disoriented, and emotionally numb. I had no clear direction or mission to guide me. My military identity was gone, and civilian life felt unfamiliar. This feeling persisted for two years. Research indicates that losing your sense of identity after separation is common. It is called "identity strain," which is the tension between who you were in the military and who you are expected to be after service (Aronson et al., 2020; McCormick et al., 2019). Without a clear mission or purpose, daily life can feel aimless, increasing the risk of depression, substance use, and suicide, especially during the first year after transition (Carroll et al., 2017; Laird & Alexander, 2019).

During this period, I kept my experiences private. McCormick et al. (2019) found that many veterans avoid discussing their service with civilians because of cultural differences, fear of being misunderstood, or a lack of trust in how their stories will be received. This silence often leads to isolation, which research shows can make reintegration harder (Laird & Alexander, 2019). I thought I was adjusting, but I was

T. Carlton, *BRAVE Theory*, https://doi.org/10.1007/978-3-032-13695-4_2

withdrawing. My body was at home, but my mind felt like it was in combat. Studies on combat trauma show that the brain can stay alert long after leaving the battlefield, with lasting changes in how stress is processed (Lanius et al., 2010). This mismatch between what the nervous system is prepared for and the demands of civilian life is one of the first hurdles many veterans face after service.

Recent research provides a more structured way to understand these differences in how military identity persists after discharge. Dolan et al. (2022) developed the Military Identity Salience (MIS) model, identifying thirteen factors that influence the prominence of military/veteran identity in civilian life. These include demographic characteristics (such as gender), service history (combat exposure, years served, rank), and post-service experiences (civilian employment, education, engagement with veteran peers, and perceptions of civilians). The MIS model emphasizes that not all veterans experience identity strain similarly; some maintain a strong military identity, which can serve as a source of belonging and structure, while others shift toward a primarily civilian identity. However, tension can heighten feelings of disconnection, mistrust, and alienation when military identity remains highly salient, and the civilian environment does not align with military values or norms.

This chapter examines how I began breaking that silence, first privately and then publicly, and how that process relates to the broader research on identity, isolation, and reintegration. It explores how finding a voice can become the starting point for rebuilding purpose after service and how understanding identity salience can help shape more effective support systems for veterans in transition.

Important: Silence functions as a coping mechanism rather than a destination. When the environment is misaligned with an individual's identity, symptoms tend to reflect the persona; the fundamental issue lies in the incongruity.

2.2 The Dream

The silence finally broke with a dream. I had been out of the military for almost two to three years, living in a state of functional withdrawal Isolation and withdrawal. I did the bare minimum to keep moving forward without real engagement. Then one night, I dreamed I was back in combat. It was the same kind of dream I had experienced hundreds of times: my rifle jammed, incoming fire, unable to act. But this one was different.

Toward the end, I saw the ones I could not save, whether directly in my care or circumstances beyond my control. They said nothing, but their faces carried a mix of sadness and something I could not fully name. Maybe pride. Maybe peace. I woke up drenched in sweat and my heart racing as always. But this time, something inside felt shifted. I didn't just feel the familiar weight of combat memories. I felt the weight of not living. I had survived, but I had not been living like it.

Survivor's guilt is a well-recognized feature in post-combat adjustment, often connected to moral injury. This psychological, social, and spiritual harm results from perceived violations of deeply held moral beliefs (Fimiani et al., 2022). For many veterans, this injury is not confined to the battlefield but extends into civilian life, manifesting as unworthiness or an unspoken obligation to "make survival matter" (McCormick et al., 2019). Such guilt can amplify the effects of earlier traumas, mainly when a veteran's life history includes ACEs. Research shows that ACEs are disproportionately common among veterans, with many reporting multiple forms of early adversity (Aronson et al., 2020; Blosnich et al., 2021; Carroll et al., 2017; Laird & Alexander, 2019; Slavin et al., 2024).

This buildup of trauma from early life adversity combined with combat exposure has been linked to higher risks of depression, PTSD, suicidal thoughts, and social withdrawal (Aronson et al., 2020; Carroll et al., 2017; Laird & Alexander, 2019; Slavin et al., 2024). The connection is not simply additive; ACEs seem to influence how later traumas are experienced, remembered, and processed, affecting vulnerability and resilience. Veterans with high ACE scores are more likely to report ongoing distress, and those burdened with survivor's guilt may feel a compounded moral and existential weight. My dream clarified that burden into a single realization: I was wasting the second chance I had been given.

Whether it was spiritual or simply my mind forcing me to confront the truth, I cannot say. Research on posttraumatic growth describes how individuals can experience positive psychological change following trauma, often marked by a re-evaluation of priorities and the development of a renewed sense of purpose (Tedeschi & Calhoun, 2004). Such moments do not erase trauma but can serve as catalysts for transformative change when acted upon. In my case, that dream became an inflection point.

From a neurobiological perspective, emotionally charged, trauma-related dreams align with what is known about the brain's response to ongoing threat exposure. Combat trauma can keep the nervous system in a heightened state of alertness, with changes in how emotional and moral memories are processed (Lanius et al., 2010). While recurring dreams often increase distress, there are cases like mine where they can help with emotional reframing and shifting focus toward action.

That night, I woke up feeling like I had another shot at life. But it wasn't enough just to survive; I felt obligated to live in a way that honored those who didn't come home. That clarity didn't solve my problems. It didn't remove the noise in my head or the weight in my chest. But it stopped the spiral. It was the first time since leaving the Navy that I actively chose to fight for my own life again. Interpreted through MIS and posttraumatic growth, the dream functioned as a disruptive cue that reoriented attention from avoidance to purpose.

2.3 Building Stability

The decision to fight for my own life again wasn't a clear plan. I didn't know what "better" looked like. I knew I couldn't keep doing nothing. Early on, my steps forward were uncoordinated and, in some ways, premature. I enrolled in a Bachelor of Science (BS) program in Exercise Science and Human Performance at California University of Pennsylvania (CalU). It felt like progress at the time. But academically, I struggled. My focus was fractured, and my energy was inconsistent. I wasn't incapable; I was failing because I was still living with untreated traumatic stress.

The research reflects this pattern. Veterans often enter civilian education or employment still carrying the physiological and cognitive effects of trauma exposure. Hyperarousal, impaired concentration, and disrupted sleep can impair performance despite high levels of discipline and motivation (Clemente-Suárez et al., 2018; Lanius et al., 2010). For those with prior ACEs layered on top of combat trauma, these challenges can be magnified, influencing academic persistence and self-perception of competence (Aronson et al., 2020; Carroll et al., 2017).

Looking back, I realize I was pushing myself forward without doing the deeper work to stabilize. My nervous system was still primed for threat. I could react accurately in high-pressure situations, but the daily demands of civilian life, like reading, writing, and meeting deadlines, were draining in a way combat never was. Research on post-combat adjustment refers to this as the "environmental mismatch" problem: the skills and states that kept you alive in war don't automatically translate into success in peace, and sometimes, they work against you (McCormick et al., 2019).

The graduate admissions staff at CalU kept me from quitting. One helped me select courses strategically, and another guided me toward the graduate program. Their willingness to see me as a whole person, rather than just a struggling student, mirrored what the literature emphasizes about reintegration: meaningful connection and recognition are critical protective factors in recovery (Bloeser et al., 2021; Cheney et al., 2018). This contrast shows how education and formal support systems can both hinder and aid recovery. On one hand, untreated traumatic stress can make academic work feel overwhelming and destabilizing; on the other, culturally competent staff who recognize the person behind the performance provide stabilizing anchors. Research consistently demonstrates that education can either be a stressor or a support depending on how help is given (Bloeser et al., 2021; Cheney et al., 2018). My own experience highlighted this dual reality: the same classroom could intensify distress or foster growth, depending on whether human connection and recognition were present.

That recognition planted a seed, even if I didn't realize it then. It would later grow into one of the core principles behind the BRAVE Theory, which states that a genuine, culturally competent human connection is essential for meaningful post-service growth. The seed the graduate staff planted took time to grow because I was still operating in survival mode, but knowing someone saw me beyond my shortcomings gave me enough stability to seek solutions. I understood now that I couldn't wait for the system to save me; it hadn't before, and I wasn't willing to risk the rest of my life on it now.

That's when I started experimenting with different coping strategies. Physical training became my first lifeline. I had always been fit, but it was different now. The gym wasn't about aesthetics this time; it was about order, control, and burning off the chaos that built up in my head. Controlled physical activity has been shown to reduce PTSD symptom severity, improve sleep quality, and enhance cognitive performance by modulating the hypothalamic–pituitary–adrenal (HPA) axis and decreasing hyperarousal (Fetzner & Asmundson, 2015).

Even with the gym, there were times when the noise in my head wouldn't shut off. That's when I found mindfulness by accident while researching one day. Sitting still didn't make sense to me, so I adapted it. I practiced in the car after workouts, focusing on my breathing, the rhythm of the road, and the tension in my chest. Over time, I noticed I was able to use the same breathing patterns during flashbacks or spikes in anxiety. Mindfulness-based interventions (MBIs) have been shown to reduce physiological arousal, decrease emotional reactivity, and improve attentional control in veterans with PTSD, with lasting effects when combined with home practice (King et al., 2013).

Mindfulness wasn't a magic cure. I still had bad days, and the progress was slow. That's something the research is clear about: recovery from combat trauma isn't linear, and no single intervention works for everyone (Steenkamp et al., 2015). Mindfulness and exercise gave me a foundation, though. It was something I could combine with other supports when they became available.

I also started working on my house. It might sound small, but turning a broken, unfinished space into something functional and complete became a metaphor for what I was trying to do with myself. Each repaired wall and finished floor became tangible proof that I could create structure out of disorder. This mirrors findings from Vaughan-Horrocks et al. (2021), who found that goal-oriented, meaningful activities, remarkably grounded in a resilience framework, can enhance self-efficacy, reduce avoidance behaviors, and promote reintegration in veterans with mental health challenges. Participants in their occupational therapy and resilience workshops reported increased participation in daily life, stronger social connections, and renewed hope for the future.

These habits didn't "fix" me but opened the door to making other kinds of progress possible. They created the conditions where I could start thinking beyond survival and toward a purpose, which is a shift that research on posttraumatic growth identifies as a critical turning point (Tedeschi & Calhoun, 2004).

2.4 Helping Others, Reclaiming Myself

Around that same time, I met someone who became a mirror for my own transformation. He was a mechanic working on my truck, weighed down literally and figuratively by poor health, repeated hospital visits, and a kind of emotional standstill I recognized immediately. I'd been there. I recognized the heaviness in every movement and resignation in his voice. I asked him to train with me. It wasn't a big pitch since I was already driving 30 minutes toward the gym, so he might as well join. What started as a few casual sessions grew into something larger. The meal planning, accountability check-ins, and eventually a friendship went far beyond the gym. He lost over 100 pounds. The transformation wasn't only physical; as he rebuilt his health, he also rebuilt his life, work, relationships, and mindset. I realized that, in helping him, I was also rebuilding myself. We weren't just lifting weights; we were also lifting each other out of inertia.

It was slow and deliberate work. There were setbacks, missed workouts, and weeks where progress seemed invisible. But we stayed the course while trusting the process. The literature on peer-supported health interventions reflects exactly what I observed happening in real time: when change is modeled by someone relatable, trust and accountability grow, making behavior change more sustainable (Hundt et al., 2015). In many ways, I couldn't let him fail because it would have meant letting myself fail, too. That mutual investment kept both of us moving forward.

Helping him taught me something that classrooms or manuals couldn't. The small, consistent changes compound into a transformation. It proved that my lived experience has value, and my scars and struggles can be tools in someone else's recovery. Research on mentorship and posttraumatic growth shows that serving as a guide for others can enhance a sense of purpose, reinforce one's coping skills, and even reduce PTSD symptoms through meaning-making (Tedeschi & Calhoun, 2004).

Renovating my home, guiding others through life changes, and starting to speak publicly about my own story gave me a kind of control I hadn't felt since combat. The silence that once defined my life had been replaced with intentional, purposeful, and connected speech. In helping others reclaim their voice, I began to claim my own. Looking back, I realize that years later, I was unknowingly trying to recreate the same kind of peer-driven, purpose-centered process when the VA system kept failing me. That dismissal was shortsighted, reinforcing the isolation I was working to overcome. The research supports this: when veterans encounter support systems that lack cultural competence or dismiss personally meaningful strategies, it can deepen disengagement and mistrust (Aronson et al., 2020; Bloeser et al., 2021; Hundt et al., 2015). These dismissals highlight the broader problem of institutional misalignment. When formal systems fail to validate or support strategies that veterans find meaningful, recovery becomes an uphill battle. The gap compelled me to work around the system, developing peer-driven approaches, relying on reciprocal mentorship, and creating accountability structures. These adaptive workarounds don't eliminate the burden but demonstrate how veterans innovate when institutions fall short, maintaining dignity and momentum even without official support.

This wasn't just about him anymore. Once I saw what was possible, I started helping more veterans, civilians, and friends. Some were stuck in the same VA system I'd wrestled with, some even worse off. I guided where I could, listened when I couldn't, and built programs out of conversations. I noticed as they grew stronger, so did I. That shift was personal and the beginning of a professional transformation. Entering the Doctor of Health Science (DHSc) program was an academic milestone and the moment I began to see myself as a systems thinker, scholar, and a leader. As I stated, the BRAVE Theory didn't emerge from textbooks; it was forged in the moments of shared struggle, mutual accountability, and the belief that survival is only the beginning.

Case Study—The Mechanic and me (Reciprocal Mentorship in Real Life)
I met a mechanic struggling, his health declining, mood flat, and lacking momentum. I asked him to train with me. It started small: show up, lift, eat cleaner, check in. He lost more than 100 pounds and regained his life. Helping him also helped me. The accountability went both ways. If he showed up, I had to show up. The work restored purpose on both sides. This is what peer trust looks like in practice: shared language, shared stakes, and measurable progress.

Teaching points: peer trust makes change sticky; small wins compound; serving others can pull you out of your inertia and rebuild identity through action.

Academic Synthesis
This chapter examined the reconstruction of identity and purpose following military service through an integration of personal experience and empirical research. The process of transition from a highly structured and mission-oriented environment to an unstructured civilian world created a profound disruption in self-concept. The literature describes this dissonance as identity strain (Aronson et al., 2020; McCormick et al., 2019), a tension between the internalized military role and the expectations of civilian life. The Military Identity Salience model (Dolan et al., 2022) provides a useful lens for interpreting this shift, emphasizing that the degree of post-service alignment between personal values and societal recognition strongly influences reintegration outcomes.

For me, the turning point occurred when unresolved memories from combat surfaced during sleep, confronting the suppressed moral and emotional conflicts that had remained dormant for years. These experiences are consistent with the concept of posttraumatic growth (Tedeschi & Calhoun, 2004), which proposes that traumatic disruption can prompt reflection, reorganization of meaning, and psychological adaptation. The sense of survivor guilt described by Fimiani et al. (2022) was particularly relevant, as it intersected with earlier experiences of instability and loss identified in the literature on adverse childhood experiences (Blosnich et al., 2021). Together, these cumulative exposures illustrate the layered nature of trauma, where developmental and combat-related stressors interact to influence long-term adjustment and recovery capacity.

Reengaging with academia provided both an avenue for personal reconstruction and a setting in which residual symptoms of hyperarousal, attentional disruption, and cognitive fatigue became visible. The experience reflected broader findings that student veterans often encounter barriers linked not to academic ability but to unaddressed physiological stress and cultural incongruence between military and academic environments (Clemente-Suárez et al., 2018; Lanius et al., 2010; McCormick et al., 2019). However, meaningful interpersonal recognition within that environment professors and peers who acknowledged both competence and struggle proved to be a stabilizing force. Research supports this observation, demonstrating that culturally competent and empathetic social support promotes adjustment and psychological recovery among veterans (Bloeser et al., 2021; Cheney et al., 2018).

Structured physical activity and adaptive mindfulness practices functioned as primary self-regulatory mechanisms during this period. Evidence indicates that such interventions improve cognitive control and reduce physiological stress markers in military and veteran populations (Fetzner & Asmundson, 2015; King et al., 2013). Parallel to these practices, engagement in task-oriented physical work, such as construction and repair, fostered tangible progress and a sense of mastery. This observation aligns with occupational therapy research suggesting that purposeful and measurable activity supports self-efficacy and behavioral regulation (Vaughan-Horrocks et al., 2021).

Mentorship and peer engagement subsequently became central to ongoing recovery and meaning-making. The process of guiding other veterans through training and reintegration not only reinforced my own coping strategies but also reflected the empirical evidence that peer-based interventions enhance motivation, accountability, and long-term psychological outcomes (Hundt et al., 2015; Tedeschi & Calhoun, 2004). Through reciprocal interaction, resilience became both a personal practice and a transferable framework for others navigating similar challenges.

Despite these gains, institutional barriers persisted. Traditional systems of care frequently failed to recognize or validate self-directed recovery strategies, resulting in frustration and partial disengagement. This pattern corresponds with findings that programmatic misalignment between veterans' lived experiences and institutional delivery models contributes to underutilization of services (Aronson et al., 2020; Bloeser et al., 2021). The evidence and lived experience together indicate that reintegration is most successful when formal support structures operate in concert with peer-driven, culturally congruent networks.

Rebuilding identity after service is not a linear process but a cyclical progression of self-assessment, behavioral adaptation, and social re-engagement. It requires simultaneous attention to psychological, physiological, and relational dimensions of recovery. The trajectory described in this chapter from identity disorientation to structured self-regulation and collaborative mentorship illustrates how lived experience can inform theory and program design. These insights serve as the conceptual foundation for Chap. 3, A Scholar Is Forged, where the personal reintegration process transitions into a systematic examination of resilience and the development of the BRAVE theoretical model.

Key Takeaways

- **Identity strain is a central reintegration challenge.** The tension between a persistent military identity and civilian expectations can drive disconnection, mistrust, and emotional withdrawal, especially when civilian environments fail to align with military values (Aronson et al., 2020; Dolan et al., 2022).
- **Catalyst events can trigger posttraumatic growth.** Symbolic or emotionally charged experiences, such as vivid dreams, can disrupt avoidance patterns, reframe survivor's guilt, and initiate purpose reconstruction (Fimiani et al., 2022; Tedeschi & Calhoun, 2004).

- **Cumulative trauma amplifies reintegration difficulty.** ACEs compound the psychological impact of combat exposure, shaping vulnerability, resilience capacity, and post-service functioning (Aronson et al., 2020; Blosnich et al., 2021).
- **Stability often requires simultaneous personal and social interventions.** Academic engagement alone may not offset untreated traumatic stress; cultural competence and human connection are critical protective factors (Bloeser et al., 2021; Cheney et al., 2018).
- **Self-directed regulation strategies work best when they are practical and meaningful**. Structured physical activity, adapted mindfulness, and goal-oriented projects like home renovation can recalibrate stress responses and reinforce self-efficacy (Fetzner & Asmundson, 2015; Vaughan-Horrocks et al., 2021).
- **Peer mentorship fosters reciprocal growth.** Trust-based, relatable peer relationships sustain behavior change, strengthen purpose, and improve mentor and mentee outcomes (Hundt et al., 2015).
- **Institutional misalignment can undermine recovery.** When formal systems dismiss or fail to support personally meaningful strategies, veterans may disengage, reinforcing isolation and mistrust (Aronson et al., 2020; Bloeser et al., 2021).

Applied Learning Prompts

Which Military Identity Salience (MIS) factors described in this chapter feel most relevant to you (or to a veteran you know), and how do they create tension with civilian roles?

1. The dream described in this chapter served as a catalyst moment. What event, conversation, or realization in your own life (or someone else's) might serve a similar purpose for growth?
2. Reflect on an educational, workplace, or institutional setting. How did support (or lack thereof) shape your ability to stabilize and move forward?
3. This chapter highlighted exercise, adapted mindfulness, and goal-based projects like home renovation. Which of these practices would be most useful for you, and why?
4. In the mechanic case study, both mentor and mentee benefited. How can reciprocity in peer mentorship strengthen outcomes for both people?
5. What is one example of institutional misalignment you've experienced (or observed) during transition? How could planning around it reduce isolation or mistrust?

References

Aronson, K. R., Perkins, D. F., Morgan, N. R., Bleser, J. A., Vogt, D., Copeland, L. A., Finley, E. P., & Gilman, C. L. (2020). The impact of adverse childhood experiences (ACEs) and combat exposure on mental health conditions among new post-9/11 veterans. *Psychological Trauma: Theory, Research, Practice, and Policy, 12*(7), 698–706. https://doi.org/10.1037/tra0000614

Bloeser, K., McCarron, K. K., Merker, V. L., Hyde, J., Bolton, R. E., Anastasides, N., Petrakis, B. A., Helmer, D. A., Santos, S., Litke, D., Pigeon, W. R., & McAndrew, L. M. (2021). Because the country, it seems though, has turned their back on me: Experiences of institutional betrayal among veterans living with gulf war illness. *Social Science & Medicine, 284*, 114211. https://doi.org/10.1016/j.socscimed.2021.114211

Blosnich, J. R., Garfin, D. R., Maguen, S., Vogt, D., Dichter, M. E., Hoffmire, C. A., Bernhard, P. A., & Schneiderman, A. (2021). Differences in childhood adversity, suicidal ideation, and suicide attempt among veterans and nonveterans. *American Psychologist, 76*(2), 284–299. https://doi.org/10.1037/amp0000755

Carroll, T. D., Currier, J. M., McCormick, W. H., & Drescher, K. D. (2017). Adverse childhood experiences and risk for suicidal behavior in male Iraq and Afghanistan veterans seeking PTSD treatment. *Psychological Trauma: Theory, Research, Practice, and Policy, 9*(5), 583–586. https://doi.org/10.1037/tra0000250

Cheney, A. M., Koenig, C. J., Miller, C. J., Zamora, K., Wright, P., Stanley, R., Fortney, J., Burgess, J. F., & Pyne, J. M. (2018). Veteran-centered barriers to VA mental healthcare services use. *BMC Health Services Research, 18*(1), 591. https://doi.org/10.1186/s12913-018-3346-9

Clemente-Suárez, V. J., Palomera, P. R., & Robles-Pérez, J. J. (2018). Psychophysiological response to acute-high-stress combat situations in professional soldiers. *Stress & Health, 34*(2), 247–252. https://doi.org/10.1002/smi.2778

Dolan, G., McCauley, M., & Murphy, D. (2022). Factors influencing the salience of military/veteran identity post discharge: A scoping review. *Journal of Veterans Studies, 8*(1), 333. https://doi.org/10.21061/jvs.v8i1.333

Fetzner, M. G., & Asmundson, G. J. G. (2015). Aerobic exercise reduces symptoms of posttraumatic stress disorder: A randomized controlled trial. *Cognitive Behaviour Therapy, 44*(4), 301–313. https://doi.org/10.1080/16506073.2014.916745

Fimiani, R., Gazzillo, F., Dazzi, N., & Bush, M. (2022). Survivor guilt: Theoretical, empirical, and clinical features. *International Forum of Psychoanalysis, 31*(3), 176–190. https://doi.org/10.1080/0803706X.2021.1941246

Hundt, N. E., Robinson, A., Arney, J., Stanley, M. A., & Cully, J. A. (2015). Veterans' perspectives on benefits and drawbacks of peer support for posttraumatic stress disorder. *Military Medicine, 180*(8), 851–856. https://doi.org/10.7205/MILMED-D-14-00536

King, A. P., Erickson, T. M., Giardino, N. D., Favorite, T., Rauch, S. A. M., Robinson, E., et al. (2013). A pilot study of group mindfulness-based cognitive therapy (MBCT) for combat veterans with posttraumatic stress disorder (PTSD). *Depression and Anxiety, 30*(7), 638–645. https://doi.org/10.1002/da.22104

Laird, C. W., & Alexander, P. (2019). Prevalence of adverse childhood experiences among veterans. *Clinical Social Work Journal, 47*(4), 384–393. https://doi.org/10.1007/s10615-019-00703-5

Lanius, R., Frewen, P., Vermetten, E., & Yehuda, R. (2010). Fear conditioning and early life vulnerabilities: Two distinct pathways of emotional dysregulation and brain dysfunction in PTSD. *European Journal of Psychotraumatology, 1*, 5467. https://doi.org/10.3402/ejpt.v1i0.5467

McCormick, W. H., Currier, J. M., Isaak, S. L., Sims, B. M., Slagel, B. A., Carroll, T. D., Hamner, K., & Albright, D. L. (2019). Military culture and post-military transitioning among veterans: A qualitative analysis. *Journal of Veterans Studies, 4*(2), 121. https://doi.org/10.21061/jvs.v4i2.121

Slavin, A. Z., Fischer, I. C., & Pietrzak, R. H. (2024). Differential associations of adverse childhood experiences and mental health outcomes in U.S. military veterans. *Journal of Psychiatric Research, 172*, 261–265. https://doi.org/10.1016/j.jpsychires.2024.02.040

Steenkamp, M. M., Litz, B. T., Hoge, C. W., & Marmar, C. R. (2015). Psychotherapy for military-related PTSD: A review of randomized clinical trials. *JAMA, 314*(5), 489–500. https://doi.org/10.1001/jama.2015.8370

Tedeschi, R. G., & Calhoun, L. G. (2004). Posttraumatic growth: Conceptual foundations and empirical evidence. *Psychological Inquiry, 15*(1), 1–18. https://doi.org/10.1207/s15327965pli1501_01

Vaughan-Horrocks, H., Reagon, C., & Seymour, A. (2021). The experiences of veterans with mental health problems participating in an occupational therapy and resilience workshop intervention: An exploratory study. *British Journal of Occupational Therapy, 84*(9), 531–540. https://doi.org/10.1177/0308022620977818

Chapter 3
A Scholar Is Forged from Lived Experience to Evidence-Based Practice

3.1 Introduction—Entering the Forge

Enrolling in the Doctor of Health Science (DHSc) program was a deliberate academic decision. By the time I applied, I had spent years in personal recovery, built resilience through adversity, and confronted systemic challenges. Acceptance into Pennsylvania Western University's program marked a change in my identity. My shift went from just surviving to preparing to lead. From the start of the first course, I began viewing my experiences as data points, evidence to analyze, patterns to recognize, and lessons to learn. The program acted as a forge where my raw insights from the field were shaped into a structured framework capable of withstanding academic scrutiny. This transformation moved me from a practitioner guided by experience to a practitioner-scholar, influencing every area of my research and professional growth.

During one of the early pre-doctoral seminars, we were assigned James Allen's As a Man Thinketh, a book written in 1901 about how thought shapes action and circumstance. At first, I read it, wrote the reflection, and moved on. It didn't strike me as anything more than a motivational text. Later, when I was deep into building the BRAVE Framework, its meaning caught up with me. The idea that mastery of the mind comes before mastery of life echoed everything. I was learning about stress regulation, attention, and recovery. What started as a pre-doctoral assignment became a reminder that real change begins with how we think. That shift in understanding shaped how I approached my research, my teaching, and eventually the way BRAVE and Mindfully Tactical were designed to train both the body and the mind to work together.

T. Carlton, *BRAVE Theory*, https://doi.org/10.1007/978-3-032-13695-4_3

3.2 First Sparks—Discovering Tactical Military Athlete Research

The Evidence-Based Theory and Practice course marked a pivotal moment in my doctoral journey. At that point, my research goals were deeply rooted in my professional background. I intended to study ACL injuries in hockey players, a subject I was very familiar with from years in athletic operations. It was safe, familiar, and ultimately uninspiring. The approach to evidence-based scholarship challenged me to look beyond what I already knew. The course's goal was to teach how to evaluate evidence quality, identify gaps in the literature, and connect research to populations and problems that matter.

Almost immediately, I started reevaluating my direction. Instead of concentrating on a narrow, sport-specific injury, I broadened my focus to tactical athlete wellness. Then I narrowed it again to tactical military athletes. This decision was both personal and strategic. The literature was fragmented: physical conditioning studies were separate from nutrition research, occupational health findings seldom linked to psychological outcomes, and few sources combined these areas into a unified approach for military-to-civilian transition. This gap was an opportunity.

The result was "The Lasting Effects of Tactical Military Demands on Health and Transition." This paper became my first applied evidence base for the physical and psychological aspects of the BRAVE model. The research explained how the operational environment places ongoing stress on tactical military athletes: musculoskeletal strain from carrying heavy loads and repetitive high-impact movements (Abt et al., 2010; Cameron et al., 2016), environmental extremes requiring careful acclimatization protocols (Farina et al., 2017), and sleep deprivation that hampers decision-making, recovery, and metabolic health (Almeida et al., 2021). Nutritional deficits are often severe during deployment, combined with lower diet quality and micronutrient shortages, further worsened by post-service health risks (Farina et al., 2017). The paper also highlighted mental health stress as both a result and a factor affecting performance, with social support emerging as a key mediator for resilience (Balcan, 2023; Flood & Keegan, 2022).

Equally important, the project highlighted solutions such as structured strength and conditioning programs, gender-specific injury prevention, environmental hydration and acclimatization strategies, targeted nutritional supplements, and intentional sleep-hygiene practices. This was my first realization that a reintegration framework could not be purely theoretical; it had to be grounded in the physiological, environmental, and cognitive realities of the populations it aimed to serve.

The next course, Health Promotion and Wellness for the Individual, provided the missing conceptual foundation for my tactical research. Here, I authored Evolutionary Wellness in a Mismatched Disease Culture. This paper introduced me to two frameworks that would become fundamental to BRAVE Theory: The Wellness Wheel and Mismatched Disease Theory. The Wellness Wheel, covering emotional, environmental, financial, intellectual, physical, social, spiritual, and occupational aspects, offers a model of interconnected health. Kwon's (2015) randomized controlled trial showed that wellness wheel counseling improved lifestyle habits and reduced depressive symptoms. Strout and Howard (2012) linked high scores across multiple wellness dimensions with protective cognitive effects in older adults. My practical experience confirmed what I had seen in the field: neglecting one wellness area often causes a decline in others, whether in a combat zone or during civilian life reintegration.

Mismatched Disease Theory frames modern chronic disease as the product of an evolutionary disconnect between human biology and today's environment (Corbett et al., 2018; Gurven & Lieberman, 2020). Tactical athletes operate in ways that align with ancestral demands during service, but post-discharge sedentary lifestyles can rapidly accelerate mismatch-related health decline. Recognizing this pattern, the World Health Organization (2022) reported that targeted interventions focused on nutrition, exercise, sleep, and stress regulation can mitigate these effects when adapted to the cultural and operational realities of veteran populations.

These two courses sparked the fire that shaped my research identity. The first course taught me about the operational demands and practical realities of tactical military service, and the second gave me the multidimensional and changing frameworks to understand why those realities matter for long-term health. This pairing set the foundation for everything that followed. BRAVE was this abstract idea emerging as the blueprint for a reintegration model connecting evidence with lived experiences.

3.3 Designing Holistic Wellness Programs

If the first two courses in the DHSc program sparked my interest, Community and Corporate Wellness is where those sparks turned into a flame. The assignment seemed simple in creating a wellness program suitable for a community or corporate setting. Most classmates chose workplace fitness initiatives, employee health campaigns, or typical wellness challenges. I saw something different, which was an opportunity to apply what I was learning about tactical athlete wellness and turn it into a practical, real-world project program.

The model I developed for this course wasn't yet called the Mindfully Tactical Foundation, but its core principles were already there. I envisioned a program that didn't separate physical training from mental resilience or nutrition from community reintegration, but instead viewed them as mutually reinforcing elements. This was the first time I truly believed that the wellness of tactical populations must be integrated, adaptable, and culturally relevant.

The literature reinforced my instincts. Studies on corporate wellness programs showed that integrated approaches that combine physical health, mental health, and organizational culture produced greater and more sustainable outcomes than siloed interventions (Baicker et al., 2010; Goetzel et al., 2019). Research from the military domain echoed this, demonstrating that physical readiness programs were most effective when combined with nutrition education, mental skills training, and environmental support (Nindl et al., 2018). Even outside tactical contexts, wellness models rooted in multiple domains of the Wellness Wheel demonstrated more substantial improvements in overall quality of life, particularly when programs emphasized self-efficacy and social connection (Kwon, 2015; Strout & Howard, 2012).

The course also prompted me to think about implementation and the realities of program delivery, buy-in, and sustainability. Community-based participatory research (CBPR) models became a key part of my thinking. CBPR stresses that communities receive programs and are active co-creators, shaping interventions to address their needs (Brush et al., 2020). For veterans, that principle meant designing a program that did not impose wellness from the outside but built it collaboratively, incorporating the voices of those who had experienced the realities of transition.

I designed the prototype program around three pillars: strength and conditioning, mindfulness training, and nutrition strategy. Each was evidence-based, adaptable, and selected for its potential to boost operational readiness in active duty and promote long-term health after service. The program also incorporated community connection as a formal element, recognizing that social isolation is one of the most consistent predictors of poor post-service outcomes (Balcan, 2023; Demers, 2011).

When I submitted the final project, I thought it would be a one-time assignment. I didn't realize it would become the foundation for a nonprofit. But in retrospect, Community and Corporate Wellness marked the moment when my research shifted from concept to prototype and from theory to an applied model. It was the first tangible blueprint of what would eventually grow into the Mindfully Tactical Foundation, a framework that fully takes shape in Chapter 4.

3.4 Foundations in Adult Learning

The Theories and Foundations of Adult Learning course was when I first saw myself as an educator. Until then, my work on tactical wellness focused on creating models and collecting evidence. In this course, my mindset shifted: How do you really teach this to adults in a lasting way?

Adult learning theory (andragogy) became my guide. Knowles (1978, 1984) argued that adult learners are self-directed, bring life experiences to the learning process, and are most engaged when content is immediately relevant to their goals. For veterans and tactical athletes, this rang true. Their buy-in comes when they see direct, practical application. That realization shaped every choice I made in the Mindfully Tactical course design.

I began with a core idea: mindfulness doesn't have to be gentle. It can be sharp-edged in tactical situations, serving as a tool for situational awareness, decision-making under stress, and recovery after intense performance. Research supported this new perspective. Studies have demonstrated that mindfulness-based interventions can enhance cognitive flexibility, lower physiological stress markers, and improve emotional regulation in military groups (Jha et al., 2010; Johnson et al., 2014). These benefits are even greater when combined with physical training and skill-based learning, boosting performance and long-term resilience (Haase et al., 2015).

I was pushed to go beyond content and think about delivery. That meant building the course on principles from experiential learning theory (Kolb et al., 2014), ensuring participants would hear about concepts, practice them, reflect on them, and apply them to real-world tactical scenarios, and embedding metacognitive strategies so learners could monitor their own mental states and performance over time (Schraw, 1998).

I designed Mindfully Tactical with progressive modules. Early sessions covered core skills like body awareness, breathing control, and self-monitoring under stress. Later modules added more advanced skills, combining physical drills with quick decision-making exercises or applying mindfulness techniques in simulated high-pressure situations. The curriculum also included peer discussions and after-action reviews, leveraging the military's feedback culture to improve learning retention.

The evidence-based guidance guided each decision. Research from the Department of Defense's Mindfulness-Based Mind Fitness Training (MMFT) program demonstrated that mindfulness training reduced working memory degradation under stress and improved attention regulation in military personnel (Stanley et al., 2011). Studies in tactical populations also showed that blended programs combining cognitive skills training with physical conditioning were more effective in sustaining performance under operational demands (Nindl et al., 2018).

By the time the course was complete, I realized something important: Mindfully Tactical was a classroom product and instruction philosophy. It fused my experience, the growing body of evidence on mindfulness and performance, and the adult learning principles that make skills transferable. The course design became a working example of how tactical education could be evidence-based and experience-driven, preparing learners to absorb and operationalize information in their own lives.

3.5 Learning Concepts for the Adult Learner

If the Theories and Foundations of Adult Learning course gave me the "why" behind how I wanted to teach, Learning Concepts for the Adult Learner gave me the "how." I took Mindfully Tactical from a conceptual framework to a fully developed undergraduate course. This required a complete pedagogical blueprint, from learning objectives and assessment strategies to week-by-week instructional design.

The first step was defining the course's purpose in measurable, evidence-based terms. Veterans and tactical athletes often thrive in structured environments, but in civilian education, they encounter more open-ended, self-directed formats. Drawing on Knowles' (1978, 1984) principles of andragogy and Brookfield's (2017) emphasis on critical reflection, I built the course to bridge that gap, offering enough structure to create security while leaving room for learner autonomy. In curriculum design, every objective had to be actionable. For example, instead of a vague aim like "students will understand mindfulness," the objective became: "Students will demonstrate the ability to implement two stress-regulation techniques in simulated high-pressure scenarios, as measured by heart rate variability and self-reported stress levels." This alignment with measurable outcomes reflected the backward design model described by Wiggins and McTighe (2005), ensuring every activity served a clear performance goal.

The content moved progressively from foundational skills to integrated application. Early modules introduced physiological awareness, breath regulation, and baseline performance tracking using wearable technology. These skills became the basis for applying mindfulness principles to tactical decision-making drills, where stress inoculation methods validated in resilience training literature (Meichenbaum, 2007) were layered into increasingly complex scenarios. Midway through the course, the emphasis shifted toward communication under pressure, combining situational awareness with verbal and non-verbal command presence strategies (Salmon et al., 2007). The course concluded with a capstone simulation requiring learners to navigate a high-pressure operational task while demonstrating both physical execution and mindful regulation, followed by structured peer and instructor debriefs.

Assessment strategies blended formative and summative measures. Learners maintained self-reflection journals, produced physiological data reports, and completed practical demonstrations. These methods aligned with evidence showing that self-monitoring and feedback loops enhance skill retention in adult learners (Fennelly-Atkinson et al., 2023). Peer evaluations mirrored the after-action review process familiar in military culture, reinforcing accountability and collaborative learning. Importantly, the course embedded cultural competence throughout. Research on veteran education consistently highlights the need to recognize military culture as both a strength and a potential barrier to learning (Dillard & Yu, 2018). Mindfully Tactical addressed this by incorporating case studies drawn from real operational contexts, creating immediate relevance while challenging learners to adapt their skills beyond the military frame.

By completing this course design, Mindfully Tactical became a scalable, replicable program that could be delivered in higher education or professional development settings. More than that, the process of building it deepened my understanding of instructional design itself. I was now designing learning experiences with the potential to shift how people think, act, and recover under pressure.

3.6 Curriculum and Course Design

The Learning Concepts for the Adult Learner course gave me the blueprint for Mindfully Tactical, and the Curriculum and Course Design course was where that blueprint became a fully operational structure. I moved beyond a single course outline into a complete curricular framework that could be implemented, evaluated, and sustained in an institutional setting. This became about engineering an educational product that could live in the real world.

The challenge was translating the philosophical and theoretical underpinnings of Mindfully Tactical into a format that would meet academic rigor, accreditation standards, and learner needs without losing the tactical authenticity that made it unique.

That meant working within backward design principles (Wiggins & McTighe, 2005) while embedding adult learning theory, experiential learning cycles (Kolb et al., 2014), and culturally responsive pedagogy. The course was broken into modular units, each with a clear performance objective, integrated assessment, and applied project component. Every learning outcome was tied directly to one or more dimensions of the BRAVE Framework, ensuring that physical, psychological, social, and economic considerations were not addressed in isolation.

One of the breakthroughs in this phase was the development of scenario-based learning modules. Rather than relying solely on classroom instruction or static case studies, learners engaged in live simulations drawn from composite veteran experiences. These scenarios integrated physical stressors such as load carriage or complex motor tasks, with decision-making under time constraints and emotional regulation challenges. The design reflected research showing that stress exposure training combined with reflective debriefing improves resilience and adaptive performance (Meichenbaum, 2007). In post-simulation debriefs, learners applied structured reflection models to identify what went well, where errors occurred, and how mindfulness and tactical preparation influenced outcomes.

Assessment strategies were refined for greater validity and practical use. Instead of depending on written exams or theoretical essays, the curriculum included skill demonstrations, reflective practice logs, and peer-reviewed leadership tasks. This comprehensive assessment method showed that performance-based measures are more effective at predicting skill transfer than just knowledge tests (Salas et al., 2017). It also made sure that learners actively applied concepts in ways that matched the demands of their operational or post-operational environments.

By the end of Curriculum and Course Design, Mindfully Tactical had grown into a comprehensive fully scaffolded program. It was designed for scalability and adaptability to various settings, such as universities, veteran transition programs, or even professional sports. The course now featured a complete syllabus, modular content outlines, an instructor's guide, and an evaluation framework for ongoing improvement. This process improved my skills as an educator and strengthened my identity as a curriculum designer capable of translating complex, multidimensional theories into structured learning experiences that work.

3.7 Research Methods in Exercise Science

By the time I took Research Methods in Exercise Science, I had designed courses, developed a curriculum, and immersed myself in tactical wellness theory. However, until then, most of my work was focused on programmatic aspects, such as how to teach, structure, and deliver. This course challenged me to adopt a new role of a disciplined investigator. It was here in this course that I started to see myself as a practitioner, educator, and subject matter expert whose work could stand up to academic scrutiny.

This course shifted my focus from conceptual understanding to developing methodological skills. I needed to master the mechanics of research design, sampling strategies, reliability, validity, and statistical analysis as essential tools for producing evidence that could influence practice. The emphasis was on aligning research questions with the most appropriate methodologies, which challenged me to refine my thinking. What had once been a general interest in "helping tactical athletes transition better" began to take shape as clearly defined problem statements and testable hypotheses.

For my major project, I conducted a review titled Integrated Mindfulness and Strength & Conditioning for Military Transition. The premise was: rather than treating physical training, mental skills, and social reintegration as separate interventions, what if they were combined into one coherent, multimodal program? I reviewed literature from both exercise science and psychology, noting how strength training could enhance neuroplasticity and stress resilience (Kraemer & Ratamess, 2005; Phillips & Schweisfurth, 2014), while mindfulness training improved attentional control, emotional regulation, and adaptive decision-making under stress (Jha et al., 2017; Kabat-Zinn, 2003). Yet, despite overlapping benefits, these modalities were rarely examined together in veteran reintegration contexts.

The review was designed as a mixed-methods approach: I analyzed quantitative data such as changes in VO_2 max, strength, heart rate variability, and perceived stress, while also synthesizing qualitative studies that captured lived experiences of transition. This approach reflected my growing belief that numbers alone could not tell the entire story; human narratives were equally essential in understanding the complexity of reintegration. I used aspects of grounded theory to illustrate how patterns might naturally emerge from qualitative data, while still maintaining the rigor of controlled physical performance testing in the quantitative research.

Writing this review was the first time I experienced what I would later call "concept-to-framework alignment," which involves taking a real problem, examining it with relevant evidence, and organizing it into a scholarly approach capable of generating new insights. It was also when I realized that my role as a researcher was to challenge, refine, and sometimes overturn those beliefs, considering the evidence.

Research Methods in Exercise Science was the intellectual link between the narrative and the evidence. It connected the personal motivations that drew me to the program with the academic discipline needed to produce reliable, actionable insights. The skills I developed here, critical evaluation, methodological alignment, and combining qualitative and quantitative methods, later became the foundation of both the BRAVE Framework and the empirical studies I had in mind for the future.

3.8 Research Methods in Exercise Science II

The transition from Research Methods in Exercise Science I to Research Methods in Exercise Science II marked where my research on veteran reintegration shifted from exploratory mapping to a more targeted focus. In the first course, my scoping review was broad, inclusive, and aimed to identify the scope of existing work across psychological, physical, social, and economic reintegration factors. That review provided a map of the terrain. In this second course, I needed to move from mapping to planning, distilling the most solid and relevant evidence into a body of work that could serve as the empirical foundation for the BRAVE Framework.

The shift in methodology was deliberate. Where the first scoping review cast a wide net, the second examination required a refined search strategy, developed in consultation with the PennWest library and guided by peer-reviewed methodological frameworks (Arksey & O'Malley, 2005; Peters et al., 2020). Search strings were rebuilt to target only peer-reviewed interventions, outcome evaluations, and longitudinal analyses directly addressing veteran reintegration. Databases including PubMed, PsycINFO, CINAHL, SPORTDiscus, and Web of Science were queried with structured Boolean combinations. Inclusion criteria tightened to focus on studies with clear methodological transparency, defined outcome measures, and populations relevant to military-to-civilian transition. Exclusion criteria eliminated studies with unclear veteran definitions, non-transferable military groups, or poor methodological quality.

From the initial pool of over 1500 titles and abstracts, only 141 studies met the final inclusion criteria. These were then systematically coded for domain (psychological, physical, social, economic), intervention type, outcome measure, study design, and OCEBM level of evidence. The process was labor-intensive, taking weeks of abstract screening, full-text reviews, and cross-referencing. Still, it ensured that what remained was relevant and defensible at the highest academic level standard.

The thematic synthesis from this evidence was notable for its consistency. In the psychological field, mindfulness-based interventions, cognitive-behavioral therapies, and meaning-centered frameworks showed measurable improvements in PTSD symptom reduction, emotional regulation, and posttraumatic growth (Kearney et al., 2021; Morland et al., 2020; Tedeschi et al., 2018). Physically, structured strength and conditioning programs, injury prevention, and tactical nutrition strategies consistently demonstrated their value in maintaining functional capacity and lowering chronic disease risk after service (Abt et al., 2010; Cameron et al., 2016). Socially, peer-led reintegration groups and community engagement programs regularly correlated with reduced isolation, better mental health outcomes, and increased employment stability (Demers, 2011; Balcan, 2023). Economically, supported employment models and financial literacy programs improved job placement, long-term retention, and career satisfaction (Bond et al., 2022; Karre et al., 2025).

At this stage, the evidence's depth and the connections' clarity changed. Patterns showed that these domains did not operate in isolation; they interacted continuously. A decline in physical health often worsens psychological distress, reducing social engagement and economic stability. Conversely, targeted improvements in one area (such as a structured exercise program) could generate upward momentum across others. This dynamic interdependence became the conceptual foundation of BRAVE's multidimensional design.

I developed a scoping review in Research Methods in Exercise Science I that mapped the breadth of available evidence on veteran reintegration and resilience-based interventions. That review later became the foundation for my published Evidence Integration Review (EIR), advancing the work from exploration to synthesis in Research Methods in Exercise Science II Completing these courses changed how I understood research and my place in it. I was no longer satisfied with only reading what others had done. I wanted to shape how evidence was gathered, interpreted, and applied in real-world contexts. The EIR became a cornerstone of that process. It informed my later publications and guided program design for veterans navigating the challenges of transition and identity reconstruction.

By the end of this second research methods course, what began as a scattered set of ideas had become a coherent, evidence-based model. The scoping review revealed what existed, and the integration review clarified what mattered most, what was effective, and how those findings could be used to build practical support systems. BRAVE was a concept becoming a structured framework with scientific grounding and operational depth that stood independently in academic and applied settings.

3.9 Leadership in Wellness Education and Professional Practice

When I entered Leadership in Wellness Education and Professional Practice, my identity as a practitioner-scholar began taking shape. I had spent the earlier part of the DHSc developing research and educational programs. Still, this course would shift my focus inward, onto the leader I was, the leader I wanted to become, and the leader my work required me to be. It was less about building programs and more about developing the person capable of leading them. This meant confronting both the philosophical foundations of my leadership and the practical skills needed to guide others in the high-stakes environments I serve.

The course began with developing my personal leadership purpose and philosophy statement, which became a guiding point for the rest of my doctoral work. In it, I articulated a purpose rooted in service and aimed to empower tactical populations, veterans, military personnel, and high-performance professionals to regain autonomy and excel in all areas of well-being. My leadership philosophy was based on transformational leadership theory (Bass, 2015), emphasizing inspiring a shared vision. Still, it also incorporated elements of servant leadership (Greenleaf, 1970), focusing on the growth, resilience, and empowerment of those I lead. These approaches were not in conflict; instead, they combined into a leadership style that was mission-driven yet people-focused, blending military decisiveness with the empathy needed for long-term wellness outcomes.

Authentic leadership theory (Avolio & Gardner, 2005) has become a guiding perspective. Through the True North and Authentic Leadership project, I mapped the crucibles that had shaped me, combat deployments, personal injury, loss, and reintegration challenges, against the five dimensions of authentic leadership: purpose, values, relationships, self-discipline, and heart. This was a deliberate alignment of lived experience with leadership practice. Research on authentic leadership emphasizes that self-awareness and relational transparency are predictive of follower trust and engagement (Walumbwa et al., 2008). In tactical wellness, trust is the currency that makes every program possible.

My Strengths Discovery process further grounded this self-examination in evidence. Using the CliftonStrengths framework, I identified top strengths reflecting my military and academic growth: strategic thinking, relator, achiever, learner, and responsibility. Strengths-based leadership literature (Rath & Conchie, 2008; Wang et al., 2023) reinforced that effective leaders don't aim to be well-rounded in every skill; instead, they build teams that collectively balance strengths while staying true to their natural talents. This meant leveraging my strategic thinking to chart the vision for programs like the WELL and PATH Initiatives, while relying on collaborators to refine operational details or manage high-volume outreach.

The course wasn't all introspective-based. The EXSC 8300 capstone project required applying leadership theory to real-world wellness practice. I examined the leadership strategies behind veteran-focused reintegration initiatives, drawing from my foundation's work and external models. The analysis incorporated concepts of emotional intelligence (Culver, 1998; Goleman, 2011), emphasizing how self-regulation and empathy serve as force multipliers in high-stress organizational settings. Emotional intelligence research consistently links these skills to improved team performance, conflict resolution, and innovation (Mayer et al., 2008), and in wellness education, these are essential for maintaining engagement over time.

Conflict resolution and consensus-building also became essential skills. Drawing from intercultural competence theory (Deardorff, 2006), I assessed how wellness leaders must navigate diverse cultural identities, especially in veteran communities where military subcultures, service branches, and personal experiences shape expectations. In practice, this involved designing communication strategies that acknowledged differences while bringing stakeholders together around shared goals, an approach supported by research showing that culturally competent leadership enhances program adherence and satisfaction (Betancourt et al., 2005).

By the end of the course, my leadership philosophy was an operational framework. I understood my strengths and limitations, had tested my leadership style in applied contexts, and had anchored my approach in peer-reviewed evidence. More importantly, I recognized that leadership in wellness education is not about commanding from the front or serving from behind but walking alongside others, creating systems where resilience can be built, tested, and sustained. This balance between vision and empathy, decisiveness and collaboration, would become the hallmark of my leadership in the following projects.

3.10 Values, Ethics, and the Promotion of Health and Wellness

In the Doctor of Health Science program, EXSC 8350 Values, Ethics, and the Promotion of Health and Wellness acted as a lens that allowed me to reevaluate my professional identity, decision-making processes, and the ethical principles I carried from the military into my civilian and academic life. Essentially, the course pushed me to examine my moral framework while providing structured models, such as Linda Fisher Thornton's 7 Lenses of Ethical Responsibility, for applying ethical principles across personal, organizational, and societal levels.

The fusion of introspection and application made this course so impactful, like the Leadership in Wellness Education and Professional Practice course. The curriculum moved beyond abstract theory, requiring sustained journaling over multiple modules to reflect on evolving insights. In these entries, I confronted foundational questions: What does ethics mean to me? Where are my blind spots? How does my leadership style reflect, or fail to reflect, my stated values? This process aligned my core strengths: bravery, honesty, teamwork, hope, zest, curiosity, and my professional practice. Yet it also exposed gaps: moments when tactical decision-making could overshadow long-term ethical considerations and when loyalty to mission threatened to mute moral dissent.

The academic literature supported these self-assessments. For example, Sherwood's (2022) analysis of deception in business negotiations echoed my belief that dishonesty damages trust even when justified as strategic. Similarly, Fatima and Elbanna's (2023) work on corporate social responsibility emphasized that ethics cannot be reduced to compliance checklists; they must be integrated into organizational culture and daily actions. These principles were not just abstract ideas to me. They were directly reflected in my leadership experiences, from mentoring veterans through my foundation to guiding a professional hockey team's strength and nutrition program.

One of the key applications of the course was the Organizational Ethics and Compliance capstone project, where I assessed the Fayetteville Marksmen hockey organization I am a part of. Using structured interviews and policy analysis, I identified strengths such as role-specific training, a tiered disciplinary system, and strong community engagement, along with weaknesses like the lack of a dedicated ethics officer and formal ethics audits. My recommendations, including appointing an Ethics Liaison, conducting structured ethics audits, implementing anonymous reporting systems, and enhancing training with scenario-based exercises, were based on Farrell et al.'s (2022) best practices for ethical program design. This project connected theoretical ethics to practical operational challenges, showing that effective leadership requires moral clarity and practical action strategies.

Equally impactful was exploring ethical blind spots. In both the literature (Bazerman & Tenbrunsel, 2011) and my personal experience, I observed how structural pressures and reward systems can normalize questionable practices. I reflected on my time in Afghanistan, where strict adherence to the Rules of Engagement (ROE) sometimes conflicted with immediate operational safety. Throughout the course, I realized that these tensions reflected broader organizational dynamics: moments when "following the rules' substitutes meaningful engagement with the deeper moral question of what is right in this context. This integration of scholarship, reflection, and application transformed my understanding of ethical leadership in health and wellness. It is insufficient to "do no harm" or meet minimum compliance. An ethical leader must anticipate evolving challenges, whether from technological progress, changing cultural norms, or systemic inequalities, and proactively develop systems that promote fairness, transparency, and accountability. Furthermore, leadership in this field is just as much about modeling behavior as it is about establishing policy.

By the end of EXSC 8350, my ethical philosophy had evolved into a more multidimensional framework: a commitment to leading with integrity and service, holding myself and others accountable across all seven lenses, and integrating ethical considerations into every operational and strategic decision. This gave me an adaptable structure grounded in both evidence-based practice and personal conviction that continues to guide my work with veterans, athletes, and organizations striving to align their mission with the greater good.

3.11 Advanced Delivery Techniques and Technology

EXSC 8450, Advanced Delivery Techniques and Technology, was pivotal in my doctoral journey. Just as my scholarly identity shifted from conceptual designer to professional presenter and course developer, this course was almost entirely practical. Unlike previous classes that relied heavily on written assignments and literature synthesis, this class focused on using advanced instructional tools, digital platforms, and presentation technologies to improve learning outcomes and professional communication.

The first significant project was a complete overhaul of my professional portfolio website. My earlier version functioned as a repository that included a digital résumé with scattered work samples. By the midpoint of this course, I had transformed it into a curated, audience-focused platform that could serve academic committees, potential collaborators, and professional stakeholders. The redesign followed established digital communication guidelines, emphasizing clarity, accessibility, and strategic visual hierarchy (Clark & Lyons, 2010). The site now reflected my evolving professional brand, integrating narrative, research artifacts, and multimedia content into a coherent representation of my work.

A second key deliverable was the creation of my research poster for the program. This was an exercise in academic distillation to translate a multi-thousand-word scholarly manuscript into a concise, visually engaging presentation without sacrificing methodological integrity or interpretive nuance (Rowe & Ilic, 2009). The process reinforced an essential skill for a scholar-practitioner: the ability to communicate complex research to multiple audiences, from subject matter experts to community stakeholders.

The course also provided me with my own Brightspace account, allowing me to pilot the Mindfully Tactical course I had designed in earlier adult learning and curriculum development classes. Implementing the course at an undergraduate level was critical in moving it from theory to application. It allowed me to test the sequencing of modules, the clarity of assessment rubrics, and the functionality of interactive components. Feedback from learners confirmed which modules were most impactful and which needed refinement, insights I later used to adapt Mindfully Tactical into the first online offering on the MindfullyTactical.org website.

Beyond my own projects, the course immersed me in a wide range of educational technologies. I explored presentation tools like Prezi and Canva for visual storytelling, Screencast-O-Matic and Loom for asynchronous content delivery, and interactive polling platforms like Mentimeter for live engagement. I also experimented with adaptive learning systems and open educational resource (OER) platforms, evaluating their applicability to tactical athlete education. The literature supports the value of these tools when used intentionally; Mayer's (2020) multimedia learning theory emphasizes that effective instructional technology is not about novelty, but about aligning visual, auditory, and kinesthetic modes with clearly defined learning goals objectives.

By the conclusion of EXSC 8450, my professional presence and instructional capacity had expanded in parallel. The portfolio website became a polished, functional hub for my academic and applied work. The research poster demonstrated that I could communicate at scholarly and public-facing levels. The Mindfully Tactical course moved from a theoretical construct to a fully implemented learning experience. My understanding of educational technology has evolved from casual familiarity to strategic integration. This ensured that every platform, presentation style, and delivery method was intentionally chosen, grounded in pedagogy and evidence.

This course strengthened a skill set that has become essential: the ability to connect content expertise, instructional design, and technological fluency to develop learning experiences that are both academically rigorous and practically engaging. It focused on choosing the right tools for the right audience at the right time, a principle guiding my teaching, research dissemination, and professional growth outreach.

3.12 Evidence-Based Project Seminar: Building the BRAVE Framework

As I began the Evidence-Based Project Seminar (EXSC 8990), my doctoral journey had already enhanced my abilities in curriculum design, methodological accuracy, and applied program development. What I had not yet done, at least not at the scale needed for this course, was to integrate all aspects of my research into a single, comprehensive scholarly work that could stand alone in the academic literature. This course served as the bridge between years of preparation and the act of asserting my voice in the peer-reviewed space.

The assignment felt monumental in scope: conduct an evidence-based project worthy of scholarly submission. For me, there was no question what that would be. I would write the structured narrative review, building fragments since my first term, synthesizing the scattered, multidimensional evidence on veteran reintegration. The working title was Building Resilience and Advancing Veteran Empowerment (BRAVE): A Holistic Framework for Reintegration. I knew this would not be a typical literature review from the start. Too often, veteran reintegration research is fragmented, with separate studies on mental health, physical rehabilitation, social reintegration, or economic stability, but very few that weave these threads together. My goal was to create a framework grounded in evidence that could speak to the interconnectedness of these domains. This meant compiling findings, connecting the dots between them, pinpointing where interventions could work together, and suggesting a framework that captured the real-life complexity of transitioning from military to civilian life.

Methodologically, I followed established guidance for structured narrative reviews, drawing on elements from both Arksey and O'Malley's (2005) scoping framework and Popay et al.'s (2006) narrative synthesis approach. The search strategy was exhaustive, covering databases including PubMed, PsycINFO, SPORTDiscus, Web of Science, and CINAHL, and was designed to capture empirical studies across four domains: psychological, physical, social, and economic reintegration. Inclusion criteria required clear definitions of veteran populations, transparent methodology, and outcome measures relevant to post-service well-being. Out of an initial pool of thousands, 157 studies met the criteria for inclusion.

The findings reinforced what my experience had already suggested: veteran reintegration is not a straightforward process, nor does it revolve around a single area of need. For example, psychological health was profoundly affected by physical function, social support, and financial stability. Physical rehabilitation programs that overlooked mental health or social connections often failed to maintain progress. Economic stability efforts were more successful when combined with mentoring and community involvement. Patterns emerged that made it clear these areas are not separate silos but interconnected systems, with changes in one area affecting others.

In the psychological domain, the most consistently effective interventions included mindfulness-based programs, trauma-focused cognitive-behavioral therapies, and meaning-centered approaches that promoted posttraumatic growth (Kearney et al., 2021; Morland et al., 2020; Tedeschi et al., 2018). This not only reduced symptom severity but also improved self-efficacy and life satisfaction. In the physical domain, structured strength and conditioning programs, tactical injury prevention protocols, and targeted nutritional strategies demonstrated strong evidence for preserving function, reducing chronic disease risk, and enhancing quality of life after service (Abt et al., 2010; Cameron et al., 2016; Gonzalez et al., 2022).

The social domain revealed that peer-led groups, community-based participatory initiatives, and programs facilitating role identity reconstruction were critical in combating isolation and fostering belonging (Balcan, 2023; Demers, 2011). Finally, in the economic domain, supported employment models, targeted vocational training, and financial literacy interventions demonstrated significant benefits for job placement and long-term career satisfaction and retention (Bond et al., 2022; Karre et al., 2025).

From this synthesis emerged the BRAVE Framework, a model that positions the veteran as an active agent in their reintegration. This model is supported by coordinated, evidence-based interventions across all four domains. BRAVE emphasized adaptability, acknowledging that the optimal intervention mix changes over time and across individual contexts.

When I submitted Building Resilience and Advancing Veteran Empowerment (BRAVE) to the Journal of Veterans Studies in my third portfolio course, it marked my official entry into scholarly discussions on veteran reintegration. Although that manuscript was not accepted for peer review immediately, it had to wait six months because my Evidence Integration Review (EIR), which I adapted in Research Methods II and submitted during Portfolio II, was accepted for publication. That acceptance was a significant milestone: it was the first time my research identity felt fully developed, both as a student synthesizing others' work and as a scholar contributing something original to the field.

This shift also laid the foundation for the development of the BRAVE work. I reorganized the original framework paper into an official theory manuscript. I submitted it to the Journal of Military Social Work and Behavioral Health. Reflecting, EXSC 8990 was the course that combined all the ideas from earlier classes, like tactical wellness research, adult learning design, methodological rigor, and leadership philosophy into a single, focused concept. BRAVE was no longer just an emerging idea but a fully developed, evidence-based model ready to be tested, refined, and, most importantly, applied in real-world settings.

3.13 Portfolio I Defense

In the first portfolio defense course, I was no longer just participating in the Doctor of Health Science program. I was now shaping the kind of work that would define my career. The portfolio sequence replaced a traditional dissertation. It allowed me to integrate my research, leadership, and educator skills into artifacts that could stand independently as scholarly, applied, and sustainable contributions.

The scholarship artifact for this course, The Lasting Effects of Tactical Military Demands on Health and Transition, represented my first attempt to distill years of lived military experience, professional tactical athlete work, and academic inquiry into a single, evidence-driven synthesis. The central thesis was that tactical military athletes, defined as service members whose occupational duties require sustained high-level physical, cognitive, and environmental performance, face cumulative demands that shape their health long after the uniform comes off.

The literature review was intentionally multidisciplinary, pulling from strength and conditioning research (Abt et al., 2010; Kraemer & Ratamess, 2005), military occupational physiology (Cameron et al., 2016), environmental acclimatization science (Farina et al., 2017), nutritional epidemiology (Farina et al., 2017), and sleep research (Abanes et al., 2022). The evidence is consistent: years of heavy load carriage, repetitive high-impact movement, and heat/cold exposure degrade musculoskeletal integrity, cardiovascular efficiency, and metabolic health. Deployment diets, often calorically insufficient, nutrient-poor, and logistically inconsistent, further compound injury risk, immune suppression, and long-term disease susceptibility. Chronic sleep restriction, common in both training and deployment environments, undermines neurocognitive performance, impairs hormonal regulation, and accelerates mental fatigue (Almeida et al., 2021).

Just as important, the paper connected these physical realities to post-service reintegration. Veterans often transition into biologically mismatched environments to the high-output lifestyles of their service years (Gurven & Lieberman, 2020). The sudden shift from daily occupational physicality to sedentary civilian roles accelerates deconditioning and can exacerbate mental health conditions. Evidence supported a multimodal prescription: structured strength and conditioning programs, targeted nutritional supplementation, individualized injury prevention protocols, deliberate sleep hygiene, and integrated mental skills training. I argued that these were not "nice-to-have" wellness options but operational necessities for sustaining health and identity during and after military service.

While the scholarship artifact identified the demands and solutions at a system level, the leadership artifact, The LINK Initiative (Leadership, Integration, Networking, Knowledge), was my direct response to an evident gap: the absence of structured, peer-driven reintegration networks. LINK was designed to reflect what research repeatedly confirms: social support is one of the most powerful protective factors against post-service decline (Demers, 2011; Balcan, 2023). Instead of waiting for veterans to "find their tribe" after discharge, LINK proactively established it.

The initiative launched as a structured peer support model incorporating four pillars:

- **Leadership**—training veterans to take active roles in guiding their peers.
- **Integration**—facilitating deliberate connection to civilian systems and communities.
- **Networking**—linking veterans to career, education, and resource opportunities.
- **Knowledge**—providing vetted, evidence-based health, education, and financial stability information.

We piloted the program in partnership with local organizations, producing a comprehensive LINK Resource Guide, hosting peer sessions, and even incorporating community outreach through events like a local charity golf tournament. This was implementation science in real time. The guiding principles drawn from contemporary leadership literature, such as ethical transparency, respect, accountability, shared purpose, and ethical risk-taking, were put into practice to resolve conflicts, foster cohesion, and sustain engagement.

The teaching artifact for this portfolio, Mindfully Tactical: Resilience Beyond the Service, brought scholarship and leadership work into the public education space. It was designed as a podcast hosted on the Mindfully Tactical Foundation's website. It served two purposes: to share evidence-based resilience strategies in an accessible format for veterans and their families, and to model open, stigma-reducing conversations about post-service mental health. Drawing from the Department of Defense findings from the Mindfulness-Based Mind Fitness Training (MMFT) program (Stanley et al., 2011) and broader resilience literature, the episode with veteran guest TJ explored mindfulness as a tactical skill and a tool for stress regulation, decision-making, and posttraumatic growth. It connected seamlessly with the BRAVE Framework's psychological and social dimensions, providing real-world context to concepts that, until then, mainly existed in manuscripts and research outlines.

Together, these three artifacts aligned my academic training and professional goals. The research assessed the demands. The leadership initiative developed a structural solution. The teaching platform shared knowledge. Equally important, the process taught me that scholarship in health science isn't complete until it is both actionable and accessible. In Portfolio Defense I (EXSC 9150), I began to see how the different aspects of my work could be combined into a stronger, unified effort. This was the first defense in my portfolio sequence and the first time I could see the BRAVE Theory taking shape in both research and reality.

3.14 Portfolio Defense II

The second portfolio defense marked the point in my doctoral journey where my research transitioned from coursework and proposal drafts to standing in the arena of peer-reviewed scholarship, strategic leadership advocacy, and applied teaching in real veteran facing environments. Here, the theories, frameworks, and programs developed in the earlier stages of my Doctor of Health Science program faced the dual tests of academic rigor and real-world application impact.

The scholarship artifact for this defense was my Evidence Integration Review of Multimodal Interventions for PTSD, Social Reintegration, and Economic Stability in Veterans, accepted for publication in the Journal of Veterans Studies. It is built on the methodological discipline refined in Research Methods I and II. This review synthesized 41 high-quality studies from PsycINFO, MEDLINE, CINAHL, and Web of Science, including randomized controlled trials (RCTs), mixed-methods investigations, and qualitative analyses. It followed PRISMA principles, and the review focused on U.S.-based interventions that integrate psychological, physical, and social domains, mindfulness-based protocols, structured physical activity programs, peer mentorship models, and vocational readiness programs.

The evidence multimodal approaches consistently outperformed single-domain interventions in improving veteran well-being. Studies on mindfulness-based interventions, such as Mindfulness-Based Stress Reduction (MBSR) and Mindfulness-Based Cognitive Therapy (MBCT), showed significant reductions in PTSD symptoms, often exceeding 30% improvement on standardized measures like the Clinician-Administered PTSD Scale (CAPS-5) (Kearney et al., 2021; Polusny et al., 2015). When combined with trauma-focused therapies like Cognitive Processing Therapy (CPT) or Prolonged Exposure (PE), these programs had synergistic effects, speeding up symptom reduction and enhancing emotional regulation. Physical activity interventions including resistance training, yoga, and multimodal exercise programs were shown to decrease chronic pain (Oliveira et al., 2018), improve sleep efficiency (LeardMann et al., 2013), and preserve functional capacity essential for post-service work activities demands.

Social reintegration outcomes were most notable in studies utilizing structured peer support, especially when facilitators shared lived military experiences (Pietrzak et al., 2010; Sayer et al., 2011). These programs helped build trust, reduce perceived stigma, and increase engagement in treatment. Employment-focused interventions, particularly those combining skills transfer with targeted job placement assistance, showed improvements in both short-term employment rates and long-term career satisfaction (Burnett-Zeigler et al., 2011; Van Til et al., 2013). Importantly, veterans who participated in vocational rehabilitation alongside mental health support were more likely to maintain employment beyond the 12-month post-program period mark.

However, the review also uncovered systemic flaws. Across different interventions, dropout rates often surpassed 25%, with adherence issues frequently due to logistical barriers like transportation, appointment availability, and other life stressors. Female veterans and racial/ethnic minority groups were notably underrepresented, which limits the generalizability of findings and worsens disparities in-service access (Lehavot et al., 2018). Furthermore, the lack of longitudinal studies hindered understanding of how durable these interventions are, as most only tracked outcomes for three to six months after the intervention, with few studies extending that period year.

When the acceptance email from the Journal of Veterans Studies arrived, it marked a significant publication milestone and confirmed that my years of field experience, academic training, and evidence synthesis had made a meaningful contribution to the scholarly discourse on veteran reintegration. This achievement is now part of a broader conversation shaping policy, program development, and institutional practices.

While the scholarship artifact provided the empirical foundation, the leadership artifact operationalized its findings through the Warrior Empowerment, Lifestyle & Leadership (WELL) Program. WELL is designed as an institutional-level, evidence-based reintegration model that integrates mentorship, academic navigation, financial literacy, and structured social connection. During this portfolio cycle, I expanded two flagship initiatives under its umbrella: the LINK Initiative (Leadership, Integration, Networking, Knowledge) and the PATH Initiative (Preparing, Advancing, Transitioning Heroes).

The LINK Initiative formalized peer-to-peer mentorship networks by training volunteers in emotional intelligence, conflict resolution, and resource navigation. Evidence supporting peer-based approaches in military populations (Resnick & Rosenheck, 2008; Pfeiffer et al., 2011) directly shaped its framework. The PATH Initiative addressed a recurring finding in my review: the lack of structured benefit navigation and proactive academic planning hampers successful transition. By placing veteran advisors within university workflows, PATH ensured that service members did not face the complex processes of GI Bill, VR&E, and degree pathway decisions alone. This approach is supported by research that links early advising to improved retention and graduation rates among veteran students (Ford & Vignare, 2015). These initiatives were formally presented to Pennsylvania Western University leadership and the North Carolina Veterans Council for institutional and state-level review, marking a deliberate shift toward policy advocacy.

The teaching artifact, the Mindfully Tactical Pilot Course, served as the direct instructional embodiment of my scholarship, translating the evidence base from my Evidence Integration Review into a live learning environment. Originally developed during my coursework in Adult Learning Theory and Course Design, the curriculum was rooted in principles of andragogy (Knowles et al., 2015) and evidence-based instructional strategies. Building on my earlier design work, I refined the course into a three-week pilot version of the eight-week Mindfully Tactical program. I ensured that the core mindfulness-based stress regulation, strategic decision-making, and resilience-building modules were maintained while enabling rapid-cycle evaluation adaptation.

The pedagogical approach aligned with transformative learning theory (Mezirow, 1997) by encouraging veterans to reflect on their assumptions critically, reframe their post-service identity, and develop actionable strategies for civilian success. Each week, integrated experiential learning components, guided mindfulness practices, tactical decision-making simulations, and peer dialogue circles to reinforce retention and real-world relevance. The content was tailored explicitly for veteran learners, featuring military-specific language, operational scenarios, and pacing designed to promote engagement and psychological safety, an element strongly supported in the literature on culturally responsive pedagogy for military populations (Hunter-Johnson, 2018; Vacchi & Berger, 2014).

The pilot evaluation was iterative. Participants representing various service eras, occupational specialties, and levels of educational readiness gave structured feedback via weekly surveys and focus group discussions. Their insights led to improvements in the course, including creating an introductory video module to enhance onboarding, adjusting pacing to better balance content density with cognitive load, and streamlining the interface to improve digital accessibility. These changes aligned with best practices in instructional design for adult learners, which focus on adaptability, learner autonomy, and accessibility (Merriam & Bierema, 2013).

The alignment with the Department of Defense's Intrepid Spirit program further confirmed its clinical and transitional importance, placing it alongside nationally recognized efforts to support medically retiring service members. Combining evidence-based resilience training with a delivery model rooted in adult learning theory, the Mindfully Tactical Pilot Course showed that research-informed educational interventions could be academically rigorous and practically meaningful for the veteran community. Portfolio Defense II thus represented a complete research-to-practice cycle: thorough evidence synthesis, strategic leadership application, and direct teaching intervention. For me personally, it confirmed that the BRAVE Framework and WELL Program were functional, adaptable, evidence-based systems capable of producing measurable change in the lives of veterans. This was scholarship in the service of those it studied, and it became the standard by which I measured every project that followed.

3.15 Portfolio Defense III

When I reached the third portfolio defense, my work had developed from individual projects into a cohesive, theory-based ecosystem for veteran reintegration. This stage was characterized by the integration of academic rigor, practical systems design, and direct policy advocacy, culminating in three interconnected artifacts: the BRAVE Theory manuscript, the V.E.T.S. Toolkit, and the Own Your Next Mission workshop for Winnebago Industries' VetNet program. Together, these works demonstrated my doctoral learning and offered tangible, scalable solutions to long-standing gaps in veteran transition support.

The BRAVE Theory manuscript, submitted to Military Behavioral Health, consolidates a decade of lived experience and three years of doctoral research into a multi-dimensional framework for veteran reintegration. It was based on the foundational evidence summarized in my EXSC 8990 narrative review. BRAVE conceptualizes reintegration across psychological, physical, social, and economic domains, mediating factors such as identity reconstruction, cultural adaptation, and environmental safety. This theoretical expansion was deeply influenced by Social Identity Theory (Turner et al., 1979), Transformative Learning Theory (Mezirow, 1997), and the Biopsychosocial Model (Engel, 1977), as well as trauma-specific frameworks like Posttraumatic Growth Theory (Tedeschi & Calhoun, 2004).

Quantitative evidence strengthened the model's core assumptions: mindfulness-based interventions reduce PTSD severity by up to 30% in veteran populations (Kearney et al., 2021), peer mentorship decreases reintegration-related depressive symptoms (Hauser et al., 2025) and supported employment programs enhance job retention by 47% (Bond et al., 2022). Qualitative findings showed that veterans experience greater long-term stability when interventions address multiple areas simultaneously, a key difference of BRAVE from isolated service approaches. The theory was intentionally designed to function as both a research roadmap and a practical guide for policymakers, service organizations, and higher education institutions.

The Veterans' Vision, Education, Translation, and Strategy (V.E.T.S.) Toolkit operationalizes BRAVE. It was developed through the Mindfully Tactical Foundation's WELL and PATH Initiatives. This resource responds to a consistent finding in the literature: access to benefits is not synonymous with successful transition.

Demers (2011) highlight that many veterans underutilize or mismanage their GI Bill and VR&E benefits due to a lack of structured planning, misaligned educational pathways, or inadequate advising.

The Toolkit's Veteran Track and Advisor Track align with BRAVE's economic and social domains. Each step—Vision, Education, Translation, and Strategy—is rooted in evidence-based planning principles. For example, Step 3's skill translation process utilizes O*NET's military-to-civilian crosswalk data. It aligns with findings from Stone & Stone (2015), which show that veterans who receive structured skill translation support are 37% more likely to find employment in their target field within one year of separation. Step 4's stackable credentialing model is backed by Carnevale et al. (2020), whose longitudinal data indicate that layered certifications increase lifetime earnings potential by 15–25% over degree-only pathways. The Toolkit's mission planning worksheets, GI Bill navigation checklists, skill translation templates, and tactical academic planners transform the abstract concepts of "post-service planning" into concrete, actionable tasks. Its integration into advisor training programs offers a scalable model for standardizing veteran academic and career advising across institutions.

The Own Your Next Mission workshop, delivered to Winnebago Industries' VetNet network, proved valuable for translating BRAVE and the V.E.T.S. Toolkit into engaging, accessible instruction. The session was grounded in adult learning theory (Knowles, 1978) and trauma-informed pedagogy (US Department of Health and Human Services, 2014), demonstrating how veterans can strategically deploy GI Bill and VR&E benefits to accelerate economic stability and personal fulfillment.

The presentation's emphasis on credential stacking and non-traditional benefit applications, which range from commercial driver's licenses to cybersecurity bootcamps, was supported by empirical data showing that diversified credentials improve reemployment speed and job satisfaction (Harrell & Berglass, 2012). Attendees were introduced to the Toolkit's vision-mapping exercises, skill translation processes, and strategic planning templates, allowing them to leave with a personalized action plan rather than passive knowledge. Feedback indicated a 92% self-reported increase in confidence navigating education benefits, affirming both the instructional approach and the underlying resource design.

Collectively, these three artifacts in Portfolio Defense III illustrate the complete translational journey from theory (BRAVE) to system (V.E.T.S. Toolkit) to instruction (Own Your Next Mission). They represent the core of the doctoral portfolio pillars:

- **Scholarship**: BRAVE contributes a peer-reviewed theoretical framework backed by multidisciplinary evidence.
- **Leadership**: The V.E.T.S. Toolkit institutionalizes transition planning as a structured, replicable process.
- **Teaching**: Own Your Next Mission delivers applied strategies directly to the veteran learner.

This integration reflects what the literature consistently calls for but rarely achieves: a coordinated, multimodal reintegration strategy that is culturally competent, evidence-driven, and practically implementable. As echoed in my own research and that of Joseph et al. (2023), proper post-service stability is achieved through single-point interventions and sustained, interconnected support systems. By the conclusion of this portfolio defense Portfolio defense process, I was able to build frameworks, tools, and learning experiences that are rooted in academic credibility and proven in practical use. In this, the BRAVE Theory, V.E.T.S. Toolkit, and Own Your Next Mission workshop weren't separate achievements but interconnected parts of a larger mission to ensure that every veteran's "next mission" is as strategically prepared and successfully executed as they undertook in uniform.

3.16 Culminating Work: The Reintegration Equation

As I completed the DHSc, I had written dozens of papers, finished hundreds of pages of research synthesis, and defended my leadership, teaching, and scholarship artifacts. However, one paper stood out as my best work so far: the third comprehensive examination, "The Reintegration Equation: Mindfulness, Epigenetics, and Tactical Recovery in Post-Service Life." This review brought together years of lived experience, academic training, and scholarly focus on the complex reintegration needs of military veterans. It reflects where my practitioner's instincts and scholar's discipline intersect, creating a precision-based model for post-service recovery grounded in high-quality empirical evidence.

The paper started by emphasizing a recurring issue I've observed in my career and research: veteran reintegration is often treated as a fragmented process. It frequently isolates mental health, physical health, social connections, and career readiness, or ignores them altogether. This division does not reflect the reality of post-service life, where psychological trauma, biological stress responses, and environmental factors are always interconnected interaction.

Building on eight rigorous studies, including randomized controlled trials, meta-analyses, and longitudinal epigenetic research, this work developed three interconnected domains:

1. **Biological Susceptibility and Epigenetic Modifiability**—The review summarized evidence indicating that resilience is not fixed. Genetic and epigenetic differences can make some veterans more responsive to intervention, rather than less. Studies like van IJzendoorn & Bakermans-Kranenburg (2015) reframe "risk genotypes" as markers of plasticity, while Domschke et al. (2025) show that psychotherapy can change DNA methylation patterns associated with anxiety and trauma response. This section challenges deficit-focused thinking by illustrating that biological sensitivity can be a key point for recovery.
2. **Mindfulness-Based Interventions as Stress Modulators**—The second domain viewed mindfulness as a coping tool and a nervous system recalibration mechanism. Research from Joyce et al. (2019), Kearney et al. (2021), and Saban et al. (2022) showed that structured mindfulness programs can reduce PTSD symptoms, lower inflammatory biomarkers, and improve emotional regulation

in military and first responder populations. The biological and psychological findings aligned, supporting mindfulness as a precise intervention for tactical populations.

3. **Precision Reintegration Through Behavioral and Social Models**—The final focus was delivering interventions, highlighting programs like STEP-Home (Fortier et al., 2024) and Kahn et al.'s (2016) digital wellness platform. Both showed the importance of tailoring reintegration strategies to the veteran's context, whether through peer-supported group settings or self-paced, technology-assisted programs. These models reinforced a recurring theme in my work: reintegration must be evidence-based and culturally competent, respecting autonomy and operational identity.

The proposed synthesis suggests that post-service recovery should be seen as a biopsychosocial balance, where factors such as biological readiness, mind-body regulation, and environmental support are customized to encourage lasting well-being. It recommends shifting from generic reintegration models to personalized approaches that take into account each veteran's individual profile and abilities change.

To me, the Reintegration Equation connected my past experiences and future endeavors by confirming with peer-reviewed proof the concepts I had been applying informally in the WELL Program and the BRAVE Framework:

- That resilience is trainable.
- That biology is not destiny.
- That culturally competent, precision-based approaches can accelerate recovery and purpose reconstruction.

More importantly, it provides a scholarly platform to promote the integrative, adaptable veteran care I wished for and often couldn't find during my transition.

Looking forward, the insights from this paper will continue to guide my research focus, from validating tools like the Transitional Resilience Index (TRI) to developing mindfulness-based interventions for tactical groups. Just as this chapter documented my journey from practitioner to scholar, the Reintegration Equation demonstrates that lived experience can influence the future of evidence-based practice when shaped through careful inquiry.

Academic Synthesis

This chapter explored the transformation from practitioner to scholar through my intentional pursuit of doctoral education, demonstrating how lived experience can be converted into structured, evidence-based practice. The narrative illustrated the adaptive challenge of transitioning from a high-intensity, operational military role to the reflective and methodologically rigorous demands of academia, aligning with Mezirow's (1997) transformative learning theory, in which critical self-reflection enables a redefinition of identity and purpose.

The sense of "otherness" described in early academic experiences is consistent with the literature on cultural incongruence between veterans and traditional educational environments, where divergent norms, communication styles, and identity salience can heighten social disconnection (McCormick et al., 2019; Dolan et al., 2022). Small academic wins functioned as incremental mastery experiences, reinforcing self-efficacy in line with Bandura's (1977) social cognitive theory and empirical findings on the role of self-efficacy in academic persistence among non-traditional students.

The inclusion of "As a Man Thinketh" as a foundational text exemplifies the use of metacognitive reframing, an approach supported by research on cognitive-behavioral mechanisms in goal achievement and resilience building (Joyce et al., 2019). This aligns with andragogical principles (Knowles, 1978), where self-directed learners engage most deeply with material that has immediate relevance to their goals and lived experiences context.

The forging of the BRAVE Framework from both experiential and empirical foundations illustrates praxis by integrating theory and practice within a cyclical feedback loop (Freire, 1970) and reflects best practices in culturally responsive pedagogy, which emphasizes validating learners' prior knowledge and lived realities as assets in the learning process (Darling-Hammond et al., 2015; Gay, 2018). The operational testing of BRAVE through the WELL Program provided an applied research environment consistent with design-based implementation research models, which advocate iterative adaptation of interventions within real-world contexts (Penuel et al., 2011).

The emotional impact of BRAVE's acceptance into scholarly discourse reinforces the literature on meaning-making and posttraumatic growth in veterans, where the reframing of personal hardship into contributions that benefit others serves as both a coping mechanism and a driver of continued engagement (Haque et al., 2023; Tedeschi & Calhoun, 2004). In this way, scholarly validation functioned as a professional achievement and an affirmation of the enduring value of military-acquired skills and experiences in civilian domains.

In synthesis, Chap.3 advanced the understanding that veteran–scholars navigate a dual transformation: mastering the epistemological shift from practitioner knowledge to evidence-based scholarship and reframing their identity within a community that often lacks cultural congruence with military norms. This process is facilitated by incremental self-efficacy gains, culturally responsive learning environments, and opportunities to operationalize research in practice settings. The trajectory from feeling out of place in the academic arena to leading evidence-based initiatives such as BRAVE exemplifies how the fusion of lived experience and scholarly rigor can yield interventions with both empirical validity and cultural authenticity.

Key Takeaways

- **Academic transition requires dual adaptation**—Moving from practitioner to scholar demands mastering new epistemological frameworks while navigating cultural incongruence between military norms and academic environments, which can heighten feelings of otherness (McCormick et al., 2019; Dolan et al., 2022).
- **Incremental mastery experiences reinforce persistence**—Small academic wins serve as critical self-efficacy boosters, building resilience and sustaining engagement in challenging learning environments (Bandura, 1977).

- **Metacognitive reframing supports transformative learning**—Exposure to reflective texts such as As a Man Thinketh can catalyze mindset shifts, aligning with evidence on cognitive-behavioral strategies for goal attainment and identity reconstruction (Joyce et al., 2019; Mezirow, 1997).
- **Adult learning principles enhance veteran education**—Andragogical models emphasize leveraging prior experience, self-direction, and immediate application, which align with effective instructional design for veteran learners (Knowles, 1978; Gay, 2018).
- **Praxis strengthens theoretical models**—Developing the BRAVE Framework through lived experience and empirical research reflects the iterative integration of theory and practice advocated in culturally responsive pedagogy (Freire, 1970; Darling-Hammond, 2015).
- **Real-world program implementation validates research**—Testing BRAVE in the WELL Program aligns with design-based implementation research, which uses iterative refinement to improve relevance and effectiveness (Penuel et al., 2011).
- **Scholarly recognition can drive meaning-making**—Acceptance of veteran-driven frameworks into academic discourse supports posttraumatic growth and reinforces the value of military-acquired skills in civilian contexts (Tedeschi & Calhoun, 2004; Haque et al., 2023).

Applied Learning Prompts

1. Select one of your own professional experiences or observed challenges. Map the steps you would take to convert it into an evidence-based framework, including literature review, methodological design, and application.
2. Using the multidomain approach from the BRAVE Framework, outline a wellness program that addresses at least three dimensions (physical, psychological, social, and economic). Include measurable outcomes for each dimension.
3. Choose a topic you teach or would like to teach. Apply Knowles' andragogical principles and Kolb's experiential learning cycle to design a culturally relevant lesson for your target learners.
4. Review a recent peer-reviewed article in your field. Identify how its findings could be translated into a leadership initiative, teaching tool, or policy advocacy effort, similar to how BRAVE was operationalized through the WELL Program.

References

Abanes, J. J., Ridner, S. H., Dietrich, M. S., Hiers, C., & Rhoten, B. (2022). Acupuncture for sleep disturbances in post-deployment military service members: A randomized controlled trial. *Clinical Nursing Research, 31*(2), 239–250. https://doi.org/10.1177/10547738211030602

Abt, J. P., Sell, T. C., Crawford, K., Lovalekar, M., Nagai, T., DeLuzio, J., Smalley, B. W., McGrail, M. A., Rowe, R. S., Cardin, S., & Lephart, S. M. (2010). Warrior model for human performance and injury prevention: Eagle tactical athlete program (ETAP) part II. *Journal of Special Operations Medicine: A Peer Reviewed Journal for SOF Medical Professionals, 10*(4), 22–33. https://doi.org/10.55460/42ci-elhp

Almeida, M. F., Piehler, T., Carstens, K. E., Zhao, M., Samadi, M., Dudek, S. M., Norton, C. J., Parisian, C. M., Farizatto, K. L. G., & Bahr, B. A. (2021). Distinct and dementia-related synaptopathy in the hippocampus after military blast exposures. *Brain Pathology, 31*(3), e12936. https://doi.org/10.1111/bpa.12936

Arksey, H., & O'Malley, L. (2005). Scoping studies: Towards a methodological framework. *International Journal of Social Research Methodology, 8*(1), 19–32. https://doi.org/10.1080/1364557032000119616

Avolio, B. J., & Gardner, W. L. (2005). Authentic leadership development: Getting to the root of positive forms of leadership. *The Leadership Quarterly, 16*(3), 315–338. https://doi.org/10.1016/j.leaqua.2005.03.001

Baicker, K., Cutler, D., & Song, Z. (2010). Workplace wellness programs can generate savings. *Health Affairs, 29*(2), 304–311. https://doi.org/10.1377/hlthaff.2009.0626

Balcan, A.-D. (2023). The mediating role of social support in the relationship between operational stress and Well-being in military personnel. *BRAIN: Broad Research in Artificial Intelligence and Neuroscience, 14*(1), 105–116. https://doi.org/10.18662/brain/14.1/409

Bandura, A. (1977). Self-efficacy: Toward a unifying theory of behavioral change. *Psychological Review, 84*(2), 191–215. https://doi.org/10.1037/0033-295X.84.2.191

Bass, B. (2015). Transformational leadership theory. In *Organizational behavior 1* (pp. 361–385). Routledge.

Bazerman, M. H., & Tenbrunsel, A. E. (2011). *Blind spots: Why we fail to do whats right and what to do about it*. Princeton University Press. https://doi.org/10.1515/9781400837991

Betancourt, J. R., Green, A. R., Carrillo, J. E., & Park, E. R. (2005). Cultural competence and health care disparities: Key perspectives and trends. *Health Affairs, 24*(2), 499–505. https://doi.org/10.1377/hlthaff.24.2.499

Bond, G. R., Al-Abdulmunem, M., Ressler, D. R., Gade, D. M., & Drake, R. E. (2022). A randomized controlled trial of an employment program for veterans transitioning from the military: Two-year outcomes. *Administration and Policy in Mental Health and Mental Health Services Research, 49*(6), 1072–1083. https://doi.org/10.1007/s10488-022-01208-z

Brookfield, S. D. (2017). *Becoming a critically reflective teacher*. John Wiley & Sons.

Brush, B. L., Mentz, G., Jensen, M., Jacobs, B., Saylor, K. M., Rowe, Z., Israel, B. A., & Lachance, L. (2020). Success in long-standing community-based participatory research (CBPR) partnerships: A scoping literature review. *Health Education & Behavior, 47*(4), 556–568. https://doi.org/10.1177/1090198119882989

Burnett-Zeigler, I., Valenstein, M., Ilgen, M., Blow, A. J., Gorman, L. A., & Zivin, K. (2011). Civilian employment among recently returning Afghanistan and Iraq National Guard veterans. *Military Medicine, 176*(6), 639. https://doi.org/10.7205/MILMED-D-10-00450

Cameron, K. L., Driban, J. B., & Svoboda, S. J. (2016). Osteoarthritis and the tactical athlete: A systematic review. *Journal of Athletic Training, 51*(11), 952–961. https://doi.org/10.4085/1062-6050-51.5.03

Carnevale, A. P., Garcia, T. I., Ridley, N., & Quinn, M. C. (2020). *The overlooked value of certificates and associates degrees: What students need to know before they go to college*. Georgetown University Center on Education and the Workforce.

Clark, R. C., & Lyons, C. (2010). *Graphics for learning: Proven guidelines for planning, designing, and evaluating visuals in training materials*. John Wiley & Sons.

Corbett, S., Courtiol, A., Lummaa, V., Moorad, J., & Stearns, S. (2018). The transition to modernity and chronic disease: Mismatch and natural selection. *Nature Reviews Genetics, 19*(7), 419–430. https://doi.org/10.1038/s41576-018-0012-3

Culver, D. (1998, November 4–7). A review of *Emotional Intelligence* by Daniel Goleman: Implications for technical education. In *FIE'98: 28th Annual Frontiers in Education Conference:*

Moving from Teacher-Centered to Learner-Centered Education (Conference proceedings). IEEE.

Darling-Hammond, L., Barron, B., Pearson, P. D., Schoenfeld, A. H., Stage, E. K., Zimmerman, T. D., Cervetti, G. N., & Tilson, J. L. (2015). *Powerful learning: What we know about teaching for understanding*. John Wiley & Sons.

Deardorff, D. K. (2006). Identification and assessment of intercultural competence as a student outcome of internationalization. *Journal of Studies in International Education, 10*(3), 241–266. https://doi.org/10.1177/1028315306287002

Demers, A. (2011). When veterans return: The role of community in reintegration. *Journal of Loss and Trauma, 16*(2), 160–179. https://doi.org/10.1080/15325024.2010.519281

Dillard, R. J., & Yu, H. H. (2018). Best practices in student veteran education: Faculty professional development and student veteran success. *The Journal of Continuing Higher Education, 66*(2), 122–128. https://doi.org/10.1080/07377363.2018.1469072

Dolan, G., McCauley, M., & Murphy, D. (2022). Factors influencing the salience of military/veteran identity post discharge: A scoping review. *Journal of Veterans Studies, 8*(1), 1–19. https://doi.org/10.21061/jvs.v8i1.333

Domschke, K., Schiele, M. A., Crespo Salvador, Ó., Zillich, L., Lipovsek, J., Pittig, A., Heinig, I., Ridderbusch, I. C., Straube, B., Richter, J., Hollandt, M., Plag, J., Fydrich, T., Koelkebeck, K., Weber, H., Lueken, U., Dannlowski, U., Margraf, J., Schneider, S., & Deckert, J. (2025). Epigenetic markers of disease risk and psychotherapy response in anxiety disorders: A longitudinal analysis of the DNA methylome. *Molecular Psychiatry*. https://doi.org/10.1038/s41380-025-03038-5

Engel, G. L. (1977). The need for a new medical model: A challenge for biomedicine. *Science, 196*(4286), 129–136. https://doi.org/10.1126/science.847460

Farina, E. K., Taylor, J. C., Means, G. E., Murphy, N. E., Pasiakos, S. M., Lieberman, H. R., & McClung, J. P. (2017). Effects of deployment on diet quality and nutritional status markers of elite U.S. Army special operations forces soldiers. *Nutrition Journal, 16*, 41. https://doi.org/10.1186/s12937-017-0262-5

Farrell, C., Hatcher, W., & Diamond, J. (2022). Reflecting on over 100 years of public administration education. *Public Administration, 100*(1), 116–128. https://doi.org/10.1111/padm.12808

Fatima, T., & Elbanna, S. (2023). Corporate social responsibility (CSR) implementation: A review and a research agenda towards an integrative framework. *Journal of Business Ethics, 183*(1), 105–121. https://doi.org/10.1007/s10551-022-05047-8

Fennelly-Atkinson, R., Teague, C. L., & Doggett, J. (2023). Closing the professional learning loop: Designing for performance improvement. In B. Hokanson, M. Schmidt, M. E. Exter, A. A. Tawfik, & Y. Earnshaw (Eds.), *Formative design in learning: Design thinking, growth mindset and community* (pp. 33–48). Springer Nature Switzerland. https://doi.org/10.1007/978-3-031-41950-8_4

Flood, A., & Keegan, R. J. (2022). Cognitive resilience to psychological stress in military personnel. *Frontiers in Psychology, 13*, 809003. https://doi.org/10.3389/fpsyg.2022.809003

Fortier, C. B., Kenna, A., Katz, D., Kim, S., Hursh, C., Beck, B., Sablone, C. A., Currao, A., Lebas, A., Jorge, R. E., & Fonda, J. R. (2024). Step-Home Transdiagnostic Group Reintegration Workshop to Improve Mental Health Outcomes for Post-9/11 Veterans: Design, Methods, and Rationale for a Randomized Controlled Behavioral Trial.*Contemporary Clinical Trials, 141*, 107536. https://doi.org/10.1016/j.cct.2024.107536

Ford, K., & Vignare, K. (2015). The evolving military learner population: A review of the literature. *Online Learning, 19*(1), 7–30.

Freire, P. (1970). The adult literacy process as cultural action for freedom. *Harvard Educational Review, 40*(2), 205–225.

Gay, G. (2018). *Culturally responsive teaching: Theory, research, and practice* (3rd ed.). Teachers College Press.

Germer, C. K., & Neff, K. (2018). Cultivating self-compassion. *Mindfulness-oriented interventions for trauma: Integrating contemplative practices*, 43–58.

Goleman, D. (2011). *Leadership: The power of emotional intelligence*. More Than Sound.

Goetzel, R. Z., Fabius, R., Roemer, E. C., Kent, K. B., Berko, J., Head, M. A., & Henke, R. M. (2019). The Stock Performance of American Companies Investing in a Culture of Health. *American Journal of Health Promotion, 33*(3), 439–447. https://doi.org/10.1177/0890117118824818

Gonzalez, D. E., McAllister, M. J., Waldman, H. S., Ferrando, A. A., Joyce, J., Barringer, N. D., Dawes, J. J., Kieffer, A. J., Harvey, T., Kerksick, C. M., Stout, J. R., Ziegenfuss, T. N., Zapp, A., Tartar, J. L., Heileson, J. L., Van Dusseldorp, T. A., Kalman, D. S., Campbell, B. I., Antonio, J., & Kreider, R. B. (2022). International Society of Sports Nutrition position stand: Tactical athlete nutrition. *Journal of the International Society of Sports Nutrition, 19*(1), 267–315. https://doi.org/10.1080/15502783.2022.2086017

Greenleaf, R. K. (1970). *The servant as leader*. Greenleaf Center.

Gurven, M. D., & Lieberman, D. E. (2020). WEIRD bodies: Mismatch, medicine and missing diversity. *Evolution and Human Behavior, 41*(5), 330–340. https://doi.org/10.1016/j.evolhumbehav.2020.04.001

Haase, L., May, A. C., Falahpour, M., Isakovic, S., Simmons, A. N., Hickman, S. D., Liu, T. T., & Paulus, M. P. (2015). A pilot study investigating changes in neural processing after mindfulness training in elite athletes. *Frontiers in Behavioral Neuroscience, 9*, 229. https://doi.org/10.3389/fnbeh.2015.00229

Haque, M. R., Franco, Z., Hossain, M. F., Frydrychowicz, W., Madiraju, P., Baker, N. D., Hooyer, K., Ahamed, S. I., Winstead, O., Curry, R., & Rubya, S. (2023). Perceptions of mental health crisis among U.S. military veteran peer mentors and potential of mobile-based peer-support interventions. *Companion Publication of the 2023 Conference on Computer Supported Cooperative Work and Social Computing*. doi:https://doi.org/10.1145/3584931.3607009.

Harrell, M. C., & Berglass, N. (2012). *Employing Americas veterans*. Center for a New American Security.

Hauser, D., McConnell, C., Lawson, K., Kobe, S., Oakley, R., Harrison, I., Smithey, C., & Yarborough, A. (2025). Community reintegration of veterans after discharge: A qualitative look. *American Journal of Qualitative Research, 9*(3), 61–81. https://doi.org/10.29333/ajqr/16535

Jha, A. P., Morrison, A. B., Parker, S. C., & Stanley, E. A. (2017). Practice is protective: Mindfulness training promotes cognitive resilience in high-stress cohorts. *Mindfulness, 8*(1), 46–58. https://doi.org/10.1007/s12671-015-0465-9

John D. Mayer, Richard D. Roberts, Sigal G. Barsade. 2008. Human Abilities: Emotional Intelligence. *Annual Review Psychology. 59*:507–536. https://doi.org/10.1146/annurev.psych.59.103006.09364

Jha, A. P., Stanley, E. A., Kiyonaga, A., Wong, L., & Gelfand, L. (2010). Examining the protective effects of mindfulness training on working memory capacity and affective experience. *Emotion, 10*(1), 54–64. https://doi.org/10.1037/a0018438

Johnson, D. C., Thom, N. J., Stanley, E. A., Haase, L., Simmons, A. N., Shih, P.-A. B., Thompson, W. K., Potterat, E. G., Minor, T. R., & Paulus, M. P. (2014). Modifying resilience mechanisms in at-risk individuals: A controlled study of mindfulness training in marines preparing for deployment. *American Journal of Psychiatry, 171*(8), 844–853. https://doi.org/10.1176/appi.ajp.2014.13040502

Joseph, J. S., Smith-MacDonald, L., Filice, M. C., & Smith, M. S. (2023). Reculturation: A new perspective on military-civilian transition stress. *Military Psychology, 35*(3), 193–203. https://doi.org/10.1080/08995605.2022.2094175

Joyce, S., Shand, F., Lal, T. J., Mott, B., Bryant, R. A., & Harvey, S. B. (2019). Resilience@work mindfulness program: Results from a cluster randomized controlled trial with first responders. *Journal of Medical Internet Research, 21*(2), e12894. https://doi.org/10.2196/12894

Kabat-Zinn, J. (2003). Mindfulness-based interventions in context: Past, present, and future. *Clinical Psychology: Science and Practice, 10*(2), 144–156. https://doi.org/10.1093/clipsy.bpg016

Kahn, J. R., Collinge, W., & Soltysik, R. (2016). Post-9/11 veterans and their partners improve mental health outcomes with a self-directed mobile and web-based wellness training program:

A randomized controlled trial. *Journal of Medical Internet Research, 18*(9), e255. https://doi.org/10.2196/jmir.5800

Karre, J. K., Perkins, D. F., Morgan, N. R., Davenport, K. E., Aronson, K. R., Maury, R. V., Bradbard, D., Armstrong, N. J., Wright, A., Sargent, R., & Andros, M. (2025). What do successful military-to-civilian transitions look like? A revised framework and a new conceptual model for assessing veteran Well-being. *Armed Forces & Society, 51*(3), 611–640. https://doi.org/10.1177/0095327X231216678

Kearney, D. J., Malte, C. A., Storms, M., & Simpson, T. L. (2021). Loving-kindness meditation vs cognitive processing therapy for posttraumatic stress disorder among veterans: A randomized clinical trial. *JAMA Network Open, 4*(4), e216604. https://doi.org/10.1001/jamanetworkopen.2021.6604

Knowles, M. S. (1978). Andragogy: Adult learning theory in perspective. *Community College Review, 5*(3), 9–20. https://doi.org/10.1177/009155217800500302

Knowles, M. S. (1984). Theory of andragogy: A critique. *International Journal of Lifelong Education.* (Details needed).

Kolb, D. A., Boyatzis, R. E., & Mainemelis, C. (2014). Experiential learning theory: Previous research and new directions. In *Perspectives on thinking, learning, and cognitive styles* (pp. 227–247). Routledge.

Kraemer, W. J., & Ratamess, N. A. (2005). Hormonal responses and adaptations to resistance exercise and training. *Sports Medicine, 35*(4), 339–361. https://doi.org/10.2165/00007256-200535040-00004

Kwon, S.-H. (2015). Wheel of wellness counseling in community-dwelling Korean elders: A randomized controlled trial. *Journal of Korean Academy of Nursing, 45*(3), 459–468. https://doi.org/10.4040/jkan.2015.45.3.459

LeardMann, C. A., Powell, T. M., Smith, T. C., Bell, M. R., Smith, B., Boyko, E. J., Hooper, T. I., Gackstetter, G. D., Ghamsary, M., & Hoge, C. W. (2013). Risk factors associated with suicide in current and former U.S. military personnel. *JAMA, 310*(5), 496–506. https://doi.org/10.1001/jama.2013.65164

Lehavot, K., Katon, J. G., Chen, J. A., Fortney, J. C., & Simpson, T. L. (2018). Post-traumatic stress disorder by gender and veteran status. *American Journal of Preventive Medicine, 54*(1), e1–e9. https://doi.org/10.1016/j.amepre.2017.09.008

McCormick, W. H., Currier, J. M., Isaak, S. L., Sims, B. M., Slagel, B. A., Carroll, T. D., Hamner, K., & Albright, D. L. (2019). Military culture and post-military transitioning among veterans: A qualitative analysis. *Journal of Veterans Studies, 4*(2), 64–79. https://doi.org/10.21061/jvs.v4i2.121

Meichenbaum, D. (2007). Stress inoculation training: A preventative and treatment approach. In *Principles and practice of stress management* (3rd ed., pp. 497–516). The Guilford Press.

Merriam, S. B., & Bierema, L. L. (2013). *Adult learning: Linking theory and practice.* John Wiley & Sons.

Mezirow, J. (1997). Transformation theory out of context. *Adult Education Quarterly, 48*(1), 60–62. https://doi.org/10.1177/074171369704800105

Morland, L. A., Wells, S. Y., Glassman, L. H., Greene, C. J., Hoffman, J. E., & Rosen, C. S. (2020). Advances in PTSD treatment delivery: Review of findings and clinical considerations for the use of telehealth interventions for PTSD. *Current Treatment Options in Psychiatry, 7*(3), 221–241. https://doi.org/10.1007/s40501-020-00215-x

Nindl, B. C., Billing, D. C., Drain, J. R., Beckner, M. E., Greeves, J., Groeller, H., Teien, H. K., Marcora, S., Moffitt, A., Reilly, T., Taylor, N. A. S., Young, A. J., & Friedl, K. E. (2018). Perspectives on resilience for military readiness and preparedness: Report of an international military physiology roundtable. *Journal of Science and Medicine in Sport, 21*(11), 1116–1124. https://doi.org/10.1016/j.jsams.2018.05.005

Oliveira, C. B., Franco, M. R., Maher, C. G., Tiedemann, A., Silva, F. G., Damato, T. M., Nicholas, M. K., Christofaro, D. G. D., & Pinto, R. Z. (2018). The efficacy of a multimodal physical activity intervention with supervised exercises, health coaching and an activity monitor on physical activity levels of patients with chronic, nonspecific low back pain (PAYBACK trial): Study protocol for a randomised controlled trial. *Trials, 19*, Article 40. doi:https://doi.org/10.1186/s13063-017-2436-z

Penuel, W. R., Fishman, B. J., Cheng, B. H., & Sabelli, N. (2011). Organizing research and development at the intersection of learning, implementation, and design. *Educational Researcher, 40*(7), 331–337.

Peters, M. D. J., Marnie, C., Tricco, A. C., Pollock, D., Munn, Z., Alexander, L., McInerney, P., Godfrey, C. M., & Khalil, H. (2020). Updated methodological guidance for the conduct of scoping reviews. *JBI Evidence Synthesis, 18*(10). https://journals.lww.com/jbisrir/fulltext/2020/10000/updated_methodological_guidance_for_the_conduct_of.4.aspx

Pfeiffer, P. N., Heisler, M., Piette, J. D., Rogers, M. A. M., & Valenstein, M. (2011). Efficacy of peer support interventions for depression: A meta-analysis. *General Hospital Psychiatry, 33*(1), 29–36. https://doi.org/10.1016/j.genhosppsych.2010.10.002

Phillips, D., & Schweisfurth, M. (2014). *Comparative and international education: An introduction to theory, method, and practice* (2nd ed.). Bloomsbury Academic.

Pietrzak, R. H., Johnson, D. C., Goldstein, M. B., Malley, J. C., Rivers, A. J., Morgan, C. A., & Southwick, S. M. (2010). Psychosocial buffers of traumatic stress, depressive symptoms, and psychosocial difficulties in veterans of operations enduring freedom and Iraqi freedom: The role of resilience, unit support, and postdeployment social support. *Journal of Affective Disorders, 120*(1–3), 188–192. https://doi.org/10.1016/j.jad.2009.04.015

Polusny, M. A., Erbes, C. R., Thuras, P., Moran, A., Lamberty, G. J., Collins, R. C., Rodman, J. L., & Lim, K. O. (2015). Mindfulness-based stress reduction for posttraumatic stress disorder among veterans: A randomized clinical trial. *JAMA, 314*(5), 456–465. https://doi.org/10.1001/jama.2015.8361

Popay, J., Roberts, H., Sowden, A., Petticrew, M., Arai, L., Rodgers, M., & Duffy, S. (2006). Guidance on the conduct of narrative synthesis in systematic reviews. *A product from the ESRC methods programme Version, 1*(1), b92.

Rath, T., & Conchie, B. (2008). *Strengths based leadership: Great leaders, teams, and why people follow*. Gallup Press.

Resnick, S. G., & Rosenheck, R. A. (2008). Integrating peer-provided services: A quasi-experimental study of recovery orientation, confidence, and empowerment. *Psychiatric Services, 59*(11), 1307–1314. https://doi.org/10.1176/ps.2008.59.11.1307

Rowe, N., & Ilic, D. (2009). What impact do posters have on academic knowledge transfer? A pilot survey on author attitudes and experiences. *BMC Medical Education, 9*, 71. https://doi.org/10.1186/1472-6920-9-71

Saban, K. L., Collins, E. G., Mathews, H. L. et al. Impact of a Mindfulness-Based Stress Reduction Program on Psychological Well-Being, Cortisol, and Inflammation in Women Veterans. *Journal of General Internal Medicine, 37*(Suppl 3), 751–761 (2022). https://doi.org/10.1007/s11606-022-07584-4

Salas, E., Reyes, D. L., & Woods, A. L. (2017). The assessment of team performance: Observations and needs. In A. A. von Davier, M. Zhu, & P. C. Kyllonen (Eds.), *Innovative assessment of collaboration* (pp. 21–36). Springer. https://doi.org/10.1007/978-3-319-33261-1_2

Salmon, P. M., Walker, G. H., Ladva, D., Stanton, N. A., Jenkins, D. P., & Rafferty, L. (2007). Measuring situation awareness in command and control: Comparison of methods study. In *Proceedings of the 14th European Conference on Cognitive Ergonomics: Invent! Explore!*. doi:https://doi.org/10.1145/1362550.1362559.

Sayer, N. A., Spoont, M., Murdoch, M., Parker, L. E., Hintz, S., & Rosenheck, R. (2011). A qualitative study of U.S. veterans' reasons for seeking Department of Veterans Affairs disability benefits for posttraumatic stress disorder. *Journal of Traumatic Stress, 24*(6), 699–707. https://doi.org/10.1002/jts.20693

Schraw, G. (1998). Promoting general metacognitive awareness. *Instructional Science, 26*(1), 113–125. https://doi.org/10.1023/A:1003044231033

Sherwood, C. N. C. (2022). A Lie Is a Lie: The Ethics of Lying in Business Negotiations. *Business Ethics Quarterly, 32*(4), 604–634. https://doi.org/10.1017/beq

Stanley, E. A., Schaldach, J. M., Kiyonaga, A., & Jha, A. P. (2011). Mindfulness-based mind fitness training: A case study of a high-stress predeployment military cohort. *Cognitive and Behavioral Practice, 18*(4), 566–576. https://doi.org/10.1016/j.cbpra.2010.08.002

Stone, C., & Stone, D. L. (2015). Factors Affecting Hiring Decisions About Veterans. *Human Resource Management Review, 25*(1), 68–79. https://doi.org/10.1016/j.hrmr.2014.06.003

Strout, K. A., & Howard, E. P. (2012). The six dimensions of wellness and cognition in aging adults. *Journal of Holistic Nursing, 30*(3), 195–204. https://doi.org/10.1177/0898010112440883

Tedeschi, R. G., & Calhoun, L. G. (2004). Posttraumatic growth: Conceptual foundations and empirical evidence. *Psychological Inquiry, 15*(1), 1–18. https://doi.org/10.1207/s15327965pli1501_01

Tedeschi, R. G., Shakespeare-Finch, J., & Taku, K. (2018). *Posttraumatic growth: Theory, research, and applications.* Routledge.

Thornton, L. F. (2013). [Introduction to] *7 Lenses: Learning the principles and practices of ethical leadership.* Leading in Context LLC.

Turner, J. C., Brown, R. J., & Tajfel, H. (1979). Social comparison and group interest in ingroup favouritism. *European Journal of Social Psychology, 9*(2), 187–204. https://doi.org/10.1002/ejsp.2420090207

US Department of Health and Human Services. (2014). SAMHSAs concept of trauma and guidance for a trauma-informed approach.

Vacchi, D. T., & Berger, J. B. (2013). Student veterans in higher education. In *Higher education: Handbook of theory and research* (Vol. 29, pp. 93–151). Springer.

van Ijzendoorn, M. H., & Bakermans-Kranenburg, M. J. (2015). Genetic differential susceptibility on trial: Meta-analytic support from randomized controlled experiments. *Development and Psychopathology, 27*(1), 151–162. https://doi.org/10.1017/S0954579414001369

Van Til, L., Fikretoglu, D., Pranger, T., Patten, S., Wang, J., Wong, M., Zamorski, M., Loisel, P., Corbière, M., Shields, N., Thompson, J., & Pedlar, D. (2013). Work reintegration for veterans with mental disorders: A systematic literature review to inform research. *Physical Therapy, 93*(9), 1163–1174. https://doi.org/10.2522/ptj.20120156

Walumbwa, F. O., Avolio, B. J., Gardner, W. L., Wernsing, T. S., & Peterson, S. J. (2008). Authentic leadership: Development and validation of a theory-based measure. *Journal of Management, 34*(1), 89–126. https://doi.org/10.1177/0149206307308913

Wang, J., van Woerkom, M., Breevaart, K., Bakker, A. B., & Xu, S. (2023). Strengths-based leadership and employee work engagement: A multi-source study. *Journal of Vocational Behavior, 142*, 103859. https://doi.org/10.1016/j.jvb.2023.103859

Wiggins, G., & McTighe, J. (2005). *Understanding by design.* ASCD.

World Health Organization. (2022, October 5). *Physical activity.* https://www.who.int/news-room/fact-sheets/detail/physical-activity

Chapter 4
The Research Journey

This chapter traces the research journey from exploratory review to framework, theory, and precision-focused synthesis. It shows how methodological choices (scoping, evidence integration, mixed-methods orientation) convert lived problems into testable models and program designs, and how identity-centered, multidomain logic (psychological, physical, social, economic) becomes operational in BRAVE. After reading, you'll be able to: (1) differentiate review types used in this chapter and explain why each was appropriate at that stage; (2) evaluate the case for multimodal, identity-centered reintegration over single-modality approaches; (3) apply evidence integration logic to combine quantitative outcomes with veteran voice; (4) translate chapter findings into a BRAVE-aligned program sequence (design, delivery, evaluation); (5) identify engagement barriers (cultural fit, logistics) and plan adaptations; and (6) formulate next-step research questions that stress precision, feasibility, and measurable impact.

4.1 Introduction—The Research Journey

When I started the Doctor of Health Science (DHSc) program, my theory wasn't fully developed, nor did I have a detailed research plan or a clear vision for a doctoral portfolio. I brought lived experience with an understanding of veterans' challenges during reintegration, and a belief that the current systems were inadequate. The questions that now shape the BRAVE model arose naturally from the work. I let the research guide me, while my background in transition and service served as a guiding compass to determine which path to take.

T. Carlton, *BRAVE Theory*, https://doi.org/10.1007/978-3-032-13695-4_4

Initially, I had no idea that the journey would lead to a multidimensional reintegration theory supported by over 600 scholarly sources and multiple peer-reviewed submissions. However, as I advanced through each course, I noticed patterns showing that psychological recovery, physical performance, social connection, and economic stability were not isolated issues but interconnected areas. The gaps in the literature were apparent, and the evidence suggested that no single-discipline approach could fully address them.

The DHSc became my journey of discovery. My personal experience helped me identify issues that a purely academic view might miss. In contrast, the educational process gave me the tools to analyze, measure, and connect those issues in ways that could withstand peer review. Scattered insights gradually became a clear, evolving model.

This chapter traces the evolution from the first exploratory paper, The Lasting Effects of Tactical Military Demands on Health and Transition, through integrative works like Integrated Mindfulness and Strength and Conditioning for Military Transition, to the comprehensive Evidence Integration Review now in press with the Journal of Veterans Studies. It follows the refinement into Building Resilience and Advancing Veteran Empowerment (BRAVE): A Holistic Framework for Reintegration, the formalization into BRAVE Theory: A Multidimensional Framework for Veteran Reintegration and Empowerment, and finally the expansion into The Reintegration Equation: Mindfulness, Epigenetics, and Tactical Recovery in Post-Service Life.

These works were sequential iterations of one question, asked in different ways and at varying levels of depth. This is how those pieces fit together and how the BRAVE model was built from the unpredictable interplay of scholarship, lived experience, and a willingness to follow where the evidence led. At the core of this progression lies a single persistent problem that guides every study: tactical athletes transitioning from military to civilian life often encounter disjointed well-being strategies, lacking a cohesive approach to address their physical and mental needs. This fragmentation contributes to preventable mental health issues, physical injuries, and barriers to social and professional reintegration, the very gaps BRAVE was designed to close.

4.2 The Lasting Effects of Tactical Military Demands on Health and Transition

This review is the actual starting point of my doctoral research journey. The Lasting Effects of Tactical Military Demands on Health and Transition was the first manuscript I wrote in the DHSc program. Through this research, I learned the importance of rigorously sourcing only the highest levels of evidence. The original draft was built using only Level of Evidence (LOE) 1 and 2 studies, each accompanied by a detailed, standalone analysis page to ensure I could reference the research and thoroughly interrogate and understand it.

When I started, my focus was still on ACL injuries in hockey players, a familiar area from my work as a strength and conditioning (S&C) coach. However, as I explored further, my interest shifted to something more personal and broader, like the tactical demands of the military. I was still healing my body from service, managing ongoing injuries, and working around physical limits in my training. That experience drew me toward examining the occupational demands unique to military service that last long after the uniform is gone. This review became my way of testing the waters: what does the research really say about the physical, physiological, and nutritional toll of service? How does military life compare to sports or other demanding professions? What is temporary, and what is lasting? The paper's original working title reflected that broad scope. The title was something along the lines of "The Psychological, Physiological, and Nutritional Demands Placed on Occupational Challenges." It was an intentionally wide net, designed to let the research guide me rather than forcing it into a pre-set frame.

A broad question, disciplined methodology, and curiosity driven by professional expertise and personal experience set the tone for everything that followed in my doctoral journey. As this chapter progresses, you will see how this initial inquiry expanded into a series of interconnected studies that ultimately shaped the BRAVE Framework and Theory. The operational realities of tactical military athletes subject the human body and mind to sustained stress levels rarely seen in civilian settings. These demands are multifaceted, involving musculoskeletal load, extreme environmental exposures, irregular sleep patterns, cognitive strain, and nutritional deficits. Over time, the cumulative impact of these conditions creates a cascade of physical, physiological, and psychological effects that endure well beyond active service, influencing the veteran's post-military health and the success of reintegration efforts.

4.2.1 Physical and Physiological Demands

Musculoskeletal injuries continue to be one of the most widespread health problems for tactical athletes, caused by the repetitive high-intensity activities, heavy load carriage, and biomechanically demanding movements needed in military duties (Abt et al., 2010; Teplova et al., 2021). These injuries range from stress fractures to chronic joint degeneration that often become lifelong conditions, limiting functional ability and employment opportunities in civilian life. Targeted prevention programs like the Eagle Tactical Athlete Program (ETAP) show that personalized, load-specific training can significantly lower injury rates. However, the ongoing demands of service mean that even the best-designed programs cannot eliminate risk, especially for groups with specific vulnerabilities, such as female soldiers in combat roles (Lovalekar et al., 2021).

Environmental extremes such as heat, cold, and high altitude increase physical stress by challenging thermoregulation, oxygen transport, and neuromuscular coordination (Farina et al., 2017). Proper acclimatization, hydration strategies, and environmental-specific training can reduce these effects, but failing in these areas can cause acute injury or long-term health issues. These exposures also directly affect cardiovascular and metabolic health later in life, highlighting the importance of ongoing monitoring and intervention after service.

4.2.2 Cognitive and Mental Health Stressors

Sleep deprivation is one of the most harmful operational hazards, impairing reaction time, decision-making, and working memory (McClung et al., 2023). Chronic lack of sleep not only affects mission performance but also raises the risk of metabolic disease, cardiovascular issues, and neurodegenerative conditions (Almeida et al., 2021). Additionally, prolonged exposure to trauma and operational stress increases vulnerability to PTSD, depression, and anxiety disorders. Emerging research suggests that cognitive resilience, which is the capacity to maintain function under sustained stress, can be trained through interventions such as mindfulness-based stress reduction (Flood & Keegan, 2022) and cognitive-behavioral strategies. Social support, both during and after service, acts as a protective mediator, mitigating the effects of operational stress on mental health outcomes (Balcan, 2023).

4.2.3 Nutritional and Metabolic Considerations

Energy deficits during deployment, often between 2500 and 4500 kcal per day, are common because of high energy expenditure and limited food access (Farina et al., 2017). This caloric imbalance speeds up muscle loss, delays recovery, and weakens immune function. Combat rations like Meals Ready to Eat (MREs) meet basic short-term needs but are nutritionally lacking for long-term use, causing calcium, vitamin D, and iron deficiencies. Evidence supports strategic supplementation such as creatine for high-intensity performance and muscle recovery, beta-alanine for buffering acidosis, caffeine for cognitive alertness, and omega-3 fatty acids for anti-inflammatory and neuroprotective effects (Gonzalez et al., 2022). Hydration protocols tailored to body weight, mission duration, and environmental conditions remain essential for maintaining physical and cognitive readiness.

4.2.4 Long-Term Implications for Reintegration

The shift from military to civilian life often heightens service-related health issues. Chronic pain, mobility problems, and metabolic conditions are common, along with ongoing cognitive and psychological difficulties. Without the structured support of the military environment, veterans may find it hard to access or stick with rehabilitation, nutrition, and mental health treatments (Karre et al., 2025). Importantly, these physical and cognitive burdens interact with the larger psychosocial context of reintegration. Physical limitations may restrict employment opportunities, while psychological health affects relationship stability and community participation. Therefore, interventions should be coordinated across the physical, mental, social, and economic areas to improve post-service quality of life.

4.2.5 *Implications for the BRAVE Framework*

This research offers solid evidence for the BRAVE Theory's Physical and Psychological Dimensions. The chronic health conditions discussed here highlight the importance of long-term, multimodal strategies beyond injury rehabilitation and performance maintenance, including lifestyle redesign for lasting civilian functioning. The tactical athlete perspective emphasizes why reintegration science must go beyond mental health and career transition to include biomechanics, nutrition, and environmental health as key parts of recovery.

4.3 Integrated Mindfulness and Strength & Conditioning for Military Transition

The second significant step in my research journey was completing the Integrated Mindfulness and Strength & Conditioning for Military Transition scoping review. This paper marked the point where my focus shifted from broadly exploring tactical athlete demands in my first review to specifically examining how integrated, multimodal approaches could address both the physical and psychological aspects of reintegration. At this point, I was no longer questioning whether military service caused lasting effects on health; that was obvious from the first review. Instead, I was focused on what could be done to reduce those effects in a sustainable, evidence-based manner. My personal experience continued to guide me, but now the literature pointed me toward specific solutions. It became clear that no single intervention, whether purely physical training or strictly psychological support, could fully address the complexity of transitioning from military to civilian life.

The review synthesized literature on two intervention areas: mindfulness-based practices and strength and conditioning, which were used either independently or together for tactical populations. The physical training literature showed that structured resistance training, mobility work, and conditioning protocols can reduce chronic musculoskeletal problems, restore functional performance, and enhance long-term quality of life for veterans (Hoffman et al., 2016; Roy et al., 2013). Strength and conditioning interventions helped regain movement ability and rebuild physical confidence, which is linked to better mental health outcomes in military populations (Friedl et al., 2015).

Psychologically, the literature on mindfulness-based interventions (MBIs) consistently shows benefits for reducing symptoms of PTSD, depression, and anxiety, while also enhancing emotion regulation and cognitive flexibility (Goldberg et al., 2020). Programs like Mindfulness-Based Stress Reduction (MBSR) and Mindfulness-Based Cognitive Therapy (MBCT) have demonstrated measurable improvements in attentional control, sleep quality, and perceived stress among both active-duty personnel and veterans (Polusny et al., 2015).

Through the scoping process, the scarcity of studies integrating these two domains into a single, cohesive program for military transition became more apparent. Although physical training and mindfulness were often studied independently, their potential integrated approaches in addressing the body's recovery needs while cultivating psychological resilience remained largely untapped in the literature. A few studies suggested that integrated programs might amplify outcomes, with participants reporting better physical health markers and improved emotional stability, social reintegration, and self-efficacy (Cushing & Braun, 2017).

The broad scope of the scoping review revealed a significant gap, and while the theoretical foundation for integration was solid, empirical evidence was scattered. Studies greatly differed in design, outcome measures, and population characteristics, making it difficult to draw definitive conclusions about effectiveness. However, the clear trend was that the effects of veterans engaged in structured physical conditioning alongside mindfulness training went beyond performance metrics, affecting identity reconstruction, stress regulation, and long-term health behaviors. This realization sharpened my research focus. The first paper highlighted the unique and enduring demands placed on tactical athletes. The second review confirmed that addressing these demands requires a holistic, integrated approach in theory and how programs are designed, implemented, and evaluated. I also began to see the importance of measuring outcomes beyond standard clinical metrics, including social participation, economic stability, and self-perceived well-being.

By the end of this review, it was clear that my next step needed to be a comprehensive, evidence integration process capable of assembling the strongest available data from various intervention types. The scope limitations, the diversity of outcome measures, and the underdeveloped integration of modalities all highlighted the need for an Evidence Integration Review (EIR). That review would synthesize best practices and lay the foundation for the theoretical and practical model that would eventually become BRAVE.

4.4 Evidence Integration Review: Multimodal Interventions for Veteran Reintegration

The Evidence Integration Review (EIR) was created to go beyond traditional systematic review limits by blending quantitative outcomes with qualitative insights, providing a more comprehensive understanding of how multimodal interventions influence veterans' reintegration. The reason for this approach was based on professional and personal knowledge that statistical effect sizes alone can't explain why many veterans disengage from (or never start) programs meant to help them. As a veteran going through my own post-service journey, I saw firsthand how large systems, including the Department of Veterans Affairs, often seemed disconnected from what veterans truly need. This disconnection strengthened my belief that veterans' voices must be systematically included in the evidence base if we want to create interventions that do more than meet administrative requirements. The aim was to document "what works," and also to understand why some programs succeed, why others fail, and how to prevent becoming part of the problem.

4.4.1 Scope and Methods

This EIR reviewed 40 U.S.-based studies published between 2014 and 2024, including randomized controlled trials (RCTs), cross-sectional analyses, and qualitative studies, with a total sample of over 7300 veterans aged 28.1 to 57.1 years. The inclusion criteria require validated outcome measures such as the PTSD Checklist for DSM-5 (PCL-5), Beck Depression Inventory-II (BDI-II), and Clinician-Administered PTSD Scale for DSM-5 (CAPS-5), while also accepting studies that reported veterans' lived experiences through thematic analysis. Multimodal interventions combine at least two therapeutic modalities, mindfulness and vocational training, or exercise and peer mentorship, which simultaneously target multiple reintegration domains. This definition excluded single-modality interventions, even if they achieved numerous psychological outcomes, to focus on true cross-domain integrated approaches.

Quantitative synthesis followed PRISMA standards, with data extraction assisted by Julius.ai for efficiency and consistency. Qualitative analysis was performed in ATLAS.ti using line-by-line coding to identify recurring themes: psychological benefits, social connection, physical health improvements, barriers to engagement, and gender-specific considerations. Thematic saturation was achieved when no new concepts appeared in additional sources, ensuring the veteran voice was authentically represented in the final synthesis.

4.4.2 Quantitative Outcomes

Multimodal interventions demonstrated measurable benefits across psychological, physical, and social domains and quantifiable benefits. Mindfulness-based interventions significantly reduced PTSD severity, with large effect sizes (e.g., $d = 0.8$ in Kearney et al., 2021) and concurrent reductions in depression and grief (Acierno et al., 2021). Vocationally integrated programs, such as the National Career Coach Program (NCCP) (Bond et al., 2022), improved monthly earnings by $703 and increased employment stability by 20%. Physical activity programs yielded resilience and mobility gains, with step counts rising by 1224 per day during incentive-driven phases (Agarwal et al., 2021) and yoga interventions producing significant satisfaction and perceived global improvement (Roseen et al., 2023). These findings affirmed that multimodal approaches can generate clinically and functionally meaningful change.

4.4.3 Qualitative Insights and the Veteran Voice

Quantitative improvements only tell part of the story. Veterans' stories reveal the deeper reasons behind engagement and attrition data, which are often missing in purely statistical reviews. Stigma, logistical barriers (e.g., transportation, scheduling), mistrust in institutions, and fears of re-traumatization frequently limited participation (Goldstein et al., 2018; Saban et al., 2022). Rural veterans faced compounded access challenges (Reinhardt et al., 2018), while female veterans highlighted the importance of safe, gender-specific spaces to address military sexual trauma (Castillo et al., 2016; Saban et al., 2022). Even in successful programs, some participants still reported ongoing emotional distress, emphasizing that symptom reduction does not always mean full reintegration.

Through my transition, and this finding reflects this, it became clear that program designers often interpret dropout as disinterest or noncompliance when it is usually a rational response to poorly aligned interventions. I deliberately included qualitative studies to elevate these contextual realities from anecdotal remarks to essential evidence. Veterans consistently expressed that they valued programs that were trauma-informed, culturally competent, flexible in delivery, and co-created with input from those who had lived the experience of service and transition.

4.4.4 Integrative Interpretation

By combining numeric results and lived experiences, the EIR shows that multimodal interventions can be practical tools for change when they target the interconnected areas of psychological health, social bonds, and economic stability while respecting the complexities of veteran identity. The convergence of quantitative and qualitative findings points toward several design imperatives:

- Trauma-informed and culturally adaptive approaches increase engagement and retention.
- Integrating vocational, social, and psychological supports yields synergistic benefits beyond single-modality programs.
- Hybrid delivery models (in-person + virtual) can mitigate geographic and scheduling barriers.
- Peer and gender-specific formats enhance trust, safety, and authenticity.

The mixed-methods approach in the EIR marked a turning point in my doctoral research journey. The earlier reviews (e.g., my EXSC 8250 scoping review) showed that integrated mindfulness and strength & conditioning methods had potential for military transition, and now this EIR broadened the scope to include more diverse multimodal designs and, importantly, the veterans' voices. Without truly understanding why veterans disengage—or never start—interventions will keep underperforming, regardless of how good their quantitative results look. This insight led me to choose a format for the Evidence Integration Review that could connect to my BRAVE Theory development, ensuring the theoretical framework is based on solid empirical data and the real experiences of the community it aims to serve.

4.5 Building BRAVE: Narrative Framework of the Four Dimensions

When I reached the point in my doctoral research where the EIR had given me a broad understanding of intervention effectiveness, I knew that the next step was to build a conceptual structure capable of integrating both the science and the lived realities of veterans. This is where the 8990 narrative review emerged as the next deliberate step toward organizing the themes emerging from years of study. My earlier work taught me the importance of asking better questions, and this review allowed me to start forming the answers. I needed to go beyond describing veterans' challenges and explore how those challenges interact across different areas. The BRAVE Framework was developed as I carefully reviewed research across four main dimensions: Psychological, Physical, Social, and Economic. These areas reflected the patterns in the evidence and the ones I observed during my service and recovery. This approach helped me see the veteran transition as a complex, interconnected process.

4.5.1 Psychological Dimension

The psychological challenges of veteran reintegration go far beyond just PTSD. While PTSD remains a significant focus in the literature (Steenkamp et al., 2015), a wider range of psychological stressors, including depression, moral injury, and identity disruption, is essential for understanding how veterans adjust after service (Bryan et al., 2018; Griffin et al., 2020). In the 8990 narrative review, I found strong evidence that supporting veterans' psychological well-being is most effective through multimodal interventions that combine therapy, mindfulness, and physical activity (Kearney et al., 2021; Taylor et al., 2020).

These interventions focused on reducing symptoms and promoting adaptive coping and resilience. Mindfulness-based approaches showed promise for improving emotional regulation and decreasing reactivity to triggers (Kearney et al., 2021), while structured exercise programs provided both physiological and psychological benefits, enhancing mood and sleep quality (Caddick & Smith, 2014). Notably, the evidence indicated that veterans often disengage from purely clinical programs when those programs fail to consider military culture, peer trust, and the need for perceived competence. These insights strengthened my belief that psychological health strategies should be culturally informed, veteran-led, and grounded in agency rather than compliance.

4.5.2 Physical Dimension

Physical health in the veteran population results from a complex interaction between the lingering effects of service-related injuries and lifestyle changes after civilian life. The review highlighted ongoing musculoskeletal problems, chronic pain syndromes, and decreased physical capacity as common post-service issues (Cameron et al., 2016; Lovalekar et al., 2021). While rehabilitation efforts are available, too many are reactive rather than preventive, concentrating on managing symptoms after injury rather than maintaining sustained performance optimization.

Evidence supports incorporating strength and conditioning principles into veteran health programs to restore baseline function and enhance resilience against future decline (Nindl et al., 2018). Structured physical activity has been shown to improve cardiovascular health, decrease pain perception, and aid psychological recovery (Caddick & Smith, 2014). These benefits were significantly increased when physical programs were combined with mindfulness training, as the mind-body connection promoted better adherence and reduced injury recurrence (Taylor et al., 2020). This reinforced the idea that veterans need training that preserves the operational mindset while adjusting it for sustainability, not just short-term results, which I have considered for years.

4.5.3 Social Dimension

The social aspect is arguably the most overlooked area in veteran reintegration. My review reaffirmed that social isolation and a sense of loss are among the most destabilizing factors after service, a conclusion I reached through personal experience (Demers, 2011; Joseph et al., 2023). Veterans often find it challenging to locate civilian communities that match the camaraderie of military units, and even when they do, these communities frequently lack the shared language, values, and trust found in military environments.

The literature shows that social connection is key to mental and physical health outcomes (Cacioppo & Cacioppo, 2014). Group-based interventions, peer mentorship, and veteran community organizations offer social support and a form of identity scaffolding that helps veterans rebuild a coherent sense of self (Griffiths et al., 2020). Programs that neglect this social reintegration aspect face higher dropout rates, lower adherence, and poorer overall results. These findings support my belief that BRAVE must incorporate social identity theory principles into its operational model. Without a sense of belonging, other interventions are consistently vulnerable to deterioration.

4.5.4 Economic Dimension

Economic stability was the fourth and final aspect identified in the review. Employment and financial security are not just practical concerns for veterans' worth, purpose, and social standing (Karre et al., 2025). The literature showed that underemployment, skill translation barriers, and the loss of structured career advancement significantly contribute to post-service stress and decreased well-being (Bond et al., 2022). Veterans in the reviewed studies expressed frustration when career transition programs provided generic advice instead of individualized pathways tailored to military-acquired skills (Cooper et al., 2018). Interventions that combined career coaching, educational guidance, and mentorship showed measurable improvements in employment results and financial stability (Clemens & Milsom, 2008). The most notable results came from programs that integrated economic planning with psychosocial and physical support services, highlighting the interconnectedness of all four BRAVE dimensions.

4.5.5 From Review to Framework

By the time I finished the 8990-narrative review, the BRAVE Framework had become a structured, evidence-based model with clear domains and cross-cutting mechanisms. This was the point in my doctoral journey when I could see how the different strands of my research were coming together. The earlier Tactical Military Athlete paper provided the physiological foundation, the Integrated Mindfulness and S&C review showed how intervention models could work in integrated approaches, and the EIR confirmed the importance of hearing veterans' voices in the program evaluation. The BRAVE Framework solidified these concepts into a model that describes the challenges of veteran reintegration and guides the design, implementation, and evaluation of solutions. It serves as the bridge to the next stage, formalizing BRAVE as a theoretical concept, which will be addressed in the following BRAVE Theory manuscript.

4.6 BRAVE Theory: A Multidimensional Framework for Veteran Reintegration and Empowerment

When I finished the BRAVE Framework Narrative Review, I was struck by a recurring pattern across the evidence base: programs achieved partial success in isolated areas, yet the overall picture of veteran reintegration remained fragmented. In the studies I examined, psychological improvements were often limited by physical challenges; vocational progress was nullified by untreated trauma; social reconnection was short-lived without financial stability. My previous synthesis clearly indicated that while interventions in a single area could make some difference, they rarely led to lasting change unless other aspects of life improved simultaneously.

In addressing these limitations, the BRAVE Theory began to emerge. I aimed to create a framework that reflected the real-world interdependence I observed in the literature and my field experience. It needed to encompass psychological, physical, economic, and social recovery as interconnected parts of a living system, all centered around the reconstruction of identity. The BRAVE Framework Narrative review concluded that reintegration is not just a set of problems to fix but an adaptive process to navigate, one that requires agency, resilience, and systemic integration. The BRAVE Theory is my response to that gap. It combines the strongest theoretical and empirical findings into a multidomain, identity-centered framework to guide program development, service delivery, and evaluation.

4.6.1 *Theoretical Foundations*

The foundational decision in BRAVE was to pull from multiple, well-established theories but adapt them for the specific realities of veteran reintegration:

- From the **Biopsychosocial Model** (Engel, 1977), I retained its holistic focus on the interaction between biological, psychological, and social systems, but found its use in post-military life incomplete. In BRAVE, I formally added the economic dimension to reflect evidence that financial instability worsens mental health issues, weakens social cohesion, and limits physical recovery (Elbogen et al.,

2022; Fortier et al., 2024). I also centered the model on identity, informed by the literature (Besemann et al., 2018) and my observation that veterans often gauge recovery not by symptom relief but by their ability to be themselves again.
- The **Social Identity Model of Identity Change (SIMIC)** (Wakefield et al., 2024) explained why some veterans adapt more easily than others: those who maintain a sense of identity continuity and establish new role-based connections tend to do better across various health and well-being measures. BRAVE extends the SIMIC model by including psychophysiological and economic adaptation, recognizing research that shows identity loss impacts neuroregulation, motivation, and employment participation.
- **Trauma Exposure Theory** (Elnitsky et al., 2017) emphasizes the need for this expansion, describing trauma as an ecological disruption that affects all areas and manifests as social withdrawal, somatic symptoms, and unstable livelihoods. BRAVE therefore integrates trauma recovery into vocational planning, social programs, and physical rehabilitation, not as separate tracks but as interconnected components.
- Finally, **Transformative Learning Theory** (Mezirow, 1997) offers the mechanism for change: identity reconstruction through critical reflection, dialogue, and reframing of life's meaning. In my practice and the literature, this is where veterans shift from surviving to thriving. This is where resilience develops as an evolving capacity influenced by experience and context (Saban et al., 2022). By integrating these frameworks, BRAVE addresses the limitations in my previous work: the lack of systemic coherence, the neglect of identity as a mediator, and the failure to consider economic realities alongside health and social outcomes.

4.6.2 Core Constructs and Mechanisms

In developing BRAVE, I decided to view reintegration as a dynamic process of reconstructing identity across four interconnected areas: psychological, physical, economic, and social. This choice was based on patterns observed in previous work, where a failure in one area often led to setbacks in the others. Across all four domains, three mediating mechanisms—identity, agency, and resilience guide the model. Identity disruption causes dysfunction; agency drives goal-oriented actions; as BRAVE describes it, resilience is the emergent quality of coherent identity, relational trust, and systemic integration.

1. **Psychological Domain**—The psychological aspect is often the most noticeable in veteran care due to diagnoses like PTSD, depression, and moral injury (Elnitsky et al., 2017; Anestis et al., 2019). However, in the research I reviewed, I observed that symptom management alone rarely led to long-lasting improvements in life. Veterans in several longitudinal studies showed reduced PTSD symptoms but still struggled to rebuild satisfying relationships or find meaningful careers (Kearney et al., 2021; Kelly et al., 2022). BRAVE addresses this gap by focusing on psychological healing through identity reconstruction and

narrative agency. This approach helps veterans shift from a fragmented sense of self to one integrated with post-service realities.

2. **Physical Domain**—Physical readiness and body agency frequently appeared in my earlier review as factors that enable or hinder reintegration. Chronic pain, TBI, and mobility limitations not only decrease functional capacity but can also undermine confidence and social participation (Abanes et al., 2022; Besemann et al., 2018). BRAVE redefines physical rehabilitation to restore autonomy, resilience, and self-efficacy. By including adaptive movement, somatic therapies, and interoceptive trust-building, this domain helps the body be seen not as a reminder of loss but as a resource for ability (Gregg et al., 2018).
3. **Economic Domain**—My previous work highlighted that economic stability is a psychological intervention. Veterans facing financial insecurity are more likely to report declining mental health, strained relationships, and reduced participation in community activities (Elbogen et al., 2022; Fortier et al., 2024). In BRAVE, economic engagement is not seen as a goal after achieving "clinical stability" but as an ongoing process from the start. This includes trauma-informed workforce integration, rebuilding vocational identity, and financial literacy incorporated into care plans.
4. **Social Domain**—Social reintegration is arguably the most delicate aspect. Veterans often lose close-knit unit bonds without forming equally meaningful civilian connections, which can lead to isolation—a known predictor of suicide (Sayer et al., 2011; Cheney et al., 2018). Based on SIMIC (Wakefield et al., 2024), BRAVE views social recovery as maintaining and growing identity, creating structured peer mentorship, civic engagement opportunities, and culturally relevant community spaces. The aim is not just "support networks" but reciprocal, purpose-driven relationships that support the entire reintegration process.

4.6.3 Operationalization of the BRAVE Theory

When I designed BRAVE, I wasn't interested in a model that would live only in theory—it had to be operational. That meant translating the four domains into structures for program design, service delivery, and evaluation.

- **Program Design**—As my previous work highlighted, most veteran programs operate in silos, mental health here, vocational rehab there, physical therapy somewhere else (Demers, 2011; Duncan et al., 2020). BRAVE rejects this fragmentation. In a BRAVE-aligned program, interventions are carefully sequenced and synchronized to advance multiple domains simultaneously. For instance, a veteran might attend Acceptance and Commitment Therapy (Kelly et al., 2022) in the morning, participate in adaptive physical training (Kearney et al., 2021) in the afternoon, and join a peer-led financial planning session (Elbogen et al., 2022) in the evening—each one reinforcing the others within an identity-focused care plan.

- **Service Delivery**—In the literature and my work, peer-led delivery consistently shows higher engagement and trust than clinician-only models (Demers, 2011). BRAVE formalizes this approach by incorporating trained veteran mentors alongside clinical staff, facilitating cultural translation, role modeling, and ongoing support. These mentors are not just "add-ons" but essential co-facilitators, guiding the intervention flow and strengthening identity reconstruction.
- **Evaluation**—BRAVE's framework monitors objective, domain-specific outcomes and subjective identity coherence. This dual approach utilizes tools like the WHO-5 for psychological health, PROMIS Physical Function scales, the CFPB Financial Well-Being Scale, the Military to Civilian Questionnaire (M2C-Q), and narrative identity measures. Combining self-reported meaning-making with functional metrics, the evaluation aligns with Transformative Learning Theory's focus on reflective growth (Mezirow, 1997).

4.6.4 Comparison with Existing Models

From the beginning, I recognized that BRAVE needed to differentiate itself from current frameworks by not ignoring their valuable insights and filling in their gaps.

The Stress Process Model (Pearlin et al., 1981) helps explain strain and role shifts but doesn't fully address veteran-specific identity disruptions or how trauma and financial instability interact. The Interpersonal Theory of Suicide (Joiner, 2005) highlights the importance of belonging and burdensomeness but overlooks the systemic and multidomain challenges veterans face. Programs such as HUD-VASH show how federal efforts can coordinate effectively, yet they are too limited, mainly focusing on housing without addressing long-term psychosocial and vocational reintegration.

While these models focus on specific components, BRAVE targets the entire system: creating a unified, testable theory in which disruptions in one area affect all others. It emphasizes the role of identity as the key factor in successful reintegration. By incorporating Ecological Systems Theory (Bronfenbrenner, 1979) and Self-Determination Theory (Ryan & Deci, 2000) within a veteran-specific framework, BRAVE shifts the focus from solving isolated issues to fostering systemic, reciprocal change.

4.6.5 Implications for Research and Practice

BRAVE provides researchers with a range of testable hypotheses. The key idea is that achieving synchronized progress in all four domains leads to more sustainable reintegration than focusing on improvements in just one area. This hypothesis could be tested using longitudinal mixed-methods studies, involving veterans as co-researchers through participatory action research (Worrell-George et al., 2022). For practitioners, BRAVE serves as both a design and diagnostic instrument. Multidisciplinary teams can utilize the framework to identify where a veteran's progress stalls, facilitating coordinated interventions across different domains instead of isolated efforts. For policymakers, it acts as a blueprint for outcome-driven funding linking investments to programs that show multidomain effectiveness and tangible identity transformation.

4.7 The Reintegration Equation: Mindfulness, Epigenetics, and Tactical Recovery in Post-Service Life

In my final paper for the DHSc, I had already mapped a research journey that began with exploring tactical occupational demands, advanced through targeted reviews on military transition, and crystallized into the BRAVE Theory. That theory laid out a multidimensional view of veteran reintegration. Still, in The Reintegration Equation, the work shifted from conceptual framing to a focused, high-quality synthesis of empirical studies that directly examine how biological susceptibility, mindfulness-based interventions, and behavioral reintegration strategies interact in post-service life.

This review was not meant to be the definitive analysis that combines the strongest quantitative and qualitative evidence to demonstrate that resilience in veterans is neither static nor mysterious. It is biological, trainable, and heavily influenced by our environment and intervention choices. My goal was to remove the guesswork often seen in veteran reintegration policy and replace it with a scholarship-based model grounded in RCTs, meta-analyses, and specific behavioral trials. The paper began by pointing out the gap where most reintegration programs focus on single issues like employment, PTSD treatment, or benefits navigation without considering the complex interaction of neurobiology, psychology, and social factors. This oversight has serious consequences, seen in higher suicide rates, ongoing health problems, and disengagement from civilian life and formal care systems. From my previous work, I understood that veterans are not a uniform group for rehabilitation. They have unique physiological stress marks, operational identities, and adaptive abilities that respond differently to the same intervention. The Reintegration Equation aimed to use this variability as a strength in design.

The initial body of literature reviewed focused on biological susceptibility and epigenetic flexibility. The meta-analysis by van IJzendoorn, M. H.,, and Bakermans-Kranenburg, M. J. (2015), including 22 RCTs with over 3200 participants, reinterpreted so-called "risk" genotypes like DRD4 and 5-HTTLPR as plasticity markers. In other words, individuals most vulnerable to stress often experience the most significant benefits when provided with supportive interventions ($r = 0.33$ for carriers versus $r = 0.08$ for non-carriers). This challenges the traditional risk model embedded in most veteran care systems. Domschke et al. (2025) expanded this idea at the molecular level, showing in a longitudinal methylome study that therapeutic improvements in anxiety disorder treatment coincided with stable, positive DNA methylation changes. Van Assche et al. (2023) confirmed similar biological embedding in cognitive training for depression, demonstrating that gains in attention and memory coincided with measurable epigenetic modifications. These studies confirm that biological responsiveness is a theoretical, tangible, and quantifiable phenomenon that can be used strategically in recovery efforts.

From this biological foundation, the review shifted to mindfulness-based interventions (MBIs) as regulators of psychophysiological stress. Joyce et al. (2019) demonstrated in the Resilience@Work program that even a six-week MBI could lower distress, burnout, and stress biomarkers in first responders, a group like veterans in operational tasks. Saban et al. (2022) showed that MBSR tailored for women veterans reduced PTSD and depression severity while also decreasing inflammatory markers and cortisol reactivity. Kearney et al. (2021) advanced the discussion by showing that loving-kindness meditation performed as well as cognitive processing therapy for PTSD in veterans, offering additional benefits in self-compassion and positive emotion. The consistent theme here is that MBIs are more than symptom management tools. They recalibrate stress physiology, improve emotional regulation, and support operational skills such as self-discipline and mission focus.

The final pillar examined was precision reintegration through behavioral and social models. Fortier et al. (2024) validated a transdiagnostic group approach in the STEP-Home program, enhancing emotional regulation and social engagement for Post-9/11 veterans regardless of specific diagnosis. Kahn et al. (2016) provided a contrasting but complementary model with Mission Reconnect, a self-guided, mobile-based wellness program for veterans and their partners that improved PTSD and depression outcomes without requiring formal clinic attendance. These studies highlighted that effective reintegration depends on what is delivered and how it is delivered; community-based, flexible, and culturally congruent methods help increase engagement and retention.

Pulling these strands together, The Reintegration Equation advocates for a precision-based reintegration model grounded in biological sensitivity, modulated by mindfulness, and embedded in flexible, socially integrated delivery systems. This evidence-based conclusion is drawn from high-quality quantitative data, reinforced by qualitative insights about identity, trust, and cultural fit. The qualitative aspect was essential to me. Veterans repeatedly told me through the literature and in lived experience why they disengaged from programs: they were treated as interchangeable cases, not as individuals with unique recovery paths, and including their voices in the scholarship ensured that the science remained rooted in real-world applicability.

This paper served as the final piece within the scope of my doctoral work. The earlier research and theory development had established the foundation; here, I validated key principles of the BRAVE Theory with specific evidence and demonstrated how those principles can be transformed into practical, testable, and implementable strategies. It confirmed that veterans are not "broken," but biologically inclined to adapt when provided with the proper intervention, environment, and agency. The

Reintegration Equation became the academic and practical proof that the multidimensional, precision-focused approach I had been developing throughout the DHSc could, and should, become the new standard in veteran reintegration science.

Academic Synthesis

This chapter outlined an iterative process: a broad initial review of tactical health needs defined the problem space; a scoping review explored the possibility of merging strength and conditioning with mindfulness for transition. My Evidence Integration Review expanded the perspective to multimodal interventions and deliberately highlighted veteran narratives as evidence; the BRAVE Framework organized recurring patterns into four interconnected domains; BRAVE Theory formalized mechanisms (identity, agency, resilience) and identified identity as the mediator across domains; and the final synthesis presented a precise approach to reintegration based on biological sensitivity, mindfulness-mediated regulation, and culturally appropriate delivery.

Methodologically, form followed function. Reviews were selected for scope exploration, scoping for mapping emerging modalities, and evidence integration to reconcile diverse designs while maintaining veteran input. The mixed-methods approach addressed blind spots in purely quantitative research (e.g., mistaking dropout for disinterest) and ensured effect sizes reflected real-world feasibility. The resulting program logic was sequenced, synchronized, and centered on identity-rejected, siloed service delivery: psychological improvements must be supported by physical autonomy, social belonging, and economic stability to last.

Practically, BRAVE operationalizes three commitments: first, designing for synchrony (advancing multiple domains simultaneously); second, delivering with cultural competence (peer mentorship, trauma-informed flexibility, hybrid access); and third, evaluating through dual lenses (objective functional metrics and subjective identity coherence). The implications are that funding and policy should prioritize multidomain outcomes; researchers should test mediating mechanisms and engagement strategies; practitioners should coordinate interventions as interconnected parts rather than separate tracks. Its limitations include diverse measures, variable program fidelity, and underrepresenting specific subgroups. Still, the overall trajectory should be move from lived experience to evidence-based, testable, teachable, and adaptable theory.

Key Takeaways

- **Method shapes insight**—Sequential review methods (narrative → scoping → evidence integration) transformed lived problems into testable models and program designs, each method chosen according to the stage's requirements (Engel, 1977; Mezirow, 1997).
- **Reintegration is multidomain by default**—Psychological, physical, social, and economic factors move together; single-modality programs underperform against interconnected needs (Cameron et al., 2016; Demers, 2011; Elbogen et al., 2022).

- **Identity is the mediator**—Lasting change tracks with identity reconstruction; symptom drops without identity work rarely translate to sustained reintegration (Bryan et al., 2018; Mezirow, 1997; Wakefield et al., 2024).
- **Mind–body pairing beats silos**—Strength & conditioning plus mindfulness improves function and regulation more reliably than either alone (Goldberg et al., 2020; Polusny et al., 2015; Taylor et al., 2020).
- **Veteran voice is evidence**—Qualitative insights explain engagement and dropout (stigma, logistics, trust) that effect sizes miss; designing with veteran input raises retention and impact (Cacioppo & Cacioppo, 2014; Cheney et al., 2018; Saban et al., 2022).
- **Precision reintegration is viable**—Biological sensitivity and epigenetic plasticity suggest some veterans gain most from the proper supports at the right time (Domschke et al., 2025; Van Assche et al., 2023; van IJzendoorn, M. H.,, & Bakermans-Kranenburg, M. J., 2015).
- **Synchronize domains, don't sequence them**—Coordinated interventions (e.g., therapy + training + peer/finance) yield additive gains in health, function, and participation (Agarwal et al., 2021; Bond et al., 2022; Roseen et al., 2023).
- **Culture and delivery matter**—Peer-led, trauma-informed, and hybrid (in-person + virtual) formats reduce barriers tied to mistrust, geography, and schedule (Demers, 2011; Duncan et al., 2020; Fortier et al., 2024).
- **Evaluate with dual lenses**—Pair objective metrics (e.g., PROMIS, PCL-5, financial well-being) with subjective identity coherence to capture real progress (Engel, 1977; Ryan & Deci, 2000).
- **Operational readiness informs rehab**—Load management, movement quality, and environmental stress adaptation remain core to post-service function and confidence (Abt et al., 2010; Lovalekar et al., 2021; Nindl et al., 2018).

Applied Learning Prompts

1. Which review approach (narrative/scoping/EIR) best fits each research question in this chapter, and why?
2. Using the evidence cited here, argue for integrating physical training and mindfulness during transition rather than delivering them separately.
3. What qualitative insights from veterans would you prioritize capturing alongside quantitative metrics in a BRAVE-aligned evaluation, and how would you collect them?
4. Sketch a BRAVE-style intervention sequence for 8–12 weeks (design, delivery, evaluation) that advances at least two domains in tandem.
5. Name two predictable drop-off points (e.g., scheduling, mistrust). For each, specify one cultural/operational adaptation to prevent attrition.
6. Propose one feasible mixed-methods study to test a BRAVE mechanism (identity, agency, or resilience). List the primary outcome(s), one qualitative question, and your follow-up window.

References

Abanes, J. J., Ridner, S. H., Dietrich, M. S., Hiers, C., & Rhoten, B. (2022). Acupuncture for sleep disturbances in post-deployment military service members: A randomized controlled trial. *Clinical Nursing Research, 31*(2), 239–250. https://doi.org/10.1177/10547738211030602

Abt, J. P., Sell, T. C., Crawford, K., Lovalekar, M., Nagai, T., Deluzio, J., Smalley, B. W., McGrail, M. A., Rowe, R. S., Cardin, S., & Lephart, S. M. (2010). Warrior model for human performance and injury prevention: Eagle tactical athlete program (ETAP) part II. *Journal of Special Operations Medicine: A Peer Reviewed Journal for SOF Medical Professionals, 10*(4), 22–33. https://doi.org/10.55460/42ci-elhp

Acierno, R., Kauffman, B., Muzzy, W., Tejada, M. H., & Lejuez, C. (2021). Behavioral activation and therapeutic exposure vs. cognitive therapy for grief among combat veterans: A randomized clinical trial of bereavement interventions. *American Journal of Hospice and Palliative Medicine®, 38*(12), 1470–1478. https://doi.org/10.1177/1049909121989021

Agarwal, A. K., Waddell, K. J., Small, D. S., Evans, C., Harrington, T. O., Djaraher, R., Oon, A. L., & Patel, M. S. (2021). Effect of gamification with and without financial incentives to increase physical activity among veterans classified as having obesity or overweight: A randomized clinical trial. *JAMA Network Open, 4*(7), e2116256. https://doi.org/10.1001/jamanetworkopen.2021.16256

Almeida, M. F., Piehler, T., Carstens, K. E., Zhao, M., Samadi, M., Dudek, S. M., Norton, C. J., Parisian, C. M., Farizatto, K. L. G., & Bahr, B. A. (2021). Distinct and dementia-related synaptopathy in the hippocampus after military blast exposures. *Brain Pathology, 31*(3), e12936. https://doi.org/10.1111/bpa.12936

Anestis, J. C., Green, B. A., Arnau, R. C., & Anestis, M. D. (2019). Psychopathic personality traits in the military: An examination of the Levenson self-report psychopathy scales in a novel sample. *Assessment, 26*(4), 670–683. https://doi.org/10.1177/1073191117719511

Balcan, A.-D. (2023). The mediating role of social support in the relationship between operational stress and Well-being in military personnel. *BRAIN: Broad Research in Artificial Intelligence and Neuroscience, 14*(1), 105–116. https://doi.org/10.18662/brain/14.1/409

Besemann, M., Hebert, J., Thompson, J. M., Cooper, R. A., Gupta, G., Brémault-Phillips, S. B., & Dentry, S. J. (2018). Reflections on recovery, rehabilitation and reintegration of injured service members and veterans from a bio-psychosocial-spiritual perspective. *Canadian Journal of Surgery, 61*(6 Suppl 1), S219–S231. https://doi.org/10.1503/cjs.015318

Bond, G. R., Al-Abdulmunem, M., Ressler, D. R., Gade, D. M., & Drake, R. E. (2022). A randomized controlled trial of an employment program for veterans transitioning from the military: Two-year outcomes. *Administration and Policy in Mental Health and Mental Health Services Research, 49*(6), 1072–1083. https://doi.org/10.1007/s10488-022-01208-z

Bronfenbrenner, U. (1979). *The ecology of human development: Experiments by nature and design.* Harvard University Press.

Bryan, C. J., Leifker, F. R., Rozek, D. C., Bryan, A. O., Reynolds, M. L., Oakey, D. N., & Roberge, E. (2018). Examining the effectiveness of an intensive, 2-week treatment program for military personnel and veterans with PTSD: Results of a pilot, open-label, prospective cohort trial. *Journal of Clinical Psychology, 74*(12), 2070–2081. https://doi.org/10.1002/jclp.22651

Cacioppo, J. T., & Cacioppo, S. (2014). Social relationships and health: The toxic effects of perceived social isolation. *Social and Personality Psychology Compass, 8*(2), 58–72. https://doi.org/10.1111/spc3.12087

Caddick, N., & Smith, B. (2014). The impact of sport and physical activity on the Well-being of combat veterans: A systematic review. *Psychology of Sport and Exercise, 15*(1), 9–18. https://doi.org/10.1016/j.psychsport.2013.09.011

Cameron, K. L., Driban, J. B., & Svoboda, S. J. (2016). Osteoarthritis and the tactical athlete: A systematic review. *Journal of Athletic Training, 51*(11), 952–961. https://doi.org/10.4085/1062-6050-51.5.03

Castillo, D. T., Chee, C. L., Nason, E., Keller, J., C'De Baca, J., Qualls, C., Fallon, S. K., Haaland, K. Y., Miller, M. W., & Keane, T. M. (2016). Group-Delivered Cognitive/Exposure Therapy for Ptsd in Women Veterans: A Randomized Controlled Trial. *Psychological Trauma: Theory, Research, Practice, and Policy, 8*(3), 404–412. https://doi.org/10.1037/tra0000111

Cheney, A. M., Koenig, C. J., Miller, C. J., Zamora, K., Wright, P., Stanley, R., Fortney, J., Burgess, J. F., & Pyne, J. M. (2018). Veteran-centered barriers to VA mental healthcare services use. *BMC Health Services Research, 18*, 591. https://doi.org/10.1186/s12913-018-3346-9

Clemens, E. V., & Milsom, A. S. (2008). Enlisted service members' transition into the civilian world of work: A cognitive information processing approach. *The Career Development Quarterly, 56*(3), 246–256. https://doi.org/10.1002/j.2161-0045.2008.tb00039.x

Cooper, L., Caddick, N., Godier, L., Cooper, A., & Fossey, M. (2018). Transition from the military into civilian life: An exploration of cultural competence. *Armed Forces & Society, 44*(1), 156–177. https://doi.org/10.1177/0095327X16675965

Cushing, R. E., & Braun, K. L. (2017). Mind–body therapy for military veterans with post-traumatic stress disorder: A systematic review. *The Journal of Alternative and Complementary Medicine, 24*(2), 106–114. https://doi.org/10.1089/acm.2017.0176

Demers, A. (2011). When veterans return: The role of community in reintegration. *Journal of Loss and Trauma, 16*(2), 160–179. https://doi.org/10.1080/15325024.2010.519281

Domschke, K., Schiele, M. A., Crespo Salvador, Ó., Zillich, L., Lipovsek, J., Pittig, A., Heinig, I., Ridderbusch, I. C., Straube, B., Richter, J., Hollandt, M., Plag, J., Fydrich, T., Koelkebeck, K., Weber, H., Lueken, U., Dannlowski, U., Margraf, J., Schneider, S., & Deckert, J. (2025). Epigenetic markers of disease risk and psychotherapy response in anxiety disorders: A longitudinal analysis of the DNA methylome. *Molecular Psychiatry*. https://doi.org/10.1038/s41380-025-03038-5

Duncan, J. M., Reed-Fitzke, K., Ferraro, A. J., Wojciak, A. S., Smith, K. M., & Sánchez, J. (2020). Identifying risk and resilience factors associated with the likelihood of seeking mental health care among U.S. Army soldiers-in-training. *Military Medicine, 185*(7–8), e1247–e1254. https://doi.org/10.1093/milmed/usz483

Elbogen, E. B., Zeber, J. E., Vogt, D., Perkins, D. F., Finley, E. P., & Copeland, L. A. (2022). Financial status and Well-being in recently separated military veterans. *Military Medicine, 188*(7–8), e2181–e2188. https://doi.org/10.1093/milmed/usac030

Elnitsky, C. A., Blevins, C. L., Fisher, M. P., & Magruder, K. (2017). Military service member and veteran reintegration: A critical review and adapted ecological model. *American Journal of Orthopsychiatry, 87*(2), 114–128. https://doi.org/10.1037/ort0000244

Engel, G. L. (1977). The need for a new medical model: A challenge for biomedicine. *Science, 196*(4286), 129–136. https://doi.org/10.1126/science.847460

Farina, E. K., Taylor, J. C., Means, G. E., Murphy, N. E., Pasiakos, S. M., Lieberman, H. R., & McClung, J. P. (2017). Effects of deployment on diet quality and nutritional status markers of elite U.S. Army special operations forces soldiers. *Nutrition Journal, 16*, 41. https://doi.org/10.1186/s12937-017-0262-5

Flood, A., & Keegan, R. J. (2022). Cognitive resilience to psychological stress in military personnel. *Frontiers in Psychology, 13*, 809003. https://doi.org/10.3389/fpsyg.2022.809003

Fortier, C. B., Kenna, A., Katz, D., Kim, S., Hursh, C., Beck, B., Sablone, C. A., Currao, A., Lebas, A., Jorge, R. E., & Fonda, J. R. (2024). STEP-home transdiagnostic group reintegration workshop to improve mental health outcomes for post-9/11 veterans: Design, methods, and rationale for a randomized controlled behavioral trial. *Contemporary Clinical Trials, 141*, 107536. https://doi.org/10.1016/j.cct.2024.107536

Friedl, K. E., Knapik, J. J., Häkkinen, K., Baumgartner, N., Groeller, H., Taylor, N. A. S., Duarte, A. F. A., Kyröläinen, H., Jones, B. H., Kraemer, W. J., & Nindl, B. C. (2015). Perspectives on aerobic and strength influences on military physical readiness: Report of an international military physiology roundtable. *Journal of Strength and Conditioning Research, 29*(11 Suppl), S10–S23. https://journals.lww.com/nsca-jscr/fulltext/2015/11001/perspectives_on_aerobic_and_strength_influences_on.3.aspx

Goldberg, S. B., Riordan, K. M., Sun, S., Kearney, D. J., & Simpson, T. L. (2020). Efficacy and acceptability of mindfulness-based interventions for military veterans: A systematic review and meta-analysis. *Journal of Psychosomatic Research, 138*, 110232. https://doi.org/10.1016/j.jpsychores.2020.110232

Goldstein, L. A., Mehling, W. E., Metzler, T. J., Cohen, B. E., Barnes, D. E., Choucroun, G. J., Silver, A., Talbot, L. S., Maguen, S., Hlavin, J. A., Chesney, M. A., & Neylan, T. C. (2018). Veterans group exercise: A randomized pilot trial of an integrative exercise program for veterans with posttraumatic stress. *Journal of Affective Disorders, 227*, 345–352. https://doi.org/10.1016/j.jad.2017.11.002

Gonzalez, D. E., McAllister, M. J., Waldman, H. S., Ferrando, A. A., Joyce, J., Barringer, N. D., Dawes, J. J., Kieffer, A. J., Harvey, T., Kerksick, C. M., Stout, J. R., Ziegenfuss, T. N., Zapp, A., Tartar, J. L., Heileson, J. L., VanDusseldorp, T. A., Kalman, D. S., Campbell, B. I., Antonio, J., & Kreider, R. B. (2022). International Society of Sports Nutrition position stand: Tactical athlete nutrition. *Journal of the International Society of Sports Nutrition, 19*(1), 267–315. https://doi.org/10.1080/15502783.2022.2086017

Gregg, B. T., Shordike, A., Howell, D. M., Kitzman, P. H., & Iwama, M. K. (2018). Student veteran occupational transitions in postsecondary education: A grounded theory. *Military Behavioral Health, 6*(1), 30–40. https://doi.org/10.1080/21635781.2017.1333063

Griffin, B. J., Purcell, N., Burkman, K., Litz, B. T., Bryan, C. J., Schmitz, M., Villierme, C., Walsh, J., & Maguen, S. (2019). Moral injury: An integrative review. *Journal of Traumatic Stress, 32*(3), 350–362. https://doi.org/10.1002/jts.22362

Griffiths, H. K., Hawkins, B. L., & Crowe, B. M. (2020). Identifying contextual factors that impact community reintegration in injured female veterans. *Journal of Military, Veteran and Family Health, 6*(1), 38–47. https://doi.org/10.3138/jmvfh-2018-0043

Hoffman, M. W., Stout, J. R., Hoffman, J. R., Landua, G., Fukuda, D. H., Sharvit, N., Moran, D. S., Carmon, E., & Ostfeld, I. (2016). Critical velocity is associated with combat-specific performance measures in a special forces unit. *Journal of Strength and Conditioning Research, 30*(2), 497–504. https://journals.lww.com/nsca-jscr/fulltext/2016/02000/critical_velocity_is_associated_with.20.aspx

Joiner, T. (2005). *Why people die by suicide*. Harvard University Press.

Joseph, J. S., Smith-MacDonald, L., Filice, M. C., & Smith, M. S. (2023). Reculturation: A new perspective on military-civilian transition stress. *Military Psychology, 35*(3), 193–203. https://doi.org/10.1080/08995605.2022.2094175

Joyce, S., Shand, F., Lal, T. J., Mott, B., Bryant, R. A., & Harvey, S. B. (2019). Resilience@work mindfulness program: Results from a cluster randomized controlled trial with first responders. *Journal of Medical Internet Research, 21*(2), e12894. https://doi.org/10.2196/12894

Kahn, J. R., Collinge, W., & Soltysik, R. (2016). Post-9/11 veterans and their partners improve mental health outcomes with a self-directed mobile and web-based wellness training program: A randomized controlled trial. *Journal of Medical Internet Research, 18*(9), e255. https://doi.org/10.2196/jmir.5800

Karre, J. K., Perkins, D. F., Morgan, N. R., Davenport, K. E., Aronson, K. R., Maury, R. V., Bradbard, D., Armstrong, N. J., Wright, A., Sargent, R., & Andros, M. (2025). What do successful military-to-civilian transitions look like? A revised framework and a new conceptual model for assessing veteran Well-being. *Armed Forces & Society, 51*(3), 611–640. https://doi.org/10.1177/0095327X231216678

Kearney, D. J., Malte, C. A., Storms, M., & Simpson, T. L. (2021). Loving-kindness meditation vs cognitive processing therapy for posttraumatic stress disorder among veterans: A randomized clinical trial. *JAMA Network Open, 4*(4), e216604. https://doi.org/10.1001/jamanetworkopen.2021.6604

Kelly, M. M., Reilly, E. D., Ameral, V., Richter, S., & Fukuda, S. (2022). A randomized pilot study of acceptance and commitment therapy to improve social support for veterans with PTSD. *Journal of Clinical Medicine, 11*(12), 3482. https://doi.org/10.3390/jcm11123482

Lovalekar, M., Hauret, K., Roy, T., Taylor, K., Blacker, S. D., Newman, P., Yanovich, R., Fleischmann, C., Nindl, B. C., Jones, B., & Canham-Chervak, M. (2021). Musculoskeletal injuries in military personnel—Descriptive epidemiology, risk factor identification, and prevention. *Journal of Science and Medicine in Sport, 24*(10), 963–969. https://doi.org/10.1016/j.jsams.2021.03.016

McClung, J. P., Beckner, M. E., & Farina, E. K. (2023). Assessing the physiological basis for resilience in military personnel. *Stress and Health, 39*(S1), 33–39. https://doi.org/10.1002/smi.3271

Mezirow, J. (1997). Transformation theory out of context. *Adult Education Quarterly, 48*(1), 60–62. https://doi.org/10.1177/074171369704800105

Nindl, B. C., Billing, D. C., Drain, J. R., Beckner, M. E., Greeves, J., Groeller, H., Teien, H. K., Marcora, S., Moffitt, A., Reilly, T., Taylor, N. A. S., Young, A. J., & Friedl, K. E. (2018). Perspectives on resilience for military readiness and preparedness: Report of an international military physiology roundtable. *Journal of Science and Medicine in Sport, 21*(11), 1116–1124. https://doi.org/10.1016/j.jsams.2018.05.005

Pearlin, L. I., Menaghan, E. G., Lieberman, M. A., & Mullan, J. T. (1981). The Stress Process. *Journal of Health and Social Behavior, 22*(4), 337–356. https://doi.org/10.2307/2136676

Polusny, M. A., Erbes, C. R., Thuras, P., Moran, A., Lamberty, G. J., Collins, R. C., Rodman, J. L., & Lim, K. O. (2015). Mindfulness-based stress reduction for posttraumatic stress disorder among veterans: A randomized clinical trial. *JAMA, 314*(5), 456–465. https://doi.org/10.1001/jama.2015.8361

Reinhardt, K. M., Noggle Taylor, J. J., Johnston, J., Zameer, A., Cheema, S., & Khalsa, S. B. S. (2018). Kripalu yoga for military veterans with PTSD: A randomized trial. *Journal of Clinical Psychology, 74*(1), 93–108. https://doi.org/10.1002/jclp.22483

Roseen, E. J., Pinheiro, A., Lemaster, C. M., Plumb, D., Wang, S., Elwy, A. R., Streeter, C. C., Lynch, S., Groessl, E., Sherman, K. J., Weinberg, J., & Saper, R. B. (2023). Yoga versus education for veterans with chronic low back pain: A randomized controlled trial. *Journal of General Internal Medicine, 38*(9), 2113–2122. https://doi.org/10.1007/s11606-023-08037-2

Roy, T. C., Lopez, H. P., & Piva, S. R. (2013). Loads worn by soldiers predict episodes of low back pain during deployment to Afghanistan. *Spine, 38*(15), 1310–1317. https://journals.lww.com/spinejournal/fulltext/2013/07010/loads_worn_by_soldiers_predict_episodes_of_low.19.aspx

Ryan, R. M., & Deci, E. L. (2000). Intrinsic and extrinsic motivations: Classic definitions and new directions. *Contemporary Educational Psychology, 25*(1), 54–67. https://doi.org/10.1006/ceps.1999.1020

Saban, K. L., Collins, E. G., Mathews, H. L., Bryant, F. B., Tell, D., Gonzalez, B., Bhoopalam, S., Chroniak, C. P., & Janusek, L. W. (2022). Impact of a mindfulness-based stress reduction program on psychological Well-being, cortisol, and inflammation in women veterans. *Journal of General Internal Medicine, 37*(3), 751–761. https://doi.org/10.1007/s11606-022-07584-4

Sayer, N. A., Spoont, M., Murdoch, M., Parker, L. E., Hintz, S., & Rosenheck, R. (2011). A qualitative study of U.S. veterans' reasons for seeking Department of Veterans Affairs disability benefits for posttraumatic stress disorder. *Journal of Traumatic Stress, 24*(6), 699–707. https://doi.org/10.1002/jts.20693

Steenkamp, M. M., Litz, B. T., Hoge, C. W., & Marmar, C. R. (2015). Psychotherapy for military-related PTSD: A review of randomized clinical trials. *JAMA, 314*(5), 489–500. https://doi.org/10.1001/jama.2015.8370

Taylor, J., McLean, L., Korner, A., Stratton, E., & Glozier, N. (2020). Mindfulness and yoga for psychological trauma: Systematic review and meta-analysis. *Journal of Trauma & Dissociation, 21*(5), 536–573. https://doi.org/10.1080/15299732.2020.1760167

Teplova, A. E., Bakker, H. A. H. M., Perry, S. I. B., van Etten-Jamaludin, F. S., Plat, M. C. J., & Bekkers, M. B. M. (2021). The impact of deployment and combat exposure on physical health among military personnel: A systematic review of incidence, prevalence, and risks. *Military Medicine, 187*(9–10), e1074–e1085. https://doi.org/10.1093/milmed/usab302

Van Assche, E., Hohoff, C., Zang, J., Knight, M. J., & Baune, B. T. (2023). Epigenetic modification related to cognitive changes during a cognitive training intervention in depression. *Progress in Neuro-Psychopharmacology and Biological Psychiatry, 127*, 110835. https://doi.org/10.1016/j.pnpbp.2023.110835

van IJzendoorn, M. H., & Bakermans-Kranenburg, M. J. (2015). Genetic differential susceptibility on trial: Meta-analytic support from randomized controlled experiments. *Development and Psychopathology, 27*(1), 151–162. https://doi.org/10.1017/S0954579414001369

Wakefield, J. R. H., Bowe, M., Këllezi, B., Haslam, C., Bentley, S. V., Milani, Z., Gair, H., & McIntosh, J. S. A. (2024). Brothers and sisters in arms: A mixed-methods investigation of the roles played by military support and social identity processes in the mental health of veterans during the transition to veterancy. *Journal of Community & Applied Social Psychology, 34*(1), e2756. https://doi.org/10.1002/casp.2756

Worrell-George, K., Shienko, L., & Buechner, B. (2022). Getting unstuck: Pathways for transforming lived experience of veterans in transition to civilian life.

Chapter 5
The Road to BRAVE

This chapter charts the road from an initial framework to a formal, testable theory. It explains how lived experience and empirical evidence were fused through an Evidence Integration Review to surface what current reintegration models do well, where they fail, and why identity reconstruction must sit at the center of any durable solution. The chapter then integrates the core theories of the Biopsychosocial Model, Trauma Exposure Theory, Social Identity Theory, SIMIC, and Transformative Learning Theory into a single, multidomain logic that connects psychological, physical, social, and economic change. After reading, you'll be able to: (1) trace how the BRAVE Framework matured into BRAVE Theory; (2) interpret key findings and limits from an evidence integration of frontline studies; (3) connect multiple theoretical traditions into an identity-centered account of reintegration; (4) evaluate practice, policy, and evaluation implications of BRAVE Theory; and (5) preview how the four BRAVE domains organize real-world program design.

5.1 Introduction—Framing the Problem

The road to BRAVE began with a question that refused to leave me alone: Why are so many veterans still struggling after transition, even when services exist on paper to help them? My own experience, combined with years of listening to peers, told me this was not a matter of isolated clinical diagnoses like posttraumatic stress disorder (PTSD) or the occasional lapse in employment. Instead, the issue emerged from a more profound and systemic disconnect. It's one where institutional silo, fragmented program delivery, and narrow definitions of "reintegration" leave veterans navigating transition in pieces, rather than as whole people.

T. Carlton, *BRAVE Theory*, https://doi.org/10.1007/978-3-032-13695-4_5

From the start, I realized that systems built to support us often focus on only one area of need at a time. A veteran might get mental health counseling but lack job planning at the same time; another might complete a job-training program but still deal with untreated trauma and lack a social network to help with change. My early review of the literature confirmed what I instinctively felt: many reintegration models only target psychological trauma (e.g., cognitive-behavioral therapy for PTSD), vocational training, or social support separately. Few models combine all three in a way that recognizes how they are interconnected (Elnitsky et al., 2017; Sayer et al., 2011). This separation goes against the reality of transition, where psychological, social, physical, and economic aspects constantly interact and influence each other (Bronfenbrenner, 1979; Engel, 1977).

The evidence revealed a consistent gap between veterans' needs and the design of existing systems. Studies have shown that when services fail to recognize the multidimensional nature of reintegration, outcomes tend to be temporary or incomplete, with progress in one area often undermined by neglect in another (Demers, 2011; Elbogen et al., 2022). For instance, economic instability can worsen mental health symptoms, just as untreated trauma can hinder educational or occupational advancement. This reciprocal influence between domains is well-supported in the literature and formed the basis for my belief that a new approach was necessary. The new approach needed to integrate various interventions into a coherent, identity-centered process.

In my portfolio work, I realized that veterans do not transition in isolated parts. Instead, we transition as whole individuals with interconnected systems of identity, experience, and environment. Despite decades of research, the current reintegration landscape treats these systems separately. The development of BRAVE was not about inventing something entirely new; instead, it was about creating a framework that respects the complexity of veteran life, incorporates existing best practices, and is rooted in empirical evidence and lived experience.

5.2 Identifying the Gaps in Reintegration Models

In reviewing veteran reintegration literature for my Evidence Integration Review, I anticipated uncovering a comprehensive body of work that captured the complexity of transition, something I experienced as multifaceted, overlapping, and identity-driven. Instead, I encountered a fragmented landscape. Most models and programs addressed discrete domains in isolation:

- Psychological health was often the sole focus, framed primarily through PTSD treatment or suicide prevention programs (Kearney et al., 2021; Steenkamp et al., 2015). While critical, these approaches tended to operate within clinical silos, rarely integrating vocational or social components that influence psychological outcomes.

- Vocational reintegration programs, such as supported employment or skills translation initiatives, targeted job placement but frequently ignored the impact of untreated trauma, chronic pain, or the loss of military identity on employment stability (Bond et al., 2022; Stone & Stone, 2015).
- Social reintegration interventions, including peer mentorship and community engagement initiatives, positively affected belonging and trust (Van Kessel, 2013) but were often disconnected from clinical care or economic planning.

The issue wasn't the absence of effective strategies but that they seldom aligned in a way that mirrored the interconnected reality of veteran lives. The evidence base reflected the institutional silos I personally observed, VA healthcare focusing on mental health separately from vocational rehab; community nonprofits organizing peer groups without clinical ties; workforce agencies unaware of the cultural and psychological hurdles veterans encounter in civilian jobs. This division conflicts with established health models. The biopsychosocial model (Engel, 1977) clearly sees health as an interaction of biological, psychological, and social factors, yet veteran reintegration programs rarely apply this approach comprehensively. Likewise, ecological systems theory (Bronfenbrenner, 1979) highlights that interconnected environments influence human functioning from individuals to policy structures. Still, many interventions focus only on micro-level changes, overlooking systemic and policy factors that can either support or hinder success.

Empirical evidence supports the need for integration. Elbogen et al. (2022) found that veterans with stable income, strong social support, and access to mental healthcare reported significantly higher life satisfaction and lower distress than those with unmet needs in even one of those domains. Conversely, deficits in any single area often undermine gains elsewhere. This phenomenon is echoed in Sayer et al.'s (2011) findings that unaddressed physical limitations or chronic health issues can derail otherwise successful psychological recovery or employment trajectories.

Another essential gap was identity reconstruction. Most reintegration models focused on symptoms or outcomes, such as PTSD reduction, job placement, or educational enrollment, without considering how identity continuity and transformation support those outcomes. Social Identity Theory and the Social Identity Model of Identity Change (SIMIC) provide clear evidence that maintaining or developing valued group memberships during transition helps prevent mental health decline and promotes adaptation (Wakefield et al., 2024). Yet, few programs measured or actively supported identity reconstruction as an outcome variable. My own experience has shown me that without a coherent sense of self after service, any gains in employment, income, or symptom relief would be fragile.

Finally, I identified a methodological limitation in the literature: short follow-up periods. Many interventions were assessed at three or six months, focusing little on long-term sustainability (Sayer et al., 2014; Van Til et al., 2013). This gap is significant. Veteran reintegration is not a one-time event but a long, ongoing process. Improvements made in the first year can fade without continuous, multidomain support, a fact shown in longitudinal studies highlighting relapse in psychological symptoms and job loss when ongoing intervention is lacking (Karre et al., 2025).

In short, my literature review confirmed what I observed in the field: we have practical tools scattered across various disciplines, but without integration, they fail to create lasting change. The veterans who do best are those with comprehensive interventions, coordinated and centered on identity. These are precisely the qualities I found missing in most models. This insight laid the groundwork for moving beyond frameworks combining services toward those explaining why and how transformation happens when these domains are aligned. That was the first conceptual step toward what would become BRAVE.

5.3 From Framework to Theory—The Convergence Process

The shift toward BRAVE started with my Evidence Integration Review (EIR). It was a systematic synthesis of 41 primary studies published from 2014 to 2024, spanning four key disciplines: clinical psychology, public health, social work, and military sociology. Each discipline brought a distinct lens:

- Clinical psychology emphasized symptom-focused interventions, especially for PTSD, depression, and anxiety, often through cognitive-behavioral therapy (CBT), acceptance and commitment therapy (ACT), or prolonged exposure protocols (Kearney et al., 2021; Steenkamp et al., 2015).
- Public health contributed models of social determinants of health, showing how housing stability, income security, and access to healthcare are critical for sustaining reintegration (Betancourt et al., 2005; Elbogen et al., 2022).
- Social work highlighted case management, peer support, and systems navigation as essential tools for bridging gaps in access and continuity of care (Elnitsky et al., 2017). Military sociology examined cultural identity, role loss, and the structural challenges of reentering civilian life after extended immersion in military culture (Demers, 2011; Sayer et al., 2011).

The EIR methodology followed the PRISMA structured process: identifying peer-reviewed studies that explicitly addressed post-9/11 veteran reintegration, extracting outcome measures across psychological, physical, social, and economic domains, and coding interventions based on whether they were single-domain, multidomain, or integrative. This enabled me to see patterns that would have been invisible within any one discipline.

The most notable pattern was the consistent advantage of multidomain interventions. Programs that combined psychological care with vocational training or linked peer support with physical rehabilitation showed the most lasting positive results. For example, interventions integrating employment services with clinical mental health support achieved significantly better job retention rates and lower psychological distress compared to isolated approaches (Adler & Gutierrez, 2023; Van Til et al., 2013). Similarly, peer mentorship combined with structured skill development increased both social connectedness and self-efficacy, outcomes that continued beyond the program period (Haslam et al., 2019).

However, I also identified critical weaknesses in the existing literature:

- **Fragmentation**—Even multidomain programs were often the product of co-located but independent services, lacking a shared theoretical framework or coordinated delivery system.
- **Short evaluation windows**—Many studies assessed outcomes at three or six months, providing little insight into long-term sustainability (Sayer et al., 2011).
- **Neglect of identity reconstruction**—Few interventions measured changes in identity or role coherence, despite Social Identity Theory and SIMIC evidence that these factors are central to adaptation (Wakefield et al., 2024).
- **Underutilization of physical health integration**—Physical rehabilitation and chronic pain management were often treated as separate from psychological or vocational recovery, despite strong evidence of bidirectional influence (Sayer et al., 2011).

By the conclusion of the EIR, I had not yet articulated BRAVE as a theory, but the scaffolding was already in place. The evidence showed that sustainable reintegration required more than co-occurring interventions; it needed a unifying conceptual model that explained why aligning psychological, physical, social, and economic systems was essential, and how this alignment supported identity reconstruction. The EIR was my pivot point. It confirmed that we had effective practices in every domain and that these practices rarely produced lasting transformation without integration. It was from this intersection of empirical synthesis and personal lived reality that the first contours of BRAVE began to take shape.

The earliest formalization of these insights emerged in the BRAVE Framework. It's a multidomain reintegration model created to guide practice by organizing interventions into four interconnected domains: psychological, physical, social, and economic. Based on the evidence synthesis in the EIR, the framework highlighted that no single domain could ensure sustainable reintegration. Instead, progress is best achieved when each domain is addressed together, reinforcing improvements across the entire system.

While the framework provided a practical roadmap for service delivery, ongoing research, which included my narrative review on multidomain reintegration, showed that an applied framework alone couldn't fully explain why some multidomain interventions succeeded while others failed. This gap led to the development of the BRAVE Theory, which elevated the model from a prescriptive guide to an explanatory framework. In its theoretical form, BRAVE places identity reconstruction as both the key mechanism and the main goal of reintegration, mediating interactions between domains. By combining the Biopsychosocial Model, Trauma Exposure Theory, Social Identity Theory, the Social Identity Model of Identity Change, and Transformative Learning Theory, BRAVE Theory offers the structural foundation that the framework previously lacked, turning a collection of best practices into a unified, evidence-based model of veteran reintegration.

5.4 Theoretical Foundations of BRAVE

The BRAVE Theory emerged as a multidimensional, identity-centered reconstruction model designed to explain and guide veteran reintegration. While the BRAVE Framework organized reintegration into four interdependent domains: psychological, physical, social, and economic, the shift from framework to theory required grounding these domains in a cohesive, evidence-based structure explaining why multidomain alignment was beneficial and necessary. My Evidence Integration Review, subsequent narrative review, and lived experience all converged on one conclusion: no single theory alone captures the layered complexity of reintegration. The actual transformation mechanisms could be made visible only by integrating multiple theoretical perspectives.

The first structural pillar is the Biopsychosocial Model (Engel, 1977), long recognized for framing health as an interaction among biological, psychological, and social systems. For veterans, these elements are inseparable; physical injuries influence mental health, psychological distress alters social relationships, and social isolation worsens both. Yet the reintegration evidence base (Besemann et al., 2018; Lugg, 2022) clarifies that the traditional model is incomplete. Economic stability, often treated as a secondary or external factor, is a primary determinant of health, directly influencing treatment adherence, recovery access, and a veteran's sense of agency. Financial instability compounds psychological stress, undermines physical recovery, and disrupts relational stability (Elbogen et al., 2022). BRAVE formally extends the BPS model into a Biopsychosocial-Economic framework, elevating economic stability to an equal footing with the other domains and positioning identity as the mediator linking these systems to role performance and well-being.

Understanding how disruptions cascade through these interconnected systems requires the second theoretical element, Trauma Exposure Theory. While much of veteran mental health research focuses narrowly on PTSD, Trauma Exposure Theory accounts for both acute and cumulative stressors and the ways they reverberate across identity, functioning, and environment over time (Elnitsky et al., 2017). Trauma is not a singular event to be compartmentalized but an ecological disruption affecting every domain. It manifests in psychological dysregulation (Kelly et al., 2022; Anestis et al., 2019), relational withdrawal, somatic symptoms, and diminished occupational capacity, often with bidirectional effects. A veteran struggling with chronic pain may experience depression, which erodes social trust and employment stability, which in turn worsens the pain. BRAVE adopts this ecological understanding, insisting that trauma recovery must be embedded within vocational, physical, and social reintegration strategies rather than siloed as a purely mental health intervention.

The third foundation lies in Social Identity Theory (Turner et al., 1975; Trepte & Loy, 2017) and the Social Identity Model of Identity Change (SIMIC) (Haslam et al., 2019; Wakefield et al., 2024). Military service constructs occupational skill and shapes a deeply held social identity rooted in hierarchy, cohesion, and shared mission. This identity offers role clarity, belonging, and purpose. Separation disrupts these anchors, often producing what BRAVE frames as identity discontinuity, a loss of coherent self-concept and valued group membership. SIMIC research demonstrates that veterans who maintain or replace these valued memberships fare better in resilience and adaptation. At the same time, those who lose them face elevated risks for social isolation, psychological distress, and disengagement. BRAVE extends SIMIC by recognizing that identity transitions are not only social but also psychophysiological and economic, influencing neuroregulation, motivation, and societal participation. This broadened view underscores that interventions must facilitate new group connections and restore identity coherence across all domains.

While SIMIC explains the social dimension of identity continuity, it does not fully account for the internal cognitive and emotional labor of integrating new experiences into a coherent worldview. This is where Transformative Learning Theory (Mezirow, 1997) becomes indispensable. TLT describes how individuals facing "disorienting dilemmas" (such as the shift from military to civilian life) engage in critical reflection, challenge prior assumptions, and reconstruct meaning. For veterans, this involves reconciling the military identity with emerging civilian roles, integrating the lessons of service (and sometimes trauma) into a new, empowered self-concept. In my own journey, and in the trajectories of veterans I have mentored, this process was not incidental; it was the core mechanism of sustainable change. BRAVE incorporates TLT by framing resilience as an emergent capacity, cultivated through narrative agency, reflective practice, and value realignment, processes that transform disruption into growth.

Integrating these four theoretical pillars transformed BRAVE from a practical framework into a predictive, explanatory model. The expanded Biopsychosocial-Economic structure maps the domains; Trauma Exposure Theory explains the systemic spread of disruption; Social Identity Theory and SIMIC illuminate the role of belonging and continuity; and Transformative Learning Theory reveals how meaning-making drives reconstruction. Together, they situate identity at the center as the mechanism through which reintegration occurs and as the outcome to be achieved. The psychological, physical, social, and economic domains are thus not isolated targets but dynamic systems whose alignment fosters agency, coherence, and purpose. Misalignment in one domain can destabilize progress in another; alignment across all can catalyze transformation. In this way, BRAVE reframes veteran reintegration not as symptom management or service delivery, but as a coordinated, identity-centered reconstruction capable of producing sustainable, life-wide change.

5.5 Identity as the Core of Reintegration—Implications for Practice and Policy

If the development of BRAVE Theory has revealed anything, identity is the core mechanism behind lasting change. In BRAVE, identity serves as a mediator, shaping how veterans engage with psychological, physical, social, and economic systems, and because of successful reintegration. This is not merely theoretical; it directly influences how programs are designed, services are delivered, and policies are evaluated.

Veteran support programs often evaluate success based on specific outcomes like reduced PTSD, employment, or stable housing. Still, they sometimes overlook whether these improvements stem from a reconstructed, coherent sense of self. BRAVE's foundation in Social Identity Theory, SIMIC, and Transformative Learning Theory emphasizes that such achievements are fragile without identity rebuilding. For example, a job driven solely by economic need without vocational purpose might not withstand stress, and psychological symptom relief without social reconnection can fade due to loneliness. However, when identity is reconstructed across multiple areas, aligning purpose with work, fostering social belonging, and ensuring financial stability, these improvements reinforce each other, creating more durable and holistic benefits.

Practically, BRAVE encourages service providers such as clinicians, vocational counselors, peer mentors, and educators to view themselves as part of an interconnected ecosystem instead of working in isolated professional silos. This approach supports the goals of the Biopsychosocial-Economic model and aligns with Bronfenbrenner's ecological systems theory. For example, a trauma-focused therapist should consider how symptom improvement relates to employability and community involvement; a workforce development expert should be aware of psychological barriers that affect job retention; and a peer mentor should recognize how physical limitations influence social participation. The aim is not for each practitioner to become a jack-of-all-trades, but to establish deliberate points of integration where services seamlessly support the veteran's reconstructing identity.

At the policy level, BRAVE directly confronts the fractured structure of veteran services. The institutional separation between VA healthcare, Department of Labor employment programs, and community-based nonprofits creates inefficiencies and hampers outcomes. Reintegration is a series of isolated tasks that involve rebuilding identity within interconnected systems. BRAVE-informed policy would prioritize:

- Formalized data-sharing agreements support interagency collaboration.
- Coordinated case management guided by multidomain assessment.
- Funding structures that acknowledge reintegration as a long-term, non-linear process, extending evaluation windows beyond the typical 3–6 months to capture sustainability.

BRAVE also redefines the veteran from being a passive recipient of services to an active participant in reintegration. This empowerment approach aligns with SIMIC's evidence that self-efficacy, role clarity, and valued group membership boost resilience (Haslam et al., 2019; Wakefield et al., 2024). Policies should thus focus on programs that incorporate leadership development, decision-making opportunities, and personal agency into service delivery, rather than providing support in ways that foster dependency. An additional implication is the need for identity-sensitive metrics in practice and policy evaluation. Assessment tools rarely measure role coherence, purpose, belonging, and agency. This omission creates a blind spot where programs seem adequate by traditional measures but still leave veterans vulnerable to destabilization. BRAVE's focus on identity emphasizes the need for validated tools to track these psychosocial variables, allowing practitioners and policymakers to differentiate between temporary stability and real reintegration.

Finally, BRAVE emphasizes that reintegration cannot be treated as a one-size-fits-all process. Veterans' reintegration experiences differ widely by service era, branch culture, combat exposure, gender, race, sexual orientation, disability status, and post-service environment. The ecological framework within BRAVE ensures that interventions are context-sensitive while still following the multidomain, identity-centered approach. A rural veteran with limited local infrastructure needs different strategic supports than an urban veteran pursuing higher education. This variability is not a barrier but a design requirement: by customizing interventions while maintaining a strong theoretical foundation, BRAVE offers both a unifying structure and the flexibility needed to address individual circumstances.

Essentially, BRAVE acts as both a diagnostic lens and a strategic guide. It emphasizes that reintegration efforts will continue to fail if viewed as a checklist of separate tasks. However, they can succeed when seen as the intentional rebuilding of a whole person across connected areas. When identity is regained and when veterans see themselves not just as former service members but as capable, connected, and purpose-driven individuals, reintegration becomes not only possible but transformative.

5.6 Defining BRAVE Theory

BRAVE Theory positions veteran identity as the mediator and the outcome of veteran reintegration, with four interdependent domains: psychological, physical, social, and economic, serving as the structural pillars of that process. These domains do not operate in isolation; they function as an integrated system in which disruption or growth in one area reverberates across the others. In this model, reintegration is understood not as a checklist of tasks to be completed, but as a dynamic rebalancing of interconnected systems in service of a coherent and empowered self-concept.

The psychological domain encompasses mental health, emotional regulation, and cognitive resilience, recognizing that trauma, stress, and identity disruption can undermine functioning even in the absence of clinical diagnoses. The physical domain addresses the realities of injury, chronic pain, and physical conditioning, acknowledging the bidirectional influence between bodily capacity and psychological well-being. The social domain reflects the importance of belonging, relational trust, and community integration, grounded in evidence from Social Identity Theory and the Social Identity Model of Identity Change, that group membership continuity is a critical protective factor. The economic domain incorporates employment, financial literacy, and resource stability, not as peripheral concerns but as core determinants of agency, opportunity, and self-efficacy.

While these domains can be examined separately for clarity, the BRAVE Theory insists that they must be addressed collectively. A veteran's progress in one area, such as securing stable employment, will be fragile if undermined by unresolved trauma, social isolation, or unmanaged physical limitations. Conversely, coordinated progress across multiple domains can produce a reinforcing cycle of stability and growth. Identity functions as the integrative mechanism, shaping how gains are perceived, internalized, and sustained. This multidomain, identity-centered structure makes BRAVE both diagnostic and prescriptive. It can explain why certain reintegration efforts fail and offer a blueprint for interventions that align domains toward lasting transformation. The next chapter examines each domain in depth, exploring how it operates individually, interacts with the others, and how intentional alignment can shift reintegration from a process of survival to one of empowerment.

Academic Synthesis

The development of the BRAVE Theory—Building Resilience and Advancing Veteran Empowerment—originated from a multi-stage research process that began with an Evidence Integration Review (EIR) synthesizing 41 primary studies published between 2014 and 2024. The EIR covered fields including clinical psychology, public health, social work, and military sociology, revealing ongoing fragmentation in veteran reintegration programs despite promising domain-specific interventions (Steenkamp et al., 2015; Betancourt et al., 2005; Elnitsky et al., 2017; Sayer et al., 2014). Patterns showed that sustainable reintegration outcomes most consistently occurred when interventions combined psychological, physical, social, and economic supports, rather than addressing these areas separately (Van Til et al., 2013; Haslam et al., 2019).

The BRAVE Framework was created to tackle this fragmentation by viewing reintegration as a process involving four connected areas: psychological, physical, social, and economic. The framework identified identity reconstruction, rather than just symptom reduction or functional improvements, as the key factor linking these areas. Its initial implementation drew from public health methods, peer mentorship models, and evaluations of veteran-specific programs, aiming to promote coordinated service delivery across different sectors.

The shift from framework to formal theory required integrating various foundational perspectives. The Biopsychosocial Model (Engel, 1977) offered a systemic view, expanded in BRAVE to explicitly include the economic aspect as an equal determinant of well-being (Besemann et al., 2018; Lugg, 2022). Trauma Exposure Theory highlighted the cumulative and cross-domain effects of both acute and chronic service-related stressors, emphasizing the need for interventions that address the ripple effects of trauma beyond psychiatric diagnosis (Elnitsky et al., 2017). The Social Identity Theory (Turner et al., 1975; Trepte & Loy, 2017) and Social Identity Model of Identity Change (Haslam et al., 2019; Wakefield et al., 2024) explained how losing group belonging disrupts role continuity and adaptation, while Transformative Learning Theory (Mezirow, 1997) outlined the reflective processes veterans need to reconcile military and civilian identities.

The BRAVE Theory integrates these models into a comprehensive, multidimensional view centered on identity in the reintegration process. It sees identity both as a mediator—through which psychological, physical, social, and economic factors influence—and as an outcome, marking the successful completion of reintegration. By viewing veterans as active participants, the theory challenges deficit-based approaches and advocates for empowerment-driven, identity-aware strategies. It highlights that progress in one domain can be hindered by weaknesses in another if there's no coordinated effort. Conversely, aligning multiple domains can foster a cycle of agency, purpose, and stability, leading to lasting positive change.

In practice, BRAVE offers a theoretical foundation for integrated program design, coordinated case management, and policy structures that promote interagency collaboration. For policymakers, it calls for evaluation metrics that include validated measures of identity reconstruction (such as role clarity, belonging, purpose, and self-efficacy) alongside functional and clinical outcomes. By situating veteran reintegration within a biopsychosocial-economic framework and grounding it in trauma, identity, and learning theories, BRAVE provides both explanatory power and practical guidance for enhancing veteran support systems.

Key Takeaways

- **Identity as Keystone**—Identity reconstruction is the central mechanism driving durable reintegration, influencing and being influenced by all four domains (Haslam et al., 2018; Wakefield et al., 2024).
- **Multidomain Superiority**—Integrated interventions yield more sustainable outcomes than siloed approaches, particularly when aligning psychological, physical, social, and economic supports (Van Til et al., 2013; Adler et al., 2023).
- **Theoretical Convergence**—The Biopsychosocial-Economic Model, Trauma Exposure Theory, Social Identity Theory/SIMIC, and Transformative Learning Theory together offer a comprehensive explanatory and predictive model (Engel, 1977; Mezirow, 1997).
- **Policy Integration Required**—Fragmented systems (e.g., VA healthcare vs. Department of Labor programs) undermine long-term outcomes; coordinated, identity-centered policy frameworks improve sustainability (Elnitsky et al., 2017).
- **Measurement Innovation**—Inclusion of identity-sensitive metrics—belonging, purpose, role clarity, and self-efficacy—is essential for evaluating program success (Haslam et al., 2019; Wakefield et al., 2024).

Applied Learning Prompts

1. Using the four theoretical foundations of BRAVE, design a hypothetical intervention for a veteran transitioning into higher education. Explain how each theory would shape program components.
2. Map the current reintegration services in your community or organization across the four BRAVE domains. Identify gaps, overlaps, and opportunities for integration.

3. Select and analyze an existing veteran reintegration policy through BRAVE Theory. What aspects align with the theory, and what modifications would increase multidomain integration and identity reconstruction?
4. Propose three identity-sensitive metrics that could be incorporated into reintegration program evaluations. Justify your choices using relevant theoretical foundations.

References

Adler, A. B., & Gutierrez, I. A. (2023). Enhancing resilience in service members and military veterans. In D. Forbes, J. I. Iverson, & R. K. McGuire (Eds.), *Veteran and military mental health: A clinical manual* (pp. 29–44). American Psychological Association. https://doi.org/10.1037/0000333-003

Anestis, J. C., Green, B. A., Arnau, R. C., & Anestis, M. D. (2019). Psychopathic personality traits in the military: An examination of the Levenson self-report psychopathy scales in a novel sample. *Assessment, 26*(4), 670–683. https://doi.org/10.1177/1073191117719511

Besemann, M., Hebert, J., Thompson, J. M., Cooper, R. A., Gupta, G., Brémault-Phillips, S. B., & Dentry, S. J. (2018). Reflections on recovery, rehabilitation and reintegration of injured service members and veterans from a bio-psychosocial-spiritual perspective. *Canadian Journal of Surgery, 61*(6), S219–S231. https://doi.org/10.1503/cjs.015318

Betancourt, J. R., Green, A. R., Carrillo, J. E., & Park, E. R. (2005). Cultural competence and health care disparities: Key perspectives and trends. *Health Affairs, 24*(2), 499–505. https://doi.org/10.1377/hlthaff.24.2.499

Bond, G. R., Al-Abdulmunem, M., Ressler, D. R., Gade, D. M., & Drake, R. E. (2022). A randomized controlled trial of an employment program for veterans transitioning from the military: Two-year outcomes. *Administration and Policy in Mental Health and Mental Health Services Research, 49*(6), 1072–1083. https://doi.org/10.1007/s10488-022-01208-z

Bronfenbrenner, U. (1979). *The ecology of human development: Experiments by nature and design.* Harvard University Press.

Demers, A. (2011). When veterans return: The role of community in reintegration. *Journal of Loss and Trauma, 16*(2), 160–179. https://doi.org/10.1080/15325024.2010.519281

Elbogen, E. B., Zeber, J. E., Vogt, D., Perkins, D. F., Finley, E. P., & Copeland, L. A. (2022). Financial status and Well-being in recently separated military veterans. *Military Medicine, 188*(7–8), e2181–e2188. https://doi.org/10.1093/milmed/usac030

Elnitsky, C. A., Blevins, C. L., Fisher, M. P., & Magruder, K. (2017). Military service member and veteran reintegration: A critical review and adapted ecological model. *Psychological Services, 14*(2), 161–170. https://doi.org/10.1037/ort0000244

Engel, G. L. (1977). The need for a new medical model: A challenge for biomedicine. *Science, 196*(4286), 129–136. https://doi.org/10.1126/science.847460

Haslam, C., Steffens, N. K., Branscombe, N. R., Haslam, S. A., Cruwys, T., Lam, B. C. P., Pachana, N. A., & Yang, J. (2019). The importance of social groups for retirement adjustment: Evidence, application, and policy implications of the social identity model of identity change. *Social Issues and Policy Review, 13*(1), 93–124. https://doi.org/10.1111/sipr.12049

Karre, J. K., Perkins, D. F., Morgan, N. R., Davenport, K. E., Aronson, K. R., Maury, R. V., Bradbard, D., Armstrong, N. J., Wright, A., Sargent, R., & Andros, M. (2025). What do successful military-to-civilian transitions look like? A revised framework and a new conceptual model for assessing veteran Well-being. *Armed Forces & Society, 51*(3), 611–640. https://doi.org/10.1177/0095327X231216678

Kearney, D. J., Malte, C. A., Storms, M., & Simpson, T. L. (2021). Loving-kindness meditation vs cognitive processing therapy for posttraumatic stress disorder among veterans: A randomized clinical trial. *JAMA Network Open, 4*(4), e216604. https://doi.org/10.1001/jamanetworkopen.2021.6604

Kelly, M. M., Reilly, E. D., Ameral, V., Richter, S., & Fukuda, S. (2022). A randomized pilot study of acceptance and commitment therapy to improve social support for veterans with PTSD. *Journal of Clinical Medicine, 11*(12), 3482. https://doi.org/10.3390/jcm11123482

Lugg, W. (2022). The biopsychosocial model—History, controversy and Engel. *Australasian Psychiatry, 30*(1), 55–59. https://doi.org/10.1177/10398562211037333

Mezirow, J. (1997). Transformation theory out of context. *Adult Education Quarterly, 48*(1), 60–62. https://doi.org/10.1177/074171369704800105

Sayer, N. A., Spoont, M., Murdoch, M., Parker, L. E., Hintz, S., & Rosenheck, R. (2011). A qualitative study of U.S. veterans' reasons for seeking Department of Veterans Affairs disability benefits for posttraumatic stress disorder. *Journal of Traumatic Stress, 24*(6), 699–707. https://doi.org/10.1002/jts.20693

Steenkamp, M. M., Litz, B. T., Hoge, C. W., & Marmar, C. R. (2015). Psychotherapy for military-related PTSD: A review of randomized clinical trials. *JAMA, 314*(5), 489–500. https://doi.org/10.1001/jama.2015.8370

Stone, C., & Stone, D. L. (2015). Factors affecting hiring decisions about veterans. *Human Resource Management Review, 25*(1), 68–79. https://doi.org/10.1016/j.hrmr.2014.06.003

Trepte, S., & Loy, L. S. (2017). Social identity theory and self-categorization theory. In P. Rössler, C. A. Hoffner, & L. van Zoonen (Eds.), *The international encyclopedia of media effects* (pp. 1–13). Wiley-Blackwell. https://doi.org/10.1002/9781118783764.wbieme00882

Turner, J. C., Brown, R. J., & Tajfel, H. (1979). Social comparison and group interest in ingroup favouritism. *European Journal of Social Psychology, 9*(2), 187–204. https://doi.org/10.1002/ejsp.2420090207

van Kessel, G. (2013). The ability of older people to overcome adversity: A review of the resilience concept. *Geriatric Nursing, 34*(2), 122–127. https://doi.org/10.1016/j.gerinurse.2012.12.011

Van Til, L., Fikretoglu, D., Pranger, T., Patten, S., Wang, J., Wong, M., Zamorski, M., Loisel, P., Corbière, M., Shields, N., Thompson, J., & Pedlar, D. (2013). Work reintegration for veterans with mental disorders: A systematic literature review to inform research. *Physical Therapy, 93*(9), 1163–1174. https://doi.org/10.2522/ptj.20120156

Wakefield, J. R. H., Bowe, M., Këllezi, B., Haslam, C., Bentley, S. V., Milani, Z., Gair, H., & McIntosh, J. S. A. (2024). Brothers and sisters in arms: A mixed-methods investigation of the roles played by military support and social identity processes in the mental health of veterans during the transition to veterancy. *Journal of Community & Applied Social Psychology, 34*(1), e2756. https://doi.org/10.1002/casp.2756

Chapter 6
The Four Dimensions of BRAVE

This chapter turns from theory to operation. It details the structure and evidence base of the four BRAVE dimensions: psychological, physical, social, and economic, showing how identity reconstruction links progress across them. The chapter draws on research from clinical psychology, public health, social work, and military sociology. The chapter demonstrates why single-track services underperform and how synchronized, trauma-informed interventions change outcomes. The Cases, including the author's reintegration and Veteran 1, compare pathways, surface constraints, and translate principles into tactics. After reading, you'll be able to: (1) explain the theoretical and empirical foundations of each BRAVE dimension; (2) analyze identity as the mechanism that coordinates change across domains; (3) assess the quality and limits of the supporting evidence base; (4) apply BRAVE to real scenarios via contrasted cases; (5) design integrated strategies that align services with identity-centered goals; and (6) identify policy and program implications across diverse veteran contexts.

6.1 Introduction

The BRAVE Theory results from an entire doctoral program's worth of combined scholarship, practice, and lived experiences. It is not based on a single manuscript but on the convergence of three major peer-reviewed works and over 600 scholarly references across health science, psychology, sociology, education, and veteran studies. Collectively, these works form the intellectual foundation of BRAVE.

T. Carlton, *BRAVE Theory*, https://doi.org/10.1007/978-3-032-13695-4_6

- Building Resilience and Advancing Veteran Empowerment (BRAVE): A Holistic Framework for Reintegration—a comprehensive narrative review synthesizing biopsychosocial and ecological perspectives, translating theory into a pragmatic reintegration model.
- BRAVE Theory: A Multidimensional Framework for Veteran Reintegration and Empowerment—a theoretical paper refining the framework into a predictive, identity-centered construct grounded in multiple established theories, including the Biopsychosocial-Economic Model, Trauma Exposure Theory, Social Identity Theory, the Social Identity Model of Identity Change (SIMIC), and Transformative Learning Theory.
- Evidence Integration Review of Multimodal Interventions for PTSD, Social Reintegration, and Economic Stability in Veterans—a PRISMA-guided systematic review of 41 studies examining interventions across psychological, social, and economic domains, providing the empirical scaffolding for BRAVE's multidomain structure.

Across these studies, a consistent finding is that veteran reintegration is not simply a checklist of separate outcomes. Instead, it is a complex, multidomain process where reconstructing identity is the primary mechanism and the final objective. The four dimensions of BRAVE: psychological, physical, social, and economic, were identified through years of research, clinical observation, and direct mentorship with transitioning veterans. These dimensions highlight the key areas where post-military life can either stabilize and develop or become unstable and break down.

The BRAVE Theory's uniqueness comes from its systems-based approach. It acknowledges each area and its mutual influences instead of viewing each separately. Psychological recovery impacts physical rehabilitation; physical ability influences employability; social belonging supports economic stability; and the veteran's evolving self-concept shapes each area. This view is based on key theories backed by empirical data and tested through real-life experience, where success or failure in reintegration depends on alignment across these areas.

This chapter will explore each domain sequentially, combining in-depth theoretical insights with practical examples. The case of Veteran 1 will guide it; a veteran whose reintegration journey exemplifies the BRAVE principles. His story illustrates how focused, multidomain interventions through mentorship, advocacy, and systems navigation can help restore agency, belonging, and purpose, even after years of slow progress. Combining scholarship and real-life experiences, the chapter emphasizes that sustainable reintegration is neither accidental nor solely the result of isolated efforts. Instead, it is achieved through deliberate, coordinated actions across all four domains, centered on rebuilding identity and fostering empowerment.

6.2 Psychological Dimension

The psychological aspect is the core element that all other facets of reintegration rely on, a conclusion supported by research across clinical psychology, military sociology, public health, and social identity theory (Elnitsky et al., 2017; Haslam et al., 2019; Sayer et al., 2011). Decades of studies focused on veterans show that unresolved psychological injuries, such as PTSD, depression, anxiety, or moral injury, consistently hinder physical rehabilitation, social reintegration, and economic stability (Bryan et al., 2018; Kearney et al., 2021; Hoge et al., 2014). The BRAVE model emphasizes this domain as part of a larger framework and as the key driver for recovery across multiple areas. Without psychological readiness, progress in other domains often remains delicate and vulnerable to setbacks when stressors recur.

The conceptual foundation of this dimension is heavily based on Transformative Learning Theory (Mezirow, 1997), which describes how identity disruption after trauma acts as a "disorienting dilemma" that forces individuals to reevaluate their worldview, values, and self-concept critically. For veterans, this process is intensified by the sudden removal from high-cohesion, high-stakes environments and the loss of clearly defined roles. Trauma Exposure Theory complements this by highlighting the neurocognitive changes due to chronic threat, such as shifts in arousal regulation, an attentional bias toward threat cues, and stress hormone dysregulation that continue beyond service and influence post-transition functioning (McEwen, 2017; Yehuda et al., 2014). Although these adaptations may be beneficial in combat, they can lead to hypervigilance, emotional numbing, or maladaptive coping in civilian settings, hindering the meaningful reconstruction of identity.

Within BRAVE, psychological recovery is viewed as identity reconstruction rather than symptom suppression. This shift aligns with the Social Identity Model of Identity Change (SIMIC) (Haslam et al., 2019; Wakefield et al., 2024), highlighting that lasting well-being during major life changes depends on maintaining or regaining meaningful group memberships. The evidence supporting SIMIC is especially relevant for veterans, who often lose access to the primary social group that previously defined their self-identity. The loss of these identity anchors is linked to increased risks of social withdrawal, unemployment, and mental health decline (Adler & Gutierrez, 2023; Stevelink et al., 2019). On the other hand, targeted interventions that promote identity continuity, such as peer networks, mentorship programs, and community reintegration efforts, are associated with better mental health outcomes and lower relapse rates (Morland et al., 2024; Sippel et al., 2015).

Long-term findings from multimodal intervention studies further support the multidomain aspect of psychological recovery. These studies show that integrated programs targeting mental health, physical activity, and social engagement lead to more lasting improvements than treatments focusing on a single area (Caddick & Smith, 2014; Steenkamp et al., 2015). This synergy is intentional; neuroplasticity research indicates that physical exercise, social bonding, and cognitive reframing activate overlapping neural pathways involving the prefrontal cortex, hippocampus, and limbic system, which boost emotional regulation and mental flexibility (Davidson & McEwen, 2012). These mechanisms explain why focusing solely on the psychological domain often does not produce sustainable results; proper recovery depends on reciprocal reinforcement from other areas.

Moral injury, a concept different from PTSD, is also key to understanding the psychological aspect. Defined as the distress caused by actions, or the lack of actions, that violate one's moral or ethical standards (Litz et al., 2009), moral injury disrupts core identity, leading to guilt, shame, and an existential crisis. Evidence indicates that moral injury responds less well to traditional cognitive-behavioral treatments and is more suited to approaches that involve meaning-making, storytelling, and re-aligning values (Currier et al., 2015; Griffin et al., 2019). In BRAVE, this highlights the need to go beyond purely clinical methods and adopt integrative strategies targeting symptoms and identity recovery.

Untreated psychological injuries' economic and social impacts also emphasize their importance within the BRAVE structure. Unresolved trauma is linked to lower employment retention, increased healthcare use, and a higher risk of homelessness (Metraux et al., 2013; Tsai et al., 2016). These results are personal tragedies and systemic inefficiencies, underscoring the need for policies incorporating psychological readiness and identity-sensitive metrics into all reintegration programs. Such metrics could include validated measures of role clarity, sense of belonging, and purpose factors strongly associated with long-term reintegration success but often missing from standard program assessments (Haslam et al., 2019; Wakefield et al., 2024).

6.3 Physical Dimension

The physical aspect of BRAVE is based on the understanding that the body is not just a functional tool but an active source of meaning, memory, and identity. In veteran reintegration, physical recovery goes hand in hand with psychological and social healing because the body bears both visible and invisible marks of service. Physical impairments, whether from combat injuries, occupational stress, or long-term wear, intersect with neurocognitive issues such as traumatic brain injury (TBI), chronic pain, and sleep problems, causing ripple effects across other areas (Carlson et al., 2011; Lew et al., 2009; Sayer et al., 2011). The disruption is physical, and for veterans trained to see their bodies as reliable tools for mission success, losing function often causes deep identity conflicts and feelings of lost control (Caddick & Smith, 2014; Keats, 2010).

The theoretical basis of the physical dimension is rooted in the Biopsychosocial Model (Engel, 1977), which places physical health within a dynamic system of psychological and social factors. In BRAVE, this model is expanded by trauma-informed care principles that recognize how bodily states are affected by hyperarousal, sensory triggers, and conditioned fear responses resulting from prolonged exposure to threat (van der Kolk, 1996). Somatic memory research shows that trauma is not only stored cognitively but also embedded within neuromuscular and autonomic patterns, manifesting as chronic tension, altered proprioception, and dysregulated stress responses (Payne et al., 2015; Scaer, 2014). This emphasizes the importance of approaching physical rehabilitation not just as orthopedic recovery, but as a process of restoring trust and communication between body and mind.

Intervention research supports a multimodal approach that combines traditional physical rehabilitation with adaptive physical activity, mindfulness-based movement, and strength training tailored to the tactical athlete identity. Exercise has been shown to enhance neuroplasticity, lower systemic inflammation, and improve mood regulation through the modulation of brain-derived neurotrophic factor (BDNF) and serotonergic systems (Cotman et al., 2007; Kandola et al., 2019). Among veterans, adaptive physical activity programs have demonstrated improvements in functional capacity and psychological well-being, especially when delivered in group settings that restore military-style camaraderie and collective identity (Brittain et al., 2024; Caddick & Smith, 2014). This dual benefit aligns with BRAVE's multidomain approach, where physical gains are used to strengthen social connection and psychological resilience.

The importance of sleep and circadian rhythm regulation in physical recovery must be highlighted. Chronic sleep disruption, frequently seen in post-deployment veterans due to hyperarousal, pain, and shift work during service, has been associated with impaired cognitive function, metabolic issues, and a higher risk of mood disorders (Mysliwiec et al., 2013; Seelig et al., 2010). Therefore, addressing sleep hygiene in the physical health domain is crucial, as restorative sleep supports neuroendocrine balance, tissue healing, and emotional stability—all vital for a veteran's overall recovery and ability to participate in other areas.

For those with significant injury or disability, adaptive movement and assistive technologies expand the possibilities of physical reintegration. Research on disability identity development indicates that reconciling bodily change with self-concept is facilitated by engaging in meaningful physical activity, even when performance goals need to be reframed (Gill, 1997; Shakespeare, 2006). In this context, the physical dimension becomes a place for reclaiming agency, not necessarily by restoring pre-injury function but by redefining capability in ways that match personal values and life goals. This reframing aligns with Transformative Learning Theory, where shifts in meaning perspective arise from critically engaging with altered realities rather than trying to return to a pre-trauma state (Mezirow, 1997).

Integrating physical training within BRAVE draws on the tactical athlete paradigm, which conceptualizes veterans as possessing performance mindsets that can be redirected toward health restoration. Research in sports science and occupational rehabilitation has shown that goal-directed, progressively overloaded physical conditioning can catalyze psychological gains by enhancing self-efficacy, fostering mastery experiences, and re-establishing a coherent performance identity (Bandura, 1977). Importantly, this process requires individualized programming sensitive to injury profiles, pain thresholds, and psychological readiness, underscoring the need for interdisciplinary collaboration between strength coaches, physical therapists, and mental health professionals.

Untreated or poorly managed physical limitations have ripple effects across social and economic areas. Chronic pain and mobility issues are strongly linked to unemployment, social withdrawal, and increased severity of mental health symptoms in veterans (Dobscha et al., 2014; Outcalt et al., 2015). Conversely, gains in physical ability often led to positive feedback loops: decreased symptom burden allows for greater social and occupational participation, which further supports identity rebuilding and self-esteem. This mutual reinforcement illustrates BRAVE's main idea that domains are not simply additive but are mutually shaping physical recovery, influencing and being influenced by progress in other areas.

6.4 Social Dimension

The social aspect in BRAVE is a key element that determines if reintegration lasts. Decades of research have shown that social connections serve as a protective factor for mental health, physical health, and long-term adjustment after trauma (Cacioppo & Cacioppo, 2014; Holt-Lunstad et al., 2010). For veterans, moving from the close-knit, high-reliability military teams to the scattered social environments of civilian life can lead to a deep sense of isolation and loss of identity (Demers, 2011; Joseph et al., 2023). Without intentional social reintegration, progress made in other areas like psychological healing, physical recovery, or economic stability is less likely to last.

From a theoretical perspective, BRAVE's social domain is rooted in Social Identity Theory (Turner et al., 1979) and its practical development in the Social Identity Model of Identity Change (SIMIC) (Haslam et al., 2019). SIMIC highlights that well-being during major life changes is affected by both maintaining existing group memberships and gaining new ones that offer meaning, belonging, and a shared social reality. For veterans, the abrupt loss of military group identity without suitable alternatives in civilian identities creates an "identity gap," which is linked to higher risks of depression, substance abuse, and suicidal thoughts (Stevelink et al., 2019).

Social reintegration in BRAVE goes beyond rejoining existing communities, including building new networks reinforcing the veteran's renewed self-image. This method aligns with the ecological systems perspective (Bronfenbrenner, 1979), which places the individual within interconnected layers of interpersonal, institutional, and societal influences. It acknowledges that belonging is not solely an interpersonal experience but is also influenced by access to community infrastructure, the cultural literacy of civilian networks in understanding veteran experiences, and the extent to which systems support reciprocal contribution rather than just passive receipt of care.

Empirical studies show that peer-to-peer support is particularly effective in bridging the cultural and experiential divide between veterans and civilian service providers. Peer mentorship programs have demonstrated clear improvements in social functioning, psychological resilience, and treatment engagement among veterans, with mentors acting as role models who normalize challenges and demonstrate adaptive coping strategies (Resnick & Rosenheck, 2008; Sayer et al., 2011). The mechanism is more than just providing information; it is about confirming identity, as veterans see their potential reflected in someone who has faced similar experiences.

Social capital, the resources embedded in one's social networks, is another key concept underpinning the social dimension (Putnam, 2000). Veterans often experience a decline in bridging social capital (connections to diverse civilian networks) after service, while they maintain or seek to rebuild bonding social capital (connections with other veterans). BRAVE focuses on strengthening both types: bonding capital supports cultural identity and mutual trust, while bridging capital enables access to new opportunities, broadens perspectives, and reduces dependence on insular networks that may unintentionally reinforce harmful patterns.

Unaddressed social disconnection can have serious effects. Loneliness is linked to higher risks of illness and death, comparable to well-known health risks like smoking and obesity (Holt-Lunstad et al., 2010). For veterans, isolation can worsen moral injury, increase PTSD symptoms, and make it harder to follow medical or job plans (Bryan et al., 2018). On the other hand, strong social bonds can reduce stress response, boost immune health, and improve mental flexibility, all of which help performance in the other BRAVE areas (Haslam et al., 2019; Uchino et al., 2018).

BRAVE promotes social reintegration through targeted strategies: structured peer mentorship; group-based adaptive activities that connect physical and social improvements; collaborative leadership roles that empower veterans as contributors, not just recipients; and community education programs to bridge the military-civilian understanding gap. This approach is supported by trauma-informed principles that recognize the importance of psychological safety in all social environments, allowing veterans to participate without fear of stigma, re-traumatization, or cultural invalidation (Elliott et al., 2005).

The veteran's ability to recover economically and psychologically often depends on whether they are part of a social environment that affirms their worth, supports their goals, and meets their needs without labeling their identity as a problem. That's why, in BRAVE, social reintegration isn't seen as just an optional addition but as a fundamental component—a key factor without which the multidomain model cannot stand. The evidence clearly shows that reintegration is just as much about who one is with as it is about what one does.

6.5 Economic Dimension

Economic stability within BRAVE is a final milestone of reintegration and a continuous, essential condition that affects and is affected by psychological, physical, and social recovery. The literature on post-service adjustment consistently highlights financial security and meaningful employment as key factors for long-term well-being, yet these are often seen as endpoints rather than evolving processes (MacLean et al., 2018; Vogt et al., 2020). Without economic stability, progress in other areas is compromised, creating a cycle of stress, disengagement, and increased risk of relapse into unhealthy coping behaviors.

The relationship between economic stability and health outcomes is well-established. Financial stress has been connected to higher allostatic load, greater risk of depression, and reduced ability for health self-management (Carlton, 2025). For veterans, economic insecurity is often worsened by service-related disabilities, skill mismatch in the civilian job market, and employer misconceptions about military experience (Stone & Stone, 2015). Underemployment, a mismatch between a veteran's abilities and their job role, stands out as a significant risk factor, damaging self-efficacy and increasing identity loss (Maguire et al., 2022).

BRAVE's economic dimension is guided by the concept of "economic identity" (Yates & Masten, 2004), which considers employment and financial agency not just as sources of income but as core parts of self-concept, autonomy, and future outlook. The model also includes trauma-informed economic development strategies, acknowledging that past adverse experiences and systemic barriers influence financial behaviors and career choices (Sherraden & Barr, 2005). This approach moves away from linear "job placement" models, focusing instead on sustainable pathways like certification pipelines, adaptive vocational training, entrepreneurship incubation, and financial literacy programs designed to meet veterans where they are regarding skills and readiness.

Evidence from vocational rehabilitation research underscores the importance of multidomain coordination in economic interventions. Studies of Veteran Readiness and Employment (VR&E) programs show higher success rates when services include mental health support, physical accommodations, and peer mentorship alongside career training (Davis et al., 2018; Rumann & Hamrick, 2010). Conversely, when vocational services operate independently from psychological and social supports, dropout rates increase and job retention decreases, even if initial placement rates are high (Haynie & Shepherd, 2011).

The economic aspect in BRAVE also connects with the broader social determinants of health (Marmot et al., 2008). Access to affordable housing, transportation, and childcare, along with protections against predatory lending, are essential factors in maintaining economic stability. These structural supports work together with individual factors such as confidence in navigating benefits systems, digital literacy, and professional networking to determine long-term sustainability. Without such systemic support, veterans may face what sociologists call "precarity," a state of ongoing insecurity that hampers goal setting and adaptive functioning (Standing, 2011).

Importantly, BRAVE frames economic reintegration not just as a protective measure against poverty but as an opportunity for posttraumatic growth. Research on meaning-centered work indicates that veterans who engage in occupations aligned with their personal values and mission report higher life satisfaction, lower burnout, and stronger social engagement (Dik et al., 2013; Steger, 2012; Steger et al., 2015). This is especially relevant for those whose military roles were closely tied to their identity; recreating a sense of purpose in civilian jobs can help buffer against existential distress and improve workforce retention.

The interdependence between the economic dimension and other BRAVE domains is both reciprocal and multiplicative. Physical capacity influences employability; psychological resilience impacts persistence in skill development; social networks affect job opportunities and access to mentorship. Conversely, economic stability supports health behaviors, funds physical rehabilitation, and enables participation in social activities that help rebuild identity. The evidence is clear: economic isolation sustains multidomain decline, while economic empowerment drives multidomain recovery.

BRAVE implements this dimension through layered strategies: personalized vocational mapping; partnerships with higher education institutions to support degree and certification completion; integration of financial coaching into health and wellness programs; and structured employer engagement to educate and motivate veteran hiring and retention. These interventions are trauma-informed, culturally competent, and flexible enough to adapt to the diverse experiences of veterans, whether reentering the workforce after injury, navigating a midlife career change, or starting a business as a form of self-directed reintegration.

The current policy landscape remains fragmented, with workforce development, disability benefits, and mental health services often functioning separately rather than together. BRAVE challenges this separation by promoting policy coordination that recognizes economic stability as a key factor and an outcome of veteran well-being. Achieving this requires integrated funding sources, shared data systems, and long-term outcome tracking that measures employment status, job quality, satisfaction, and how well roles match the veteran's reconstructed identity.

In summary, the economic aspect within BRAVE is not a final phase or an isolated factor. Instead, it is a core element that constantly engages with and supports the psychological, physical, and social aspects. The research highlights that reintegration remains fragile and incomplete without intentional, comprehensive economic strategies. When such strategies are in place, veterans are better equipped to survive in civilian life and flourish with a sense of agency, purpose, and lasting stability.

6.6 Integrated Case Study

The best way to demonstrate how BRAVE functions is to showcase it in real people's lives. This section presents two cases: mine and Veteran 1's. Although we started from different points, with various injuries and barriers, both of us had to navigate through the exact four domains: psychological, physical, social, and economic. While the specifics may differ, the process remains consistent, illustrating how adaptable BRAVE is when used as an integrated system rather than a simple checklist.

I want to illustrate the messy, non-linear reality of reintegration, the setbacks, breakthroughs, and moments when one area has to carry others until they can catch up. I've seen firsthand how a success in one area can ripple into others: how achieving mental clarity opens the door to physical progress, how physical skills boost confidence for social connections, how a sense of belonging makes it easier to pursue economic goals, and how financial stability quiets the noise enough to focus on healing. The research supports this (Haslam et al., 2019; Liu et al., 2019; Mezirow, 1997), but experiencing it and witnessing it in someone else solidifies it in a way no academic article ever can.

These two stories run in parallel here for a reason. Veteran 1's path shows what it looks like to apply BRAVE from the outside, as someone I've mentored and walked beside. My path shows what it looks like from the inside out, building BRAVE while living it. Together, they give a complete picture of what this framework can do when it becomes a map, compass, and sometimes, a lifeline.

6.6.1 Veteran 1

When I first met Veteran 1, he was spinning his wheels. He was physically there but emotionally checked out. On paper, he had survived the unimaginable: an accident that left him paraplegic, with rods in his neck, and years of navigating a system that told him "no" more often than "yes." He was stuck. His GI Bill was used up, his request for Veteran Readiness & Employment (VR&E) had been denied. I approached with empathy, knowing his situation in my own way, because I'd been there myself. BRAVE shouldn't be a forceful push but a supportive framework that meets you at your current level and gradually builds capacity in areas capable of progress, even if some parts are still struggling. For Veteran 1, this meant beginning with the psychological aspect.

The psychological work wasn't clinical therapy, but it was intensely therapeutic. It was about reframing his narrative, shifting it from "I've been written off" to "I still have options." The literature clearly states that identity reconstruction is central to posttraumatic growth (Haslam et al., 2019; Tedeschi & Calhoun, 2004), and without it, gains in other areas rarely last. We had to address the loss of self that came with his injury and years of systemic rejection. Trust was built gradually, through consistent follow-up and small victories. Over time, he began to see the possibility of a future worth pursuing.

He was often seen as permanently broken in the physical dimension, but BRAVE challenges that view. Using adaptive training based on trauma-informed physical rehab and tactical athlete principles, he transformed his body from a symbol of limitation into an asset. Even with paraplegia, he continued to train for deadlifts, seated presses, and targeted conditioning, which rebuilt his strength and his sense of control over his movements. According to research on somatic recovery, physical rehab is essential for mood regulation, cognitive enhancement, and boosting self-efficacy (Van der Kolk, 1996; Varela & Melvin, 2023).

The social domain was perhaps the most delicate. Years of isolation had diminished his sense of belonging. We intentionally reconnected him, not through the superficial "support groups," but through meaningful roles. As he advanced, he became "Patient Zero" for the WELL Program BRAVE's applied tactical reintegration model, helping shape its early systems. This shift from recipient to contributor aligns with the Social Identity Model of Identity Change (SIMIC): sustained identity continuity and the development of new, valued social roles establish the basis for lasting reintegration (Haslam et al., 2009; Wakefield et al., 2024).

Finally, the economic dimension had to expand beyond "find a job" thinking. We prioritized education first because it was the key to vocational options and renewed self-worth. I attended his VR&E appeal meeting with him, and we made the case for full academic funding together. The result was approval not only for a bachelor's degree, but also for a master's program and Certified Mental Performance Counselor (CMPC) certification. We also used prior credits to earn his AA in Automotive Technology, closing gaps that had remained unresolved for years. This was about employability and creating a path with stability, purpose, and agency, precisely as the literature on economic empowerment and veteran transition highlights (Elbogen et al., 2022; Savoca & Rosenheck, 2000).

Veteran 1's story isn't a straightforward success story; none are. There were setbacks, times when one area advanced while another fell behind, and moments when it felt like starting over. But that's the point, BRAVE is not a step-by-step checklist. It's an adaptive, interconnected system. By working simultaneously across all four areas, each improvement strengthened the others. Over time, he regained capacity and built a new identity rooted in capability, belonging, and a vision for the future. Today, Veteran 1 excels academically and mentors other veterans navigating the same maze he once believed was impassable. His progress affirms BRAVE's core idea: reintegration works when it is seen as rebuilding a whole person across connected areas, with identity at the center.

6.6.2 My Case

Veteran 1's story demonstrates that BRAVE is effective in harsh conditions; mine shows it was initially shaped there. I didn't aim to develop a formal framework, let alone one supported by over 600 scholarly sources, significant publications, and years of doctoral work. My goal was to survive. Like many veterans, I discovered that survival without a sense of identity is essentially ongoing erosion.

When I left the military, I faced a psychological landscape as challenging as any deployment. I wore the visible signs of service and the lingering moral injuries that persisted long after combat. Research shows that moral injury can disrupt core identity and beliefs even more profoundly than physical wounds (Currier et al., 2015; Litz et al., 2009). My internal struggle was heightened because many of my actions were within ROE but felt incompatible with the values I upheld during service. The silence after combat was more overwhelming than the chaos itself. Like Veteran 1, my turning point wasn't in therapy but in reconstructing my narrative, intentionally reframing my story to find purpose amid pain. BRAVE's foundation in Mezirow's Transformative Learning Theory stemmed directly from this process, emphasizing that perspective transformation is a vital survival tool, not just an academic concept.

Physically, my injuries differed from Veteran 1's, but the psychological impact was remarkably alike. Years of chronic pain, disrupted sleep, and repeated blast exposure made my body unreliable at best and hostile at worst. The literature on somatic trauma confirms that the body stores injury but also the meaning of that injury (Shipherd, 2007; Van der Kolk, 1996). I couldn't train the way I did as a Navy Corpsman embedded with Marines, and losing that physical ability directly challenged my identity as a tactical athlete. Rebuilding physically followed the same principles that would later support BRAVE's adaptive rehabilitation model: trauma-informed movement, gradual reconditioning, and viewing the body as a partner instead of an obstacle. Veteran 1 had to learn how to perform complex lifts from a chair; I had to relearn how to trust my stability. We both had to reclaim agency in movement to regain control of our lives.

Social reintegration was perhaps my deepest point of fracture. Before separation, my identity was rooted in a tight-knit brotherhood where each role was clear and every action mattered. After service, I found myself in spaces where no one understood what a corpsman was, let alone what it meant to serve in combat. Research in the Social Identity Model of Identity Change (SIMIC) underscores that losing a valued group identity without creating a new one is a major predictor of poor post-transition adjustment (Haslam et al., 2009; Wakefield et al., 2024). Like Veteran 1, I experienced the hollow echo of isolation. But my path out was different. I started building the community I couldn't find. The WELL Program and the Mindfully Tactical Foundation became my social lifeline and the platform on which I could support others. In SIMIC terms, I replaced my social identity and expanded it into one that could connect civilian and veteran worlds.

Economically, I held one advantage over Veteran 1: I started my reintegration with more accessible educational benefits. However, advantage doesn't automatically mean simplicity. Transitioning from tactical operations to academia caused a cultural shock. My skills, sharpened for triage in combat, were not suited for understanding APA formatting or IRB protocols. Research on veteran employment suggests that veterans often face underemployment, regardless of their formal education, without intentional efforts to translate military skills into civilian roles (Elbogen et al., 2022; Savoca & Rosenheck, 2000). My economic reintegration involved a layered strategy: utilizing the GI Bill for advanced degrees, accumulating performance science and conditioning credentials, and transforming my lived experience into academic authority. This approach reflected the BRAVE economic model's focus on long-term capacity building over quick solutions.

Comparing my case to Veteran 1's highlights BRAVE's universality and adaptability. Both of us started with fractured identities, both needed psychological reframing before progress in other areas could stick, and both discovered that physical rehabilitation was as much about agency as it was about strength. Social reconnection proved crucial for each of us, but my approach was to build the system from scratch, while his was to enter one already forming and shape it with his lived experience. Economically, I began with relatively better resource access, while he had to rebuild from systemic rejection to secure full academic funding. Still, in both cases, the four domains supported each other's gains in one, creating leverage in another, and setbacks in one were mitigated by stability elsewhere.

The academic synthesis of these parallel paths is revealing. BRAVE is not a prescriptive sequence. It is an adaptive, multidimensional system grounded in identity reconstruction and sustained by cross-domain integration. The evidence from transformative learning theory to SIMIC, from trauma-informed rehabilitation to economic empowerment research, confirms that lasting reintegration requires more than just symptom management or box-checking outcomes. It requires rebuilding a coherent, empowered self across interconnected domains. Veteran 1's trajectory demonstrates how BRAVE functions when applied to a veteran facing complex physical and systemic barriers; mine illustrates how it operates when the main issues are moral injury, cultural displacement, and the need to repurpose tactical skills into academic and professional leadership. Together, these cases prove BRAVE is not only a theory but a real, repeatable practice.

Academic Synthesis

This chapter applies BRAVE as a multidimensional, identity-focused framework for veteran reintegration, linking the psychological, physical, social, and economic areas as interconnected systems rather than separate parts. This structure results from integrating over 600 scholarly sources across the BRAVE Theory, BRAVE Framework, and the Evidence Integration Review, along with practical insights from lived experience and applied practices. The model is guided by the Biopsychosocial Model (Engel, 1977), Trauma Exposure Theory (Brewin et al., 1996), the Social Identity Model of Identity Change (Haslam et al., 2009), and Transformative Learning Theory (Mezirow, 1997), offering both a conceptual foundation and a practical pathway from theory to implementation.

The psychological dimension acts as both the foundation and a limiting factor for progress in other areas. Extensive evidence shows that unresolved psychological injuries such as PTSD, depression, and moral injury disrupt identity continuity, impair self-efficacy, and increase risk factors for maladaptive coping (Currier et al., 2015; Litz et al., 2009). BRAVE's focus on identity reconstruction rather than symptom suppression aligns with trauma-informed care models and transformative learning theory, reframing reintegration as a process of meaning-making instead of just clinical stabilization. This dimension's importance in the model reflects findings from the EIR's multimodal intervention review and clinical outcome studies, which indicate that psychological readiness is a key factor influencing the success of physical rehabilitation, social reintegration, and vocational programs.

The physical dimension explores the reciprocal influence between body function and psychological state, supported by research in psychophysiology, neurorehabilitation, and adaptive sport science (Caddick & Smith, 2014; Shipherd et al., 2007; Van der Kolk, 2014). Chronic pain, TBI, and physical disability affect not only functional ability but also identity and perceived control. BRAVE rejects the mechanistic view of the body as a separate system, instead viewing physical rehabilitation as a process that restores identity. This is consistent with evidence showing that trauma-informed movement, somatic therapies, and adaptive athletic training improve both physiological and psychosocial outcomes.

The social dimension draws on SIMIC and social identity theory to address the rupture in belonging that occurs when veterans transition from tightly bonded military units to fragmented civilian networks. Loss of valued group membership without replacement is strongly associated with reduced well-being and increased risk of psychological distress (Haslam et al., 2009; Wakefield et al., 2024). BRAVE's approach prioritizes role restoration, peer mentorship, and community integration not as adjunctive supports but as core reintegration mechanisms. Empirical evidence supports this, with peer-led programs demonstrating superior engagement and sustainability compared to non-peer models.

The economic aspect redefines vocational reintegration and financial stability as both results and catalysts of comprehensive recovery. Studies consistently connect financial instability to poor physical health, decreased social involvement, and worse mental health outcomes (Elbogen et al., 2022; Savoca & Rosenheck, 2000). BRAVE's approach goes beyond just placing people in jobs; it focuses on building capacity by including skill development, education pathways, and trauma-informed career growth. This aligns with workforce development research that highlights the importance of long-term employability over simple job placement.

Essentially, these four domains function not as linear steps but as an interconnected, mutually supportive system. Progress in one area promotes improvements in others, while weaknesses in any single part can weaken stability throughout the system. This interdependence aligns with ecological and systems-based models of health and performance, which highlight cross-domain feedback loops in complex adaptive systems (Bronfenbrenner, 1979; Masten & Obradović, 2008).

The case studies of Veteran 1 and the author serve as real-world evidence supporting BRAVE's theoretical ideas. Veteran 1's experience shows how the model applies to complex cases involving physical disability, systemic benefit exclusion, and social isolation. Meanwhile, the author's reintegration highlights different challenges, such as moral injury, cultural displacement, and the need to shift tactical skills into academic and professional contexts. Both examples reveal that psychological reframing is often essential before making progress in other areas; that physical rehab should be rooted in identity; that social reintegration depends on gaining meaningful roles; and that economic stability is not just a goal but a vital foundation for ongoing success.

In summary, this chapter demonstrates that BRAVE's strength is its flexibility across different reintegration profiles while staying true to its multidimensional framework. Its foundation in established theory, extensive empirical data, and lived experience positions it as both a scholarly contribution to the reintegration literature and a practical tool for practitioners. By integrating the psychological, physical, social, and economic aspects through an identity-focused perspective, BRAVE advances beyond typical programmatic efforts toward a cohesive, scalable model for restoring wholeness after service.

Key Takeaways

- **Reintegration is a multidomain, interconnected process**—The psychological, physical, social, and economic dimensions function as a dynamic system, where progress or setbacks in one domain directly influence the others.
- **Identity reconstruction is central**—Psychological recovery is not simply symptom reduction but the reframing of personal identity, aligning with trauma-informed and transformative learning models (Haslam et al., 2009; Mezirow, 1997).
- **Physical rehabilitation is identity restoration**—Evidence shows that trauma-informed movement and adaptive training improve physical capacity and psychosocial well-being (Caddick & Smith, 2014; Van der Kolk, 2014).
- **Social reintegration depends on belonging and role restoration**—Peer mentorship and community integration enhance identity continuity and are more sustainable than non-peer interventions (Wakefield et al., 2024).
- **Economic stability is foundational, not final**—Long-term career capacity building, skills translation, and financial literacy reduce systemic risk factors and improve quality of life (Elbogen et al., 2022; Savoca & Rosenheck, 2000).
- **Case evidence validates theory**—Veteran 1's and the author's trajectories demonstrate BRAVE's adaptability and effectiveness across different reintegration profiles, reinforcing its utility as both a scholarly model and practical tool.
- **Systemic coordination is critical—**Fragmented services fail to account for the multidimensional nature of reintegration; BRAVE offers a framework for aligning interventions across domains and sectors.

Applied Learning Prompts

1. Elect a veteran reintegration case (real or hypothetical) and map its challenges and supports across the four BRAVE dimensions. Identify interdependencies between domains and propose at least one multidomain intervention strategy.
2. Using Mezirow's Transformative Learning Theory and the Social Identity Model of Identity Change (SIMIC), analyze how identity reconstruction influences outcomes in each domain. Apply these theories to either Veteran 1's or the author's case study in this chapter.
3. Design a coordinated support plan that integrates services from healthcare, vocational, and community sectors to address all four domains simultaneously. Justify your integration points using evidence from the BRAVE Framework and Evidence Integration Review.
4. Create a financial and vocational trajectory plan for a veteran facing physical limitations and skill translation barriers. Include career coaching, credentialing pathways, and financial literacy elements, and explain how these economic strategies reinforce psychological, physical, and social recovery.

References

Adler, A. B., & Gutierrez, I. A. (2023). Enhancing resilience in service members and military veterans. In *Veteran and military mental health: A clinical manual* (pp. 29–44).

Bandura, A. (1977). Self-efficacy: Toward a unifying theory of behavioral change. *Psychological Review, 84*(2), 191–215. https://doi.org/10.1037/0033-295X.84.2.191

Brewin, C. R., Dalgleish, T., & Joseph, S. (1996). A dual representation theory of posttraumatic stress disorder. *Psychological Review, 103*(4), 670–686. https://doi.org/10.1037/0033-295X.103.4.670

Brittain, I., Bunds, K., & Bocarro, J. (2024). The contribution of sport in the rehabilitation process of disabled military veterans: A case study of the 2016 Invictus Games. *Journal of Global Sport Management, 9*(1), 62–85.

Bronfenbrenner, U. (1979). *The ecology of human development: Experiments by nature and design.* Harvard University Press.

Bryan, C. J., Leifker, F. R., Rozek, D. C., Bryan, A. O., Reynolds, M. L., Oakey, D. N., & Roberge, E. (2018). Examining the effectiveness of an intensive, 2-week treatment program for military personnel and veterans with PTSD: Results of a pilot, open-label, prospective cohort trial. *Journal of Clinical Psychology, 74*(12), 2070–2081. https://doi.org/10.1002/jclp.22651

Cacioppo, J. T., & Cacioppo, S. (2014). Social relationships and health: The toxic effects of perceived social isolation. *Social and Personality Psychology Compass, 8*(2), 58–72. https://doi.org/10.1111/spc3.12087

Caddick, N., & Smith, B. (2014). The impact of sport and physical activity on the well-being of combat veterans: A systematic review. *Psychology of Sport and Exercise, 15*(1), 9–18. https://doi.org/10.1016/j.psychsport.2013.09.011

Carlson, E. B., Smith, S. R., Palmieri, P. A., Dalenberg, C., Ruzek, J. I., Kimerling, R., & Spain, D. A. (2011). Development and validation of a brief self-report measure of trauma exposure: The Trauma History Screen. *Psychological Assessment*, 23(2), 463–477. https://doi.org/10.1037/a0022294

Carlton, T. (2025). Evidence integration review of multimodal interventions for PTSD, social reintegration, and economic stability in veterans. *Journal of Veterans Studies, 11*(2), 15–27. https://doi.org/10.21061/jvs.v11i2.683

Cotman, C. W., Berchtold, N. C., & Christie, L.-A. (2007). Exercise builds brain health: Key roles of growth factor cascades and inflammation. *Trends in Neurosciences, 30*(9), 464–472. https://doi.org/10.1016/j.tins.2007.06.011

Currier, J. M., Holland, J. M., & Malott, J. (2015). Moral injury, meaning making, and mental health in returning veterans. *Journal of Clinical Psychology, 71*(3), 229–240. https://doi.org/10.1002/jclp.22134

Davidson, R. J., & McEwen, B. S. (2012). Social influences on neuroplasticity: Stress and interventions to promote well-being. *Nature Neuroscience, 15*(5), 689–695. https://doi.org/10.1038/nn.3093

Davis, L. L., Kyriakides, T. C., Suris, A., Ottomanelli, L., Drake, R. E., Parker, P. E., Mueller, L., Resnick, S. G., Toscano, R., Blansett, C. M., McCall, K. P., & Huang, G. D. (2018). Veterans individual placement and support toward advancing recovery: Methods and baseline clinical characteristics of a multisite study. *Psychiatric Rehabilitation Journal, 41*(1), 55–66. https://doi.org/10.1037/prj0000250

Demers, A. (2011). When veterans return: The role of community in reintegration. *Journal of Loss and Trauma, 16*(2), 160–179. https://doi.org/10.1080/15325024.2010.519281

Dik, B. J., Byrne, Z. S., & Steger, M. F. (2013). Purpose and meaning in the workplace. *American Psychological Association.* https://doi.org/10.1037/14183-000

Dobscha, S. K., Denneson, L. M., Kovas, A. E., Teo, A., Forsberg, C. W., Kaplan, M. S., Bossarte, R., & McFarland, B. H. (2014). Correlates of suicide among veterans treated in primary care: Case—Control study of a nationally representative sample. *Journal of General Internal Medicine, 29*(4), 853–860. https://doi.org/10.1007/s11606-014-3028-1

Elbogen, E. B., Zeber, J. E., Vogt, D., Perkins, D. F., Finley, E. P., & Copeland, L. A. (2022). Financial status and well-being in recently separated military veterans. *Military Medicine, 188*(7–8), e2181–e2188. https://doi.org/10.1093/milmed/usac030

Elliott, D. E., Bjelajac, P., Fallot, R. D., Markoff, L. S., & Reed, B. G. (2005). Trauma-informed or trauma-denied: Principles and implementation of trauma-informed services for women. *Journal of Community Psychology, 33*(4), 461–477. https://doi.org/10.1002/jcop.20063

Elnitsky, C. A., Blevins, C. L., Fisher, M. P., & Magruder, K. (2017). Military service member and veteran reintegration: A critical review and adapted ecological model. *American Journal of Orthopsychiatry, 87*(2), 114–128. https://doi.org/10.1037/ort0000244

Engel, G. L. (1977). The need for a new medical model: A challenge for biomedicine. *Science, 196*(4286), 129–136. https://doi.org/10.1126/science.847460

Gill, C. J. (1997). Four types of integration in disability identity development. *Journal of Vocational Rehabilitation, 9*(1), 39–46. https://doi.org/10.3233/JVR-1997-9106

Griffin, B. J., Purcell, N., Burkman, K., Litz, B. T., Bryan, C. J., Schmitz, M., Villierme, C., Walsh, J., & Maguen, S. (2019). Moral injury: An integrative review. *Journal of Traumatic Stress, 32*(3), 350–362. https://doi.org/10.1002/jts.22362

Haslam, C., Steffens, N. K., Branscombe, N. R., Haslam, S. A., Cruwys, T., Lam, B. C. P., Pachana, N. A., & Yang, J. (2019). The importance of social groups for retirement adjustment: Evidence, application, and policy implications of the social identity model of identity change. *Social Issues and Policy Review, 13*(1), 93–124. https://doi.org/10.1111/sipr.12049

Haslam, S. A., Jetten, J., Postmes, T., & Haslam, C. (2009). Social identity, health and well-being: An emerging agenda for applied psychology. *Applied Psychology: An International Review, 58*(1), 1–23. https://doi.org/10.1111/j.1464-0597.2008.00379.x

Haynie, J. M., & Shepherd, D. (2011). Toward a Theory of Discontinuous Career Transition: Investigating Career Transitions Necessitated by Traumatic Life Events. *Journal of Applied Psychology, 96*(3), 501–524. https://doi.org/10.1037/a0021450

Hoge, C. W., Grossman, S. H., Auchterlonie, J. L., Riviere, L. A., Milliken, C. S., & Wilk, J. E. (2014). PTSD treatment for soldiers after combat deployment: Low utilization of mental health care and reasons for dropout. *Psychiatric Services, 65*(8), 997–1004. https://doi.org/10.1176/appi.ps.201300307

Holt-Lunstad, J., Smith, T. B., & Layton, J. B. (2010). Social relationships and mortality risk: A meta-analytic review. *PLOS Medicine, 7*(7), Article e1000316. https://doi.org/10.1371/journal.pmed.1000316

Joseph, J. S., Smith-MacDonald, L., Filice, M. C., & Smith, M. S. (2023). Reculturation: A new perspective on military-civilian transition stress. *Military Psychology, 35*(3), 193–203. https://doi.org/10.1080/08995605.2022.2094175

Kandola, A., Ashdown-Franks, G., Hendrikse, J., Sabiston, C. M., & Stubbs, B. (2019). Physical activity and depression: Towards understanding the antidepressant mechanisms of physical activity. *Neuroscience & Biobehavioral Reviews, 107*, 525–539. https://doi.org/10.1016/j.neubiorev.2019.09.040

Kearney, D. J., Malte, C. A., Storms, M., & Simpson, T. L. (2021). Loving-kindness meditation vs cognitive processing therapy for posttraumatic stress disorder among veterans: A randomized clinical trial. *JAMA Network Open, 4*(4), Article e216604. https://doi.org/10.1001/jamanetworkopen.2021.6604

Keats, P. A. (2010). Soldiers working internationally: Impacts of masculinity, military culture, and operational stress on cross-cultural adaptation. *International Journal for the Advancement of Counselling, 32*(4), 290–303. https://doi.org/10.1007/s10447-010-9107-z

Lew, H. L., Tun, C., & Cifu, D. X. (2009). Prevalence of chronic pain, posttraumatic stress disorder, and persistent postconcussive symptoms in OIF/OEF veterans: Polytrauma clinical triad. *Journal of Rehabilitation Research & Development, 46*(6), 697–702. https://doi.org/10.1682/JRRD.2009.01.0006

Litz, B. T., Stein, N., Delaney, E., Lebowitz, L., Nash, W. P., Silva, C., & Maguen, S. (2009). Moral injury and moral repair in war veterans: A preliminary model and intervention strategy. *Clinical Psychology Review, 29*(8), 695–706. https://doi.org/10.1016/j.cpr.2009.07.003

Liu, Y., Collins, C., Wang, K., Xie, X., & Bie, R. (2019). The prevalence and trend of depression among veterans in the United States. *Journal of Affective Disorders, 245*, 724–727. https://doi.org/10.1016/j.jad.2018.11.031

MacLean, M. B., VanTil, L., Sweet, J., Poirier, A., & McKinnon, K. (2018). Factors Associated with Work Satisfaction among Veterans. *Journal of Military, Veteran and Family Health, 4*(1), 33–41. https://doi.org/10.3138/jmvfh.2017-0013

Maguire, A. M., Keyser, J., Brown, K., Kivlahan, D., Romaniuk, M., Gardner, I. R., & Dwyer, M. (2022). Veteran families with complex needs: A qualitative study of the veterans' support system. *BMC Health Services Research, 22*(1), 74. https://doi.org/10.1186/s12913-021-07368-2

Marmot, M., Friel, S., Bell, R., Houweling, T. A. J., & Taylor, S. (2008). Closing the gap in a generation: Health equity through action on the social determinants of health. *The Lancet, 372*(9650), 1661–1669. https://doi.org/10.1016/S0140-6736(08)61690-6

Masten, A. S., & Obradović, J. (2008). Disaster preparation and recovery: Lessons from research on resilience in human development. *Ecology and Society, 13*(1), Article 9. http://www.jstor.org/stable/26267914

McEwen, B. S. (2017). Neurobiological and systemic effects of chronic stress. *Chronic Stress, 1*, 2470547017692328. https://doi.org/10.1177/2470547017692328

Metraux, S., Clegg, L. X., Daigh, J. D., Culhane, D. P., & Kane, V. (2013). Risk factors for becoming homeless among a cohort of veterans who served in the era of the Iraq and Afghanistan conflicts. *American Journal of Public Health, 103*(S2), S255–S261. https://doi.org/10.2105/AJPH.2013.301432

Mezirow, J. (1997). Transformation theory out of context. *Adult Education Quarterly, 48*(1), 60–62. https://doi.org/10.1177/074171369704800105

Morland, L. A., Wachsman, T., Webster, K., Fitzpatrick, S., Valela, R., Crenshaw, A. O., Monson, C. M., & Knopp, K. C. (2024). A pilot of Couple HOPES within the U.S. Veterans Affairs healthcare system: PTSD and relationship outcomes in veteran couples. *Psychological Services, 21*(3), 509–517. https://doi.org/10.1037/ser0000752

Mysliwiec, V., Gill, J., Lee, H., Baxter, T., Pierce, R., Barr, T. L., Krakow, B., & Roth, B. J. (2013). Sleep disorders in U.S. military personnel: A high rate of comorbid insomnia and obstructive sleep apnea. *Chest, 144*(2), 549–557. https://doi.org/10.1378/chest.13-0088

Outcalt, S. D., Kroenke, K., Krebs, E. E., Chumbler, N. R., Wu, J., Yu, Z., & Bair, M. J. (2015). Chronic pain and comorbid mental health conditions: Independent associations of posttraumatic stress disorder and depression with pain, disability, and quality of life. *Journal of Behavioral Medicine, 38*(3), 535–543. https://doi.org/10.1007/s10865-015-9628-3

Payne, P., Levine, P. A., & Crane-Godreau, M. A. (2015). Somatic experiencing: Using interoception and proprioception as core elements of trauma therapy. *Frontiers in Psychology, 6*, Article 93. https://doi.org/10.3389/fpsyg.2015.00093

Putnam, R. D. (2000). Bowling alone: America's declining social capital. In L. Crothers & C. Lockhart (Eds.), *Culture and politics: A reader* (pp. 223–234). Palgrave Macmillan. https://doi.org/10.1007/978-1-349-62397-6_12

Resnick, S. G., & Rosenheck, R. A. (2008). Integrating peer-provided services: A quasi-experimental study of recovery orientation, confidence, and empowerment. *Psychiatric Services, 59*(11), 1307–1314. https://doi.org/10.1176/ps.2008.59.11.1307

Rumann, C. B., & Hamrick, F. A. (2010). Student veterans in transition: Re-enrolling after war zone deployments. *The Journal of Higher Education, 81*(4), 431–458. https://doi.org/10.1080/00221546.2010.11779060

Savoca, E., & Rosenheck, R. (2000). The Civilian Labor Market Experiences of Vietnam-Era Veterans: The Influence of Psychiatric Disorders. *The Journal of Mental Health Policy and Economics, 3*(4), 199–207. https://doi.org/10.1002/mhp.102

Sayer, N. A., Spoont, M., Murdoch, M., Parker, L. E., Hintz, S., & Rosenheck, R. (2011). A qualitative study of U.S. veterans' reasons for seeking Department of Veterans Affairs disability benefits for posttraumatic stress disorder. *Journal of Traumatic Stress, 24*(6), 699–707. https://doi.org/10.1002/jts.20693

Scaer, R. (2014). *The Body Bears the Burden: Trauma, Dissociation, and Disease*. Routledge.

Seelig, A. D., Jacobson, I. G., Smith, B., Hooper, T. I., Boyko, E. J., Gackstetter, G. D., Gehrman, P., Macera, C. A., Smith, T. C., & Team, M. C. S. (2010). Sleep Patterns before, During, and after Deployment to Iraq and Afghanistan. *Sleep, 33*(12), 1615–1622. https://doi.org/10.1093/sleep/33.12.1615

Shakespeare, T. (2006). Disability rights and wrongs. *Routledge*. https://doi.org/10.4324/9780203640080

Sherraden, M., & Barr, M. S. (2005). Institutions and inclusion in saving policy. In *Building Assets, Building Credit: Creating Wealth in Low-Income Communities* (pp. 286–315). Brookings Institution Press.

Shipherd, J. C. (2007). Veterans seeking treatment for posttraumatic stress disorder: What about comorbid chronic pain? *Journal of Rehabilitation Research & Development*. https://doi.org/10.1682/JRRD.2006.06.0065

Sippel, L. M., Pietrzak, R. H., Charney, D. S., Mayes, L. C., & Southwick, S. M. (2015). How does social support enhance resilience in the trauma-exposed individual? *Ecology and Society, 20*(4), Article 22. http://www.jstor.org/stable/26270277

Standing, G. (2011). *The Precariat: The New Dangerous Class*. Bloomsbury academic.

Steenkamp, M. M., Litz, B. T., Hoge, C. W., & Marmar, C. R. (2015). Psychotherapy for military-related PTSD: A review of randomized clinical trials. *JAMA, 314*(5), 489–500. https://doi.org/10.1001/jama.2015.8370

Steger, M. F. (2012). Making meaning in life. *Psychological Inquiry, 23*(4), 381–385. https://doi.org/10.1080/1047840X.2012.720832

Steger, M. F., Owens, G. P., & Park, C. L. (2015). Violations of war: Testing the meaning-making model among Vietnam veterans. *Journal of Clinical Psychology, 71*(1), 105–116. https://doi.org/10.1002/jclp.22121

Stevelink, S. A. M., Jones, N., Jones, M., Dyball, D., Khera, C. K., Pernet, D., MacCrimmon, S., Murphy, D., Hull, L., Greenberg, N., MacManus, D., Goodwin, L., Sharp, M.-L., Wessely, S., Rona, R. J., & Fear, N. T. (2019). Do serving and ex-serving personnel of the UK Armed Forces seek help for perceived stress, emotional or mental health problems? *European Journal of Psychotraumatology, 10*(1), 1556552. https://doi.org/10.1080/20008198.2018.1556552

Stone, C., & Stone, D. L. (2015). Factors affecting hiring decisions about veterans. *Human Resource Management Review, 25*(1), 68–79. https://doi.org/10.1016/j.hrmr.2014.06.003

Tedeschi, R. G., & Calhoun, L. G. (2004). Posttraumatic growth: Conceptual foundations and empirical evidence. *Psychological Inquiry, 15*(1), 1–18. https://doi.org/10.1207/s15327965pli1501_01

Tsai, J., Link, B., Rosenheck, R. A., & Pietrzak, R. H. (2016). Homelessness among a nationally representative sample of U.S. veterans: Prevalence, service utilization, and correlates. *Social Psychiatry and Psychiatric Epidemiology, 51*(6), 907–916. https://doi.org/10.1007/s00127-016-1210-y

Turner, J. C., Brown, R. J., & Tajfel, H. (1979). Social comparison and group interest in ingroup favouritism. *European Journal of Social Psychology, 9*(2), 187–204. https://doi.org/10.1002/ejsp.2420090207

Uchino, B. N., Trettevik, R., Kent de Grey, R. G., Cronan, S., Hogan, J., & Baucom, B. R. W. (2018). Social support, social integration, and inflammatory cytokines: A meta-analysis. *Health Psychology, 37*(5), 462–471. https://doi.org/10.1037/hea0000594

van der Kolk, B. (1996). The Body Keeps the Score: Approaches to the Psychobiology of Posttraumatic Stress Disorder. In Van Der Kolk Ba, Mcfarlane Ac, Weisaeth L (Eds), *Traumatic Stress: The Effects of Overwhelming Experience on Mind*.

Varela, A. J., & Melvin, A. (2023). The Theatre of Depression: A Role for Physical Therapy. *Physiotherapy Theory and Practice, 39*(7), 1325–1341. https://doi.org/10.1080/09593985.2022.2041136

Vogt, D. S., Tyrell, F. A., Bramande, E. A., Nillni, Y. I., Taverna, E. C., Finley, E. P., Perkins, D. F., & Copeland, L. A. (2020). U.S. military veterans' health and well-being in the first year after service. *American Journal of Preventive Medicine, 58*(3), 352–360. https://doi.org/10.1016/j.amepre.2019.10.016

Wakefield, J. R. H., Bowe, M., Këllezi, B., Haslam, C., Bentley, S. V., Milani, Z., Gair, H., & McIntosh, J. S. A. (2024). Brothers and sisters in arms: A mixed-methods investigation of the roles played by military support and social identity processes in the mental health of veterans during the transition to veterancy. *Journal of Community & Applied Social Psychology, 34*(1), Article e2756. https://doi.org/10.1002/casp.2756

Yates, T. M., & Masten, A. S. (2004). Fostering the future: Resilience theory and the practice of positive psychology. In *Positive psychology in practice* (pp. 521–539). John Wiley & Sons. https://doi.org/10.1002/9780470939338.ch32

Yehuda, R., Pratchett, L. C., Elmes, M. W., Lehrner, A., Daskalakis, N. P., Koch, E., Makotkine, I., Flory, J. D., & Bierer, L. M. (2014). Glucocorticoid-related predictors and correlates of post-traumatic stress disorder treatment response in combat veterans. *Interface Focus, 4*(5), 20140048. https://doi.org/10.1098/rsfs.2014.0048

Chapter 7
The Birth of MTF

This chapter traces the development of the Mindfully Tactical Foundation (MTF) from a personal insight into a structured, mission-driven organization. It examines how principles of transformative learning and adult education can spark veteran-focused, evidence-based programs that connect theory with lived experience. The chapter details the Foundation's growth from its conceptual origins in the WELL Program, which focuses on empowerment, lifestyle wellness, and leadership, to its evolution into an active nonprofit addressing various aspects of reintegration. Readers will learn how initiatives like LINK, PATH, and the V.E.T.S. Toolkit were created to fill systemic gaps in social capital, academic preparedness, and career transition. Using biopsychosocial and ecological systems perspectives, the chapter illustrates how peer mentorship, cultural adaptation, and strategic planning promote engagement, belonging, and long-term sustainability. After reading, you'll be able to: (1) explain how transformative and adult learning theories can catalyze program creation; (2) describe the developmental stages of MTF from concept to operation; (3) analyze the WELL Program as a model for multidimensional reintegration; (4) evaluate LINK, PATH, and the V.E.T.S. Toolkit as mechanisms for bridging institutional gaps; (5) assess how BRAVE theory unifies program design and evaluation; (6) apply biopsychosocial and ecological frameworks to veteran reintegration; and (7) identify how mentorship and cultural adaptation sustain post-service initiatives.

T. Carlton, *BRAVE Theory*, https://doi.org/10.1007/978-3-032-13695-4_7

7.1 The Spark: From Classroom Insight to Conceptualization

The Mindfully Tactical Foundation (MTF) began with me sitting in a doctoral-level adult learning theory course, grappling with how theory could impact the real world I knew. The class was deeply engaged in discussions of transformative learning and andragogy when the idea hit me with the clarity and urgency of a field order: How do we make mindfulness tactical? I wrote "Mindfully Tactical" in the margin of my notepad, not knowing that those words would become the focus of my doctoral work and much of my future professional identity.

At that time, mindfulness was not new to me, but I still saw it as belonging in wellness workshops and therapy offices, not in the dust, chaos, and split-second decisions of tactical environments. I had already begun to use pieces of it on my own, small practices tailored to meet my immediate needs. As a combat veteran, I had witnessed the high cost of hesitation and distraction in operational settings, and I was starting to realize that mindfulness could be more than a way to slow down and relax. It could sharpen the mind for action. In Mezirow's (1997) terms, this was my disorienting dilemma. It was a clash between what I believed mindfulness was and what I was demonstrating it could be. Disorienting dilemmas disrupt our established ways of thinking, forcing us to reflect, challenge assumptions, and reframe our worldview (Kitchenham, 2008; Taylor & Miflin, 2008). At this point, I began to see mindfulness as a survival, performance, and resilience tool in high-stakes situations.

Knowles' (1978, 1984) principles of andragogy explain why that moment resonated so strongly. Adult learners are self-directed and bring a lifetime of experience into the classroom. They are most motivated when learning is relevant to their current needs and challenges. As a doctoral student and veteran, I was actively looking for tools to solve real problems I'd seen in the field: the cognitive overload of sustained operations, the decision fatigue after combat, the loss of mission focus in the face of transition. Merriam & Bierema (2013) and Johnson et al. (2014) reinforce that adults remain engaged when new knowledge connects directly to pressing, real-world challenges. In my case, the reintegration struggles and identity dislocation of post-9/11 veterans.

The research on mindfulness in military and tactical populations provided me with a strong foundation. Jha et al. (2017) demonstrated that mindfulness-based training can improve working memory, attentional stability, and emotional regulation in active-duty service members, even under prolonged operational stress. In a combat zone or during an emergency response, these skills can be the difference between decisive action and fatal hesitation. However, King et al. (2013) caution that mindfulness must be culturally adapted for military audiences. Without the proper framing, service members may see it as incompatible with the warrior ethos or, worse, as a sign of weakness (Caddick & Smith, 2014; Stanley et al., 2011). This aligns with my own experience: the only way mindfulness would be adopted in my world would be if it were presented not as a retreat from toughness but as an enhancement.

That's when the concept of cognitive armor made sense to me. Stanley et al. (2011) believe mindfulness could serve as a protective layer for the mind, much like body armor protects the body. Framing it this way connected it to the military identity and operational mindset, preserving the mission-driven orientation while adding tools for focus, regulation, and clarity. Hoge et al. (2014) and Caddick and Smith (2014) suggest that the most effective reintegration programs protect valued elements of the military self while supporting adaptation to civilian roles. In "Mindfully Tactical," I saw a way to do precisely that.

This was also linked to research on posttraumatic growth (Tedeschi & Calhoun, 2004). My doctoral program was a process of reintegration. It was a space where I could transform my personal experiences, including trauma, into something that benefits others. Higher education can serve as a bridge for veterans by connecting academic learning to identity rebuilding and skill transfer (DiRamio & Jarvis, 2011; Elliott, 2015). For me, the adult learning classroom was both a reflective space and a testing ground, where theory met lived experience, and I could experiment with reframing my past into a mission for the future. In that way, the inception of MTF marked the convergence of my personal and professional identities, supported by transformative learning theory, adult learning principles, and the emerging science of mindfulness in high-stakes environments. It was where my reintegration journey merged with a scholarly vision, and "Mindfully Tactical" transformed from three words in a notebook to the foundation of a veteran-centered, research-informed initiative framework.

7.2 From Course Project to Organizational Blueprint

What began as a spark in one classroom found its first real form in another. My Community and Corporate Wellness course's assignment was designing a corporate wellness program. But by then, "Mindfully Tactical" had already taken root. I wasn't interested in submitting a neatly bound theoretical plan that would be graded, and I shelved or forgot. I wanted to see if this idea could survive in the real world, and what emerged was the first working model of the MTF.

In many ways, this reflected the shift from "idea generation" to "prototyping" discussed in applied learning literature (Kolb et al., 2014; Lave & Wenger, 1991). Academic theories were raw materials I could shape into something functional. Every decision I made in that course had to answer two questions: Would this truly help a veteran in transition? And could I implement it outside the classroom? That perspective forced me to bridge the gap between acquiring knowledge and applying real-life skills.

The nonprofit filing process came next. I had no legal background, formal guidance, or mentor to walk me through it step-by-step. It involved some trial and error. It would have been easy to postpone or outsource, but as I worked through each form, I realized that this was more than just an administrative task. It was self-efficacy in action. It was the belief that I could navigate uncharted territory and make this venture real (Bandura, 1977). Research shows that entrepreneurial self-efficacy strongly predicts whether a venture survives and thrives (Newman et al., 2019). For veterans, that confidence is often built in operational environments where problem-solving under resource constraints is a daily reality (Chen & Shen, 2023). The same adaptive skills that once helped me coordinate medical evacuations under fire are now helping me handle IRS filings and state incorporation documents.

Defining MTF's mission and scope meant deciding what we would offer, who we would serve, and how we would measure impact. This was my informal needs assessment phase. I was an approach echoed in program development literature (Kettner et al., 2015). I had experience and a growing body of veteran reintegration research to guide me. Studies consistently identify mental health, career readiness, and social connection as top priorities for veterans post-service (Elbogen et al., 2022; Elnitsky et al., 2017). Those needs became the pillars around which I built the first iteration of our services. Still, I avoided locking MTF into a rigid structure too soon. The early days involved listening, adjusting, and letting the organization evolve. This approach aligns with the adaptive cycle model in resilience theory (Holling, 2001), which describes how new systems benefit from a phase of rapid experimentation before settling into stability. In practice, this meant testing ideas in small settings, taking feedback seriously, and pivoting when the evidence or community voice pointed in a new direction. This is necessary in the nonprofit world, where responsiveness often determines relevance (Maier et al., 2016).

From the beginning, I understood that MTF needed to combine mindfulness with tactical performance. I had seen firsthand how high-stress professions benefit from training that addresses mental resilience and operational skills. Research on integrative health approaches for tactical groups supports multi-component models that combine stress management, cognitive skills training, and peer support (Shonin et al., 2014). In military settings, programs that blend performance psychology with adaptive coping strategies have shown measurable improvements in focus, emotional regulation, and job performance (Crane et al., 2024; Jha et al., 2017). These findings were a design mandate.

Looking back, the creation of MTF through that class project was an early test of leadership under new conditions. McCauley et al. (2010) describe how leaders develop through challenging assignments that demand vision creation, strategic problem-solving, and resource coordination. In that sense, my doctoral coursework served as a leadership incubator, offering a safe but demanding space to practice building something that could stand up in the real world. By the time the semester ended, MTF had become an established entity with paperwork filed, a mission defined, and services taking shape. The shift from an academic exercise to an organizational blueprint was complete. It marked the beginning of an evolving, veteran-centered operation that would continue to adapt, expand, and be influenced by research and lived experience.

7.3 Mission Alignment and Foundational Values

From the moment the MTF shifted from idea to reality, I knew it had to represent something larger. I didn't need to search far for the foundation of those values. Honor, Courage, and Commitment principles had been ingrained in my DNA during my military service. I wanted that same operational ethos to carry into this new mission area. For many veterans, the consistency of values between service and post-service roles offers a stabilizing influence. Research indicates that such consistency reinforces personal coherence, lessens identity disruption, and enhances the legitimacy of new roles in the eyes of both the veteran and the community (Demers, 2011; Smith & True, 2014).

Honor means serving veterans with integrity, respect, and an unwavering commitment to evidence-based practice. In the nonprofit sector, values-based governance has been shown to maintain stakeholder trust, attract mission-aligned partners, and protect the organization's fidelity to its mission (Brown & Moore, 2001; Light, 2004). In veteran services, honor translates into culturally competent care, ethical program design, and transparency in outcomes reporting (Burnett-Zeigler et al., 2011; Cheney et al., 2018). For MTF, we would never offer a service simply because it needed to be supported by research and relevant to the lived experience of those we served.

Courage involved the willingness to face the uncomfortable truths about veteran reintegration. It meant recognizing that existing systems often fall short and being prepared to design bold, sometimes unconventional solutions to address those gaps. Adaptive leadership theory describes this as operating in the "productive zone of disequilibrium" (Heifetz et al., 2009), where real progress happens by sitting with difficult problems rather than resorting to quick technical fixes. In nonprofit innovation, this type of courage has been linked to programs that challenge norms and better tackle complex, systemic barriers, especially in underserved populations (Salamon, 2015; Weerawardena et al., 2010). For MTF, this meant being ready to challenge the status quo, even if it involved taking paths that weren't always popular or widely understood at first.

Commitment has always been the core theme of my work. It's the refusal to turn away when things get tough, the discipline to show up every day for the mission. In organizational psychology, commitment is seen as both an attitude and a behavior. Emotional investment is paired with the perseverance to carry out long-term strategies despite obstacles. For many veterans, including me, commitment is connected to "service as identity" (Dolan et al., 2022), which is the belief that duty to others doesn't end when the uniform is removed. At MTF, that commitment is reflected in how we support veterans throughout the transition process, from immediate stabilization to long-term care empowerment.

Building these values into MTF's operational DNA was an essential operational step. Symbolically, it established cultural continuity for veterans, reducing the cognitive dissonance that can arise when transitioning into civilian systems with unfamiliar norms (Hajjar, 2014; Joseph et al., 2023). Functionally, these values serve as a decision-making guide, directing resource allocation, program design, and partnership development. Nonprofit governance literature describes this as using values as “strategic filters” or ensuring that every new initiative aligns with the mission at its core (Bryson, 2018; Stone & Ostrower, 2007). By blending the traditions of military service with the flexibility of evidence-based program design, MTF holds a unique position grounded in the core values veterans cherish, yet adaptable enough to address the realities of modern reintegration. Whether it’s a tactical mindfulness workshop, a strategic planning class, or a veteran-to-veteran mentoring program, those values honor, courage, and commitment pervade everything we do. They form the operational heartbeat of the Foundation and reflect the people it serves.

7.4 Programmatic Evolution: From Mindfulness to a Comprehensive Ecosystem

From the beginning, MTF was born from a single driving question that had circled in my mind since that spark in the classroom: How could mindfulness be adapted to effectively work in the high-stakes environments faced daily by tactical athletes and military veterans? I wanted to understand how it could be lived, trained, and applied under pressure. That question shaped the earliest version of MTF, which focused on targeted mindfulness workshops designed to enhance attentional control, emotional regulation, and operational focus in unpredictable, high-stress situations.

The foundation was established through research showing that mindfulness training can enhance working memory, situational awareness, and resilience under stress for military and first responder populations (Jha et al., 2010, 2017). However, I also understood that simply integrating clinical mindfulness into a tactical environment wouldn’t be effective. Veterans and tactical athletes might view practices deemed as “soft” or unrelated to performance with skepticism. The key was cultural adaptation. Instead of presenting “breath meditation” in abstract terms, I referred to it as tactical breathing drill, a language already familiar to anyone with experience in marksmanship training or combat casualty care. This strategy involved speaking in a dialect my community already comprehended. Research supports that customizing the language, structure, and delivery of interventions to match the target population’s culture significantly boosts engagement, retention, and perceived relevance (Cushing & Braun, 2017; Kearney et al., 2021; King et al., 2013).

Over time, I realized that mindfulness alone, while powerful, was only one piece of a much larger reintegration puzzle. Veterans were navigating interconnected challenges across psychological, physical, social, and economic domains. That’s when MTF began evolving into a multimodal ecosystem. This shift aligned with the biopsychosocial model (Engel, 1977) and ecological systems theory (Bronfenbrenner, 1979), highlighting that lasting change requires addressing the entire environment in which a person exists, not just isolated symptoms. The veteran reintegration literature reinforced this idea: multi-layered, comprehensive interventions outperform single-modality approaches, especially for those dealing with cumulative trauma and identity disruption (Elnitsky et al., 2017; Sayer et al., 2011).

One of the most natural expansions came through strategic planning classes. Military service sharpened my decision-making and mission analysis skills in high-pressure, uncertain situations. Why not translate those same principles into civilian life planning? The performance psychology literature shows that high-pressure planning, rapid adaptation, and scenario analysis can directly impact employment success, educational attainment, and leadership roles in the community (Gucciardi et al., 2016; Hays, 2009). These classes focused on training decision-making skills, using scenario-based exercises to prepare veterans to navigate complex civilian challenges with the same tactical precision they once applied.

Then came the wellness events. I wanted them to be more than workouts and create spaces where veterans could connect, train, and talk without the stigma that sometimes surrounds mental health. Group-based physical activity paired with psychoeducation has been shown to boost social connectedness and reduce feelings of isolation (Caddick & Smith, 2014; Kline, 2016), and our events reflected those findings. Importantly, we placed more value on connection over competition, which research shows is a stronger predictor of long-term engagement in veteran wellness programs than performance outcomes alone (McGuire, 2025). Accessibility was another non-negotiable. I knew from experience that not every veteran can get to an in-person session. That's why we built an online learning and resource platform with our recorded workshops, interactive tools, and a growing content library so veterans could access resources anywhere, anytime. Studies show that when digital platforms maintain opportunities for interaction and personalization, they can expand reach without sacrificing impact (Glueckauf et al., 2018; Morland et al., 2017). For isolated veterans, they can even function as "virtual peer networks" (Lehavot et al., 2018), blending skill development with community support.

By 2024, MTF had expanded beyond its original tactical mindfulness workshops. It had become a fully integrated service ecosystem, connecting individual skill development with systemic reintegration support. This reflected a broader trend in veteran program innovation: niche pilot initiatives often develop into multidisciplinary platforms as organizations respond to emerging needs, participant feedback, and changing evidence (Demers, 2011). Throughout all of this, it never lost its roots. Tactical mindfulness remained at its core and my core. Still, it was now part of a larger resilience and reintegration framework designed to ensure that the ability to perform under pressure was matched by the capacity to thrive in civilian life.

7.5 The WELL Program as the Operational Backbone

The Warrior Empowerment, Lifestyle, and Leadership (WELL) Program represents the operational core of the Mindfully Tactical Foundation (MTF). While the early stages of MTF focused on tactical mindfulness and targeted workshops, WELL emerged as the comprehensive framework that unified all initiatives under a structured, evidence-based model. Its creation was informed by over 600 studies reviewed during the Doctor of Health Science (DHSc) program, integrating theoretical constructs from identity theory, biopsychosocial health models, and resilience science into a practical system for veteran reintegration.

At its core, WELL recognizes a key aspect of transition: veterans change jobs and experience an identity transformation (Demers, 2011; Smith & True, 2014). Military identity is often prominent, linked to roles, missions, and the community. Losing this identity can cause disorientation, role confusion, and emotional distress (Dolan et al., 2022; McCormick et al., 2019). The WELL Program explicitly addresses this change, making identity reconstruction a central part of the reintegration process task.

1. ***Warrior Empowerment***

Empowerment within WELL is defined as the capacity for self-advocacy, informed decision-making, and strategic action in post-service life. This dimension is grounded in self-determination theory (Ryan & Deci, 2000), which posits that autonomy, competence, and relatedness are essential to sustained motivation and well-being. Peer support plays a central role here, as veteran-to-veteran mentorship has been shown to reduce stigma, increase trust in services, and enhance goal attainment (Haque et al., 2023; Resnick & Rosencheck, 2008). Practical empowerment in WELL is achieved through structured mentorship programs, decision-making workshops, and leadership development exercises, each adapted from tactical mission planning frameworks. This adaptation reflects the transfer of military planning skills to civilian contexts, which increases self-efficacy and vocational clarity among transitioning service members (Kintzle & Castro, 2018).

2. ***Lifestyle Wellness***

The second pillar recognizes that mental, physical, and emotional well-being are deeply interconnected and must be addressed simultaneously. This aligns with the biopsychosocial model (Engel, 1977) and trauma-informed care principles, which emphasize holistic assessment and intervention for populations with complex service-related exposures (Elnitsky et al., 2017).

Lifestyle interventions in WELL combine:

- Mindfulness and stress-regulation training for attention, emotional balance, and physiological recovery (Jha et al., 2017; Polusny et al., 2015).
- Physical readiness programming rooted in tactical strength and conditioning has been shown to improve physical health markers and mood, sleep, and resilience in veteran populations (Kline et al., 2016; Nindl et al., 2016).
- Nutrition and recovery education adapted from sports performance science to address fatigue, inflammation, and long-term cardiovascular risk (Crum-Cianflone et al., 2014).

Lifestyle wellness also includes facilitated peer groups that function as psychosocial buffers, reducing isolation and fostering belonging—a critical protective factor against depression and suicidality in post-service life (Kuwert et al., 2014).

3. ***Leadership Development***

The final pillar of WELL redefines veterans as community leaders and change agents, leveraging their operational experience and resilience to create local impact. This aligns with transformative learning theory (Mezirow, 1997), which suggests that critical reflection and adopting new roles can lead to significant changes in worldview and purpose. Leadership development in WELL includes public speaking training, community engagement activities, and opportunities to lead peer initiatives. Research on generativity, which is the concern for establishing and guiding the next generation, shows that veterans who apply their skills to mentorship, civic engagement, and advocacy report higher life satisfaction and lower rates of post-service distress (Anthis & LaVoie, 2006; Tedeschi et al., 2018).

The WELL Program applies the principle that reintegration is an ongoing process, not a one-time event, requiring continuous adaptation, feedback, and goal adjustment. By focusing on empowerment, lifestyle, and leadership as interconnected areas, WELL reflects multidomain intervention models proven effective in enhancing quality of life for veterans with both visible and invisible wounds (Caddick & Smith, 2014; Elnitsky et al., 2017). Critically, WELL is a scalable and adaptable platform designed to be customized for various veteran subgroups, from recently separated service members to those who have been in civilian life for many years but still seek purpose. This flexibility exemplifies best practices in program design, with modular components enabling personalized pathways without sacrificing the integrity of the overall framework (Chinman et al., 2013).

7.6 The LINK and PATH Initiatives: Translating WELL into Targeted Action

Within the WELL Program, the Leadership, Integration, Networking, and Knowledge (LINK) Initiative and the Preparing, Advancing, Transitioning Heroes (PATH) Initiative serve as tactical extensions of the operational framework. They turn the WELL pillars into mission-specific actions, focusing on the social and educational areas most vital for veteran reintegration. Both initiatives arose from identified and confirmed gaps in empirical research related to the post-service landscape and are based on the idea that reintegration results improve when structured, peer-led systems address these specific areas simultaneously (Demers, 2011; Elnitsky et al., 2017).

The LINK Initiative was created to combat the loss of social capital that often happens when military members separate from service. Social capital theory (Coleman, 1988; Putnam, 2000) highlights the importance of networks, trust, and reciprocal exchanges in helping individuals access resources and opportunities and build collective resilience. For many veterans, the close-knit cohesion of military units is replaced in civilian life by disconnected, impersonal networks—a change that can cause social withdrawal, mistrust, and a reduced sense of belonging (Kuwert et al., 2014; McCormick et al., 2019).

LINK operationalizes social capital rebuilding through:

- Veteran-to-veteran peer networks that replicate the relational structure of military units, leveraging trust and shared experience to foster emotional safety (Haque et al., 2023).
- Community engagement events—such as MTF's outreach with Pine Forest basketball—that integrate veterans into broader civilian networks while simultaneously showcasing veteran leadership.
- Leadership immersion opportunities where veterans take point on planning, execution, and after-action reviews, aligning with adult learning principles that emphasize experiential learning and relevance (Knowles, 1978, 1984; Mezirow, 1997).

These mechanisms align with empirical findings showing that peer-led social interventions can reduce loneliness, improve mental health, and facilitate employment and educational transitions in veteran populations (Resnick et al., 2016; Van Kessel, 2013).

The PATH Initiative emphasizes academic reintegration, based on the understanding that higher education can serve as a period of developmental recalibration for veterans when the right supports are provided. Research on veteran students identifies several barriers to academic success, including navigating the GI Bill and Veteran Readiness and Employment (VR&E) benefits, managing service-related disabilities, and adjusting to classroom cultures that may lack military awareness (Rumann & Hamrick, 2010; Vacchi & Berger, 2013).

PATH addresses these barriers through four primary mechanisms:

1. **Benefit Navigation**—Hands-on guidance for maximizing GI Bill and VR&E usage, aligned with findings that benefit underutilization often stems from bureaucratic complexity and lack of institutional expertise (Carlton, 2025).
2. **Academic Mentorship**—Pairing veterans with peers or faculty mentors who have navigated similar challenges, supporting both role modeling and institutional acclimatization (Barry et al., 2017).
3. **Goal Alignment**—Structured planning sessions to translate career objectives into academic pathways, reflecting the importance of perceived relevance in adult learner persistence (Kasworm, 2014; Knowles, 1980).
4. **Purpose Recovery**—Encouraging veterans to see education not only as a credentialing process but as a vehicle for identity reconstruction and purpose-driven leadership (Demers, 2011; Mezirow, 1997).

Programs like PATH resonate with the literature on high-impact educational practices (Kuh, 2008), demonstrating that tailored advising, active learning, and community integration significantly improve outcomes for non-traditional students, including veterans.

LINK and PATH target domains like social/community integration and academic/career advancement. However, both operate within WELL's overarching philosophy that reintegration is multidimensional, iterative, and reinforced by peer-led, culturally competent approaches. Their design reflects an ecological systems perspective (Bronfenbrenner, 1979), situating veterans within overlapping contexts such as personal, social, institutional, and policy levels, ensuring interventions address all relevant areas layers.

The combined effect is a synchronized reinforcement loop:

- **LINK** enhances belonging, reduces isolation, and creates a supportive network that can bolster educational persistence.
- **PATH** equips veterans with academic clarity and resources, enabling them to contribute meaningfully to the very networks strengthened by LINK.

Both initiatives are designed to create mutually reinforcing support systems beyond isolated programs, aligning with current best practices in veteran reintegration program design (Caddick & Smith, 2014; Elnitsky et al., 2017).

7.7 The V.E.T.S. Toolkit: A Tactical Guide to Civilian Success

The Vision, Education, Translation, and Strategy (V.E.T.S.) Toolkit emerged due to a problem I experienced, studied, and repeatedly observed in the veteran community: the transition out of military service is often navigated without a clear, actionable plan. The idea for this toolkit was born during my DHSc research, when I started viewing post-service transition as a mission that requires the same clarity of purpose, operational planning, and resource allocation that characterized my military career. This approach was based on evidence. Veterans are more likely to transition successfully to civilian life when the strategies they use resemble familiar military structures and decision-making processes, which helps create a sense of continuity and eases transition-related anxiety (Cooper et al., 2018; Elnitsky et al., 2017).

From the beginning, my goal was to create something that combined the rigor of academic research with the credibility of lived experience. The "Vision" component tackles one of the most well-documented yet often underestimated reintegration challenges: losing a unifying mission and sense of identity. Research indicates that having purpose in life acts as a protective factor against depression, unhealthy coping strategies, and social withdrawal among veterans (Ryff, 2014; Smith & True, 2014). In my own experience, the lack of a mission after leaving the Navy created a void that no amount of busywork could fill. The exercises in this section are intentionally based on frameworks from purpose-in-life studies and self-determination theory (Ryan & Deci, 2000), helping veterans critically reflect, identify their core values, and craft a personal mission statement that can support them through the transition turbulence. This approach echoes Mezirow's (1997) transformative learning theory, where disorienting dilemmas catalyze shifting perspectives through structured reflection dialogue.

The "Education" component developed from my mistakes and the many stories I've heard from veterans who never fully accessed the benefits they earned. Many either misunderstood their eligibility or found the processes too complicated to navigate without help. This aligns with findings that underuse of GI Bill and Veteran Readiness & Employment (VR&E) benefits results from both institutional opacity and a lack of targeted outreach (DiRamio & Jarvis., 2011). In this section, education is seen as an operational asset connected to the individual's vision, adaptable to changing circumstances, and capable of supporting long-term employment goals. The approach draws on Knowles' (1978, 1984) andragogical principles, emphasizing self-directed learning that is immediately relevant, and Savickas' (2005) career construction theory, which views veterans' educational choices as narrative steps toward their envisioned civilian identity.

"Translation," converting military skills into civilian value, is arguably the most personally meaningful part of the toolkit. Early in my transition, I faced the frustrating reality that few outside the military could interpret my role as a Corpsman or recognize its transferable value. This experience is not unique; research shows that veterans' skills often remain unrecognized in civilian job markets because of differences in terminology, perception, and validation processes (Harrell & Berglass, 2012). In the toolkit, translation is treated as both a language and strategic process, using competency mapping to match Military Occupational Specialties with civilian job descriptions, reframe achievements into industry-standard metrics, and incorporate narrative-based resume development. These approaches are based on human capital theory (Becker, 1975) and supported by research indicating that narrative formats enhance employer understanding and engagement (Gould-Williams et al., 2014).

Finally, "Strategy" executes the transition process through detailed planning, implementation, and review. Drawing from the military decision-making process (Fisher, 2020), the toolkit guides veterans through phased goal setting, contingency planning, and tracking measurable outcomes. Research on implementation intentions (Gollwitzer, 1999) supports this method, showing that clear "if–then" planning significantly boosts goal achievement. The after-action review method (Keiser & Arthur., 2021) is included to ensure that both successes and setbacks are analyzed for lessons, promoting adaptability and ongoing improvement. This cyclical process aligns with Bronfenbrenner's (1979) ecological systems theory by acknowledging that successful reintegration requires coordinated adjustments at the environment's personal, social, institutional, and policy levels.

What makes the V.E.T.S. Toolkit unique is its dual origin. It is both the direct result of doctoral-level research informed by the empirical findings of over 600 studies in my DHSc work and a summation of the lived experiences of veterans, including myself. It does not expect veterans to conform to purely civilian frameworks, nor does it romanticize military culture; instead, it creates a hybrid operational environment where evidence-based strategies meet the practical constraints and cultural nuances of post-service life. Early use of the toolkit within the Mindfully Tactical Foundation has produced promising results, including better benefit utilization, more aligned job placements with veterans' stated career goals, and significant increases in self-efficacy, echoing Bandura's (1977) assertion that mastery experiences are the strongest source of self-belief.

In essence, the V.E.T.S. Toolkit is a plan for the next chapter of life, one that veterans can carry out with the same discipline, adaptability, and purpose that defined their service. It is a tangible example of how scholarly research, personal history, and cultural competence can create knowledge and actionable pathways to resilience and success.

7.8 Mentorship and Collaborative Support Networks

From the earliest days of building the Mindfully Tactical Foundation, I realized that the work could not be sustained alone. My doctoral program reinforced a principle I had practiced in the military: while individual skill and discipline are essential, long-term success almost always depends on the team you surround yourself with. Mentorship, both given and received, has continuously influenced MTF's path. It was both a professional necessity and a lifeline. The support of trusted advisors and my closest friend in the DHSc program, Dr. Tyton Brunner, transformed the foundation from a vision into a structured, actionable plan reality.

The role of mentorship in veteran reintegration is well-documented, with evidence showing that veterans who participate in structured, trust-based mentoring relationships experience improved psychosocial well-being, greater goal achievement, and fewer feelings of isolation (Cozza., 2014; Smith et al., 2020). In my experience, mentorship was not just a one-way process; it was reciprocal. While advisors challenged me to think more critically about program design and applying evidence-based practices, Tyton and I had daily conversations that enhanced our perspectives. This dynamic aligns with Kram's (1988) seminal work and Kram and Isabella's (1985) influential work on developmental relationships, emphasizing the dual roles of career development and psychosocial support.

Veteran-specific mentorship, especially peer-to-peer models, uses shared cultural understanding to fill trust gaps often present with non-veteran service providers (Blaisure et al., 2012). Tyton's insights into the realities of building resilience in transitional populations were invaluable, not only for improving the WELL Program but also for strengthening my resilience when doctoral work and nonprofit demands conflicted. The research confirms what I intuitively felt: peer mentors who have overcome similar challenges can uniquely model adaptive coping strategies and normalize transition difficulties (Van Kessel, 2013).

The collaborative networks created through MTF also go beyond individual mentorships. In the veteran support system, coalitions and partnerships expand the reach and longevity of programs. Community-based participatory research (CBPR) models highlight the importance of co-creating with stakeholders, ensuring interventions are developed for veterans and with them (Wallerstein et al., 2017). MTF's outreach efforts, like the LINK Initiative's partnership with Pine Forest basketball, demonstrate this approach by involving veterans in community settings that promote mutual visibility and engagement respect.

Theoretically, these mentorship and collaboration structures can be understood through Wenger's (1998) communities of practice framework. In this model, learning and identity development happen through active engagement in a shared domain. For MTF, that domain is pursuing post-service purpose, resilience, and leadership. Every interaction with a mentor, colleague, or community partner strengthens a sense of belonging and competence, which are key factors in transformative learning (Mezirow, 1997) and ecological reintegration models (Bronfenbrenner, 1979).

Mentorship also acts as a bridge between theory and practice. The BRAVE Theory, for instance, might be based on more than 600 studies, but its practical impact was sped up through iterative feedback and real-world insights from my network. This reflects Schön's (Bamberger & Schön, 1983) idea of the "reflective practitioner," where ongoing dialogue between action and reflection sharpens both the practitioner's skills and the program's effectiveness. In practice, my mentors validated my ideas, challenged them, dismantled them when necessary, and helped rebuild them stronger. That iterative process became a key element of MTF's growth and adaptability. Mentorship and collaboration are more than support mechanisms; they function as strategic assets. They build resilience, expand operational capacity, and ensure that no one (especially the founder) works in isolation. These relationships transformed MTF into a connected, evidence-based movement. And for the veterans we serve, they demonstrate that transition is, and always has been, a team effort.

7.9 Theoretical Backbone: The Birth of BRAVE

When the Mindfully Tactical Foundation was established, I realized its strength couldn't rely solely on programs, workshops, or my personal experience. To ensure its sustainability and academic credibility, it needed a theoretical framework that could both explain why it worked and steer its development. This understanding became the driving force behind the Building Resilience and Advancing Veteran Empowerment (BRAVE) Theory. The BRAVE Theory is a multidimensional model derived from reviewing over 600 peer-reviewed studies I examined during my DHSc journey.

The moment BRAVE started taking shape felt like the initial "Mindfully Tactical" spark. It was a point where scattered insights converged into a coherent whole. In academic terms, this represented a classic example of what Mezirow (1997) describes in transformative learning theory: "a disorienting dilemma." In this case, realizing MTF lacked a unifying framework triggered critical reflection and the reconstruction of meaning. I had been gathering knowledge across biopsychosocial, ecological, and trauma-informed domains; BRAVE emerged when I recognized that these were not separate tracks but interconnected dimensions of the same reintegration process.

From a research perspective, the BRAVE Theory is rooted in multiple well-established frameworks. Its biopsychosocial foundation is based on Engel's (1977) model, which views health outcomes as the result of dynamic interactions among biological, psychological, and social systems. For veterans, these systems are further influenced by the specific exposures of military service, such as operational stress, physical injuries, and cultural identity disruptions (Elnitsky et al., 2017; Sayer et al., 2011). The ecological aspect reflects Bronfenbrenner's (1979) ecological systems theory, highlighting how reintegration is affected by interconnected environments like family, community, institutions, and policy.

BRAVE's psychological aspect is heavily based on trauma theory and resilience research. Studies by Bonanno (2004) and Southwick and Charney (2018) show that resilience is not a fixed trait but a dynamic process that can be developed through specific interventions. Mindfulness, which is already a core part of MTF's identity, has empirical support in tactical populations through research by Jha et al. (2017), showing its ability to enhance attentional control, emotional regulation, and operational performance under stress. King et al. (2013) further emphasize the importance of culturally tailoring mindfulness-based interventions to match military and veteran communities' values and communication styles; a principle integrated into every BRAVE-based program.

The social dimension incorporates the Social Identity Model of Identity Change (SIMIC), which highlights the protective effects of maintaining and building valued group memberships during life transitions (Haslam et al., 2018). For veterans, structured peer networks and community involvement (core elements of the WELL Program and its initiatives) help close the identity gap that arises when leaving service (Demers, 2011; Joseph et al., 2023). The economic dimension reflects research on financial well-being and stability as key factors for successful reintegration (Elbogen et al., 2022), recognizing that without economic security, progress in other areas is often unsustainable.

Methodologically, the BRAVE Theory serves both as a conceptual framework for understanding veteran reintegration and as an operational plan for program development. This dual purpose reflects the "theory-to-practice" translation model promoted in applied health sciences (Craig, 2013). Each aspect (psychological, physical, social, economic) interacts dynamically, with mediating factors such as self-efficacy, perceived control, and access to resources shaping overall resilience trajectories.

For me, developing BRAVE was a deeply personal journey. I saw my own transition reflected in its dimensions, with variables explaining both my struggles and progress. This connection between lived experience and empirical evidence strengthened the framework's authenticity. It also allowed me to present BRAVE to academic peers, veteran stakeholders, or policymakers with both scholarly rigor and personal conviction.

In practice, BRAVE became the guiding compass for every MTF initiative, ensuring that no matter how diverse our programs became (from mindfulness workshops to career readiness toolkits), they all contributed to strengthening at least one dimension of the model. The theory provided a language for explaining our work and a method for measuring its impact, laying the groundwork for future research such as the planned Resilience Index study. In this way, BRAVE is the theoretical backbone of MTF and its long-term strategic anchor, ensuring that our mission remains evidence-driven, culturally relevant, and operationally effective.

Academic Synthesis

This chapter traced the development of the Mindfully Tactical Foundation (MTF) from a moment of personal insight into an evidence-based nonprofit framework rooted in doctoral research. The narrative demonstrated how a single transformative learning experience in an adult education course (Mezirow, 1997) sparked a shift from a conceptual interest in mindfulness to creating a veteran-centered, research-informed operational model. This process aligns with Knowles' (1978, 1984) andragogical principles, especially the focus on self-direction, relevance to life experience, and immediate applicability. The creation of MTF exemplifies the theory-to-practice translation described by Craig (2013), where academic concepts such as mindfulness integration in tactical populations (Jha et al., 2017) and cultural adaptation for military settings (King et al., 2013) were transformed into programs with measurable results. The chapter emphasized how veteran reintegration challenges documented in the literature, including identity loss, systemic navigation barriers, and social disconnection (Demers, 2011; Joseph et al., 2023), directly shaped MTF's mission and service delivery.

The WELL Program was developed as the organizational framework, emphasizing empowerment, lifestyle wellness, and leadership through initiatives like LINK, PATH, and the V.E.T.S. Toolkit. These programs were explicitly aligned with evidence indicating that peer support networks (Haslam et al., 2019), educational mentorship (Cheney et al., 2018), and structured career transition resources (Elbogen et al., 2022) help ensure long-term reintegration success. The program structure reflected the multidimensional aspects of veteran well-being, consistent with Engel's (1977) biopsychosocial model and Bronfenbrenner's (1979) ecological systems theory. The culmination of this process was the creation of the BRAVE Theory, a comprehensive conceptual framework that integrates psychological, physical, social, and economic dimensions. BRAVE's design incorporates trauma-informed resilience science (Bonanno, 2004; Southwick & Charney, 2018), identity continuity models (Haslam et al., 2019), and socioeconomic stability research (Elbogen et al., 2022). The framework functions both as a descriptive model and a prescriptive guide, ensuring that all MTF initiatives are evidence-based, culturally relevant, and strategically effective.

In summary, this chapter showed that the birth of MTF was an iterative, research-driven process based on real experience. Integrating transformative learning with multidisciplinary scholarship, the organization grew from a classroom idea to a fully operational, theoretically supported nonprofit. This path illustrates how doctoral-level research can act as both the intellectual basis and operational guide for sustainable, mission-focused community interventions.

Key Takeaways

- **Transformative insight can catalyze organizational creation**—A triggering moment of reflection in an adult learning environment can initiate a paradigm shift, aligning personal experience with scholarly theory to form a mission-driven concept (Knowles, 1980; Mezirow, 1997).
- **Theory-to-practice translation strengthens program relevance**—Applying evidence from mindfulness in tactical contexts (Jha et al., 2017) and cultural adaptation models (King et al., 2013) ensured MTF programming met both operational demands and population-specific needs.
- **Veteran reintegration requires multidimensional support**—Programs addressing identity continuity, systemic navigation, and peer connection reflect research showing that veterans benefit most from integrated biopsychosocial interventions (Demers, 2011; Haslam et al., 2018; Joseph et al., 2023).
- **Peer-led initiatives enhance engagement and retention**—Veteran-to-veteran mentorship and networked support, as in the LINK Initiative, align with evidence that shared lived experience fosters trust, accountability, and sustained participation (Cheney et al., 2018; Haslam et al., 2019).
- **Educational empowerment is central to post-service resilience**—PATH Initiative strategies that connect veterans to higher education and mentorship are supported by literature linking academic re-engagement to purpose restoration and improved life satisfaction (Cheney et al., 2018).
- **Career translation tools close critical reintegration gaps**—The V.E.T.S. Toolkit addresses skill translation, career strategy, and benefit utilization, reinforcing findings that structured career planning improves economic outcomes for transitioning veterans (Elbogen et al., 2022).
- **A unifying theoretical framework ensures coherence**—The BRAVE Theory integrates psychological, physical, social, and economic domains of resilience, drawing on trauma-informed, identity-based, and ecological models to guide program design (Bonanno, 2004; Bronfenbrenner, 1979; Southwick & Charney, 2018).
- **Doctoral research can directly shape sustainable community impact**—MTF demonstrates that scholarship, when intentionally aligned with lived experience and practical delivery models, can produce scalable, culturally relevant, and evidence-based interventions.

Applied Learning Prompts

1. Think of a moment in your professional or personal life that shifted your perspective on a key challenge. Using Mezirow's transformative learning framework, outline how you could translate that insight into a practical program, service, or intervention.
2. Using the WELL Program's three pillars—Warrior Empowerment, Lifestyle Wellness, and Leadership—design a hypothetical initiative for a different population (e.g., first responders, collegiate athletes). Identify how each pillar would address their unique biopsychosocial needs.

3. Draft a mini-V.E.T.S.-style framework for a population you work with or study. Define one step each for Vision, Education, Translation, and Strategy, and describe how it could improve long-term outcomes for that group.
4. Choose one theoretical model from this chapter (e.g., Biopsychosocial Model, Ecological Systems Theory, or BRAVE Theory) and apply it to evaluate an existing reintegration or transition program. Identify at least two strengths and two gaps revealed by this framework.

References

Anthis, K., & LaVoie, J. C. (2006). Readiness to change: A longitudinal study of changes in adult identity. *Journal of Research in Personality, 40*(2), 209–219. https://doi.org/10.1016/j.jrp.2004.12.004

Bamberger, J., & Schön, D. A. (1983). Learning as reflective conversation with materials: Notes from work in progress. *Art Education, 36*(2), 68–73. https://doi.org/10.1080/00043125.1983.11653404

Bandura, A. (1977). Self-efficacy: Toward a unifying theory of behavioral change. *Psychological Review, 84*(2), 191–215. https://doi.org/10.1037/0033-295X.84.2.191

Barry, A. E., Whiteman, S. D., & MacDermid Wadsworth, S. (2017). Mental health and academic functioning of student servicemembers and veterans in higher education: The importance of social support. In *What's next for student veterans* (pp. 59–75).

Becker, G. S. (1975). Investment in human capital: Effects on earnings. In *Human capital: A theoretical and empirical analysis, with special reference to education* (2nd ed., pp. 13–44). National Bureau of Economic Research.

Blaisure, K. R., Saathoff-Wells, T., Dombro, A. L., Pereira, C. A., & Wadsworth, S. M. M. (2012). *Serving military families in the 21st century: Theories, research, and application.* Routledge.

Bonanno, G. A. (2004). Loss, trauma, and human resilience: Have we underestimated the human capacity to thrive after extremely aversive events? *American Psychologist, 59*(1), 20. https://doi.org/10.1037/0003-066X.59.1.20

Bronfenbrenner, U. (1979). *The ecology of human development: Experiments by nature and design.* Harvard University Press.

Brown, L. D., & Moore, M. H. (2001). Accountability, strategy, and international nongovernmental organizations. *Nonprofit and Voluntary Sector Quarterly, 30*(3), 569–587. https://doi.org/10.1177/0899764001303012

Bryson, J. M. (2018). *Strategic planning for public and nonprofit organizations: A guide to strengthening and sustaining organizational achievement*. John Wiley & Sons.

Burnett-Zeigler, I., Valenstein, M., Ilgen, M., Blow, A. J., Gorman, L. A., & Zivin, K. (2011). Civilian employment among recently returning Afghanistan and Iraq National Guard veterans. *Military Medicine, 176*(6), 639. https://doi.org/10.7205/milmed-d-10-00450

Caddick, N., & Smith, B. (2014). The impact of sport and physical activity on the well-being of combat veterans: A systematic review. *Psychology of Sport and Exercise, 15*(1), 9–18. https://doi.org/10.1016/j.psychsport.2013.09.011

Carlton, T. (2025). Evidence integration review of multimodal interventions for PTSD, social reintegration, and economic stability in veterans. *Journal of Veterans Studies, 11*(2). https://doi.org/10.21061/jvs.v11i2.683

Chen, S., & Shen, T. (2023). Resource constraints and firm innovation: When less is more? *Chinese Journal of Population, Resources and Environment, 21*(3), 172–180. https://doi.org/10.1016/j.cjpre.2023.09.006

Cheney, A. M., Koenig, C. J., Miller, C. J., Zamora, K., Wright, P., Stanley, R., Fortney, J., Burgess, J. F., & Pyne, J. M. (2018). Veteran-centered barriers to VA mental healthcare services use. *BMC Health Services Research, 18*(1), 591. https://doi.org/10.1186/s12913-018-3346-9

Chinman, M., Acosta, J., Ebener, P., Burkhart, Q., Malone, P. S., Paddock, S. M., Clifford, M., Corsello, M., Duffey, T., Hunter, S., Jones, M., Lahti, M., Phillips, A., Savell, S., Scales, P. C., & Tellett-Royce, N. (2013). Intervening with practitioners to improve the quality of prevention: One-year findings from a randomized trial of Assets-Getting to Outcomes. *The Journal of Primary Prevention, 34*(3), 173–191. https://doi.org/10.1007/s10935-013-0302-7

Coleman, J. S. (1988). Social capital in the creation of human capital. *American Journal of Sociology, 94*, S95–S120. https://doi.org/10.1086/228943

Cooper, L., Caddick, N., Godier, L., Cooper, A., & Fossey, M. (2018). Transition from the military into civilian life: An exploration of cultural competence. *Armed Forces & Society, 44*(1), 156–177. https://doi.org/10.1177/0095327X16675965

Cozza, S. J. (2014). Supporting America's military children and families. *Applied Developmental Science, 18*(1), 1–4. https://doi.org/10.1080/10888691.2014.866399

Craig, R. T. (2013). Communication theory and social change. *Communication & Social Change, 1*(1), 5–18. https://doi.org/10.4471/csc.2013.01

Crane, M. F., Hazel, G., Kunzelmann, A., Kho, M., Gucciardi, D. F., Rigotti, T., Kalisch, R., & Karin, E. (2024). An exploratory domain analysis of deployment risks and protective features and their association to mental health, cognitive functioning and job performance in military personnel. *Anxiety, Stress, & Coping, 37*(1), 16–28. https://doi.org/10.1080/10615806.2023.2228707

Crum-Cianflone, N. F., Fairbank, J. A., Marmar, C. R., & Schlenger, W. (2014). The Millennium Cohort Family Study: A prospective evaluation of the health and well-being of military service members and their families. *International Journal of Methods in Psychiatric Research, 23*(3), 320–330. https://doi.org/10.1002/mpr.1446

Cushing, R. E., & Braun, K. L. (2017). Mind–body therapy for military veterans with post-traumatic stress disorder: A systematic review. *The Journal of Alternative and Complementary Medicine, 24*(2), 106–114. https://doi.org/10.1089/acm.2017.0176

Demers, A. (2011). When veterans return: The role of community in reintegration. *Journal of Loss and Trauma, 16*(2), 160–179. https://doi.org/10.1080/15325024.2010.519281

DiRamio, D., & Jarvis, K. (2011). *Veterans in higher education: When Johnny and Jane come marching to campus* (ASHE Higher Education Report, Vol. 37, No. 3). John Wiley & Sons.

Dolan, G., McCauley, M., & Murphy, D. (2022). Factors influencing the salience of military/veteran identity post discharge: A scoping review. *Journal of Veterans Studies, 8*(1). https://doi.org/10.21061/jvs.v8i1.333

Elbogen, E. B., Zeber, J. E., Vogt, D., Perkins, D. F., Finley, E. P., & Copeland, L. A. (2022). Financial status and well-being in recently separated military veterans. *Military Medicine, 188*(7–8), e2181–e2188. https://doi.org/10.1093/milmed/usac030

Elliott, M. (2015). Predicting problems on campus: An analysis of college student veterans. *Analyses of Social Issues and Public Policy, 15*(1), 105–126. https://doi.org/10.1111/asap.12066

Elnitsky, C. A., Blevins, C. L., Fisher, M. P., & Magruder, K. (2017). Military service member and veteran reintegration: A critical review and adapted ecological model. *American Journal of Orthopsychiatry, 87*(2), 114–128. https://doi.org/10.1037/ort0000244

Engel, G. L. (1977). The need for a new medical model: A challenge for biomedicine. *Science, 196*(4286), 129–136. https://doi.org/10.1126/science.847460

Fisher, T. S. (2020). *Clarifying the relationship of design thinking to the military decision-making process*. University of South Florida.

Glueckauf, R. L., Maheu, M. M., Drude, K. P., Wells, B. A., Wang, Y., Gustafson, D. J., & Nelson, E.-L. (2018). Survey of psychologists' telebehavioral health practices: Technology use, ethical issues, and training needs. *Professional Psychology: Research and Practice, 49*(3), 205–219. https://doi.org/10.1037/pro0000188

Gollwitzer, P. M. (1999). Implementation intentions: Strong effects of simple plans. *American Psychologist, 54*(7), 493–503. https://doi.org/10.1037/0003-066X.54.7.493

Gould-Williams, J. S., Bottomley, P., Redman, T., Snape, E., Bishop, D. J., Limpanitgul, T., & Mostafa, A. M. S. (2014). Civic duty and employee outcomes: Do high commitment human resource practices and work overload matter? *Public Administration, 92*(4), 937–953. https://doi.org/10.1111/padm.12019

Gucciardi, D. F., Peeling, P., Ducker, K. J., & Dawson, B. (2016). When the going gets tough: Mental toughness and its relationship with behavioural perseverance. *Journal of Science and Medicine in Sport, 19*(1), 81–86. https://doi.org/10.1016/j.jsams.2014.12.005

Hajjar, R. M. (2014). Emergent Postmodern Us Military Culture. *Armed Forces & Society, 40*(1), 118–145. https://doi.org/10.1177/0095327x12465261

Haque, M. R., Franco, Z., Hossain, M. F., Frydrychowicz, W., Madiraju, P., Baker, N. D., Hooyer, K., Ahamed, S. I., Winstead, O., Curry, R., & Rubya, S. (2023). Perceptions of mental health crisis among U.S. military veteran peer mentors and potential of mobile-based peer-support interventions. In *Companion Publication of the 2023 Conference on Computer Supported Cooperative Work and Social Computing* (Minneapolis, MN, USA). https://doi.org/10.1145/3584931.3607009

Harrell, M. C., & Berglass, N. (2012). *Employing America's veterans*. Center for a New American Security.

Haslam, C., Steffens, N. K., Branscombe, N. R., Haslam, S. A., Cruwys, T., Lam, B. C. P., Pachana, N. A., & Yang, J. (2019). The importance of social groups for retirement adjustment: Evidence, application, and policy implications of the Social Identity Model of Identity Change. *Social Issues and Policy Review, 13*(1), 93–124. https://doi.org/10.1111/sipr.12049

Hays, P. A. (2009). Integrating evidence-based practice, cognitive–behavior therapy, and multicultural therapy: Ten steps for culturally competent practice. *American Psychological Association*. https://doi.org/10.1037/a0016250

Heifetz, R. A., Grashow, A., & Linsky, M. (2009). *The practice of adaptive leadership: Tools and tactics for changing your organization and the world*. Harvard Business Press.

Hoge, C. W., Grossman, S. H., Auchterlonie, J. L., Riviere, L. A., Milliken, C. S., & Wilk, J. E. (2014). PTSD treatment for soldiers after combat deployment: Low utilization of mental health care and reasons for dropout. *Psychiatric Services, 65*(8), 997–1004. https://doi.org/10.1176/appi.ps.201300307

Holling, C. S. (2001). Understanding the complexity of economic, ecological, and social systems. *Ecosystems, 4*(5), 390–405. https://doi.org/10.1007/s10021-001-0101-5

Jha, A. P., Morrison, A. B., Parker, S. C., & Stanley, E. A. (2017). Practice is protective: Mindfulness training promotes cognitive resilience in high-stress cohorts. *Mindfulness, 8*(1), 46–58. https://doi.org/10.1007/s12671-015-0465-9

Johnson, D. C., Thom, N. J., Stanley, E. A., Haase, L., Simmons, A. N., Shih, P.-A.B., Thompson, W. K., Potterat, E. G., Minor, T. R., & Paulus, M. P. (2014). Modifying resilience mechanisms in at-risk individuals: A controlled study of mindfulness training in Marines preparing for deployment. *American Journal of Psychiatry, 171*(8), 844–853. https://doi.org/10.1176/appi.ajp.2014.13040502

Joseph, J. S., Smith-MacDonald, L., Filice, M. C., & Smith, M. S. (2023). Reculturation: A new perspective on military-civilian transition stress. *Military Psychology, 35*(3), 193–203. https://doi.org/10.1080/08995605.2022.2094175

Kasworm, C. E. (2014). Paradoxical understandings regarding adult undergraduate persistence. *The Journal of Continuing Higher Education, 62*(2), 67–77. https://doi.org/10.1080/07377363.2014.916587

Kearney, D. J., Malte, C. A., Storms, M., & Simpson, T. L. (2021). Loving-kindness meditation vs cognitive processing therapy for posttraumatic stress disorder among veterans: A randomized clinical trial. *JAMA Network Open, 4*(4), Article e216604. https://doi.org/10.1001/jamanetworkopen.2021.6604

Keiser, N. L., & Arthur, W., Jr. (2021). A meta-analysis of the effectiveness of the after-action review (or debrief) and factors that influence its effectiveness. *Journal of Applied Psychology, 106*(7), 1007–1025. https://doi.org/10.1037/apl0000821

Kettner, P. M., Moroney, R. M., & Martin, L. L. (2015). *Designing and managing programs: An effectiveness-based approach.* Sage Publications.

King, A. P., Erickson, T. M., Giardino, N. D., Favorite, T., Rauch, S. A. M., Robinson, E., Kulkarni, M., & Liberzon, I. (2013). A pilot study of group mindfulness-based cognitive therapy (MBCT) for combat veterans with posttraumatic stress disorder (PTSD). *Depression & Anxiety, 30*(7), 638–645. https://doi.org/10.1002/da.22104

Kintzle, S., & Castro, C. A. (2018). Examining veteran transition to the workplace through Military Transition Theory. In *Occupational stress and well-being in military contexts* (Vol. 16). Emerald Publishing Limited. https://doi.org/10.1108/S1479-355520180000016009

Kitchenham, A. (2008). The evolution of John Mezirow's transformative learning theory. *Journal of Transformative Education, 6*(2), 104–123. https://doi.org/10.1177/1541344608322678

Kline, D. M. S. (2016). Can restorative practices help to reduce disparities in school discipline data? A review of the literature. *Multicultural Perspectives, 18*(2), 97–102. https://doi.org/10.1080/15210960.2016.1159099

Knowles, M. S. (1978). Andragogy: Adult learning theory in perspective. *Community College Review, 5*(3), 9–20. https://doi.org/10.1177/009155217800500302

Knowles, M. S. (1984). Theory of andragogy: A critique. *International Journal of Lifelong Education.*

Kolb, D. A., Boyatzis, R. E., & Mainemelis, C. (2014). Experiential learning theory: Previous research and new directions. In *Perspectives on thinking, learning, and cognitive styles* (pp. 227–247). Routledge.

Kram, K. E., & Isabella, L. A. (1985). Mentoring alternatives: The role of peer relationships in career development. *Academy of Management Journal, 28*(1), 110–132. https://doi.org/10.5465/256064

Kram, K. E. (1988). *Mentoring at work: Developmental relationships in organizational life.* University Press of America.

Kuh, G. D. (2008). High-impact educational practices. *Peer Review, 10*(4), 30.

Kuwert, P., Glaesmer, H., Eichhorn, S., Grundke, E., Pietrzak, R. H., Freyberger, H. J., & Klauer, T. (2014). Long-term effects of conflict-related sexual violence compared with non-sexual war trauma in female World War II survivors: A matched pairs study. *Archives of Sexual Behavior, 43*(6), 1059–1064. https://doi.org/10.1007/s10508-014-0272-8

Lave, J., & Wenger, E. (1991). *Situated learning: Legitimate peripheral participation.* Cambridge University Press.

Lehavot, K., Katon, J. G., Chen, J. A., Fortney, J. C., & Simpson, T. L. (2018). Post-traumatic stress disorder by gender and veteran status. *American Journal of Preventive Medicine, 54*(1), e1–e9. https://doi.org/10.1016/j.amepre.2017.09.008

Light, P. C. (2004). *Sustaining nonprofit performance: The case for capacity building and the evidence to support it.* Rowman & Littlefield.

Maier, F., Meyer, M., & Steinbereithner, M. (2016). Nonprofit organizations becoming business-like: A systematic review. *Nonprofit and Voluntary Sector Quarterly, 45*(1), 64–86. https://doi.org/10.1177/0899764014561796

McCauley, C. D., Kanaga, K., & Lafferty, K. (2010). Leader development systems. In *The Center for Creative Leadership handbook of leadership development* (p. 29).

McCormick, W. H., Currier, J. M., Isaak, S. L., Sims, B. M., Slagel, B. A., Carroll, T. D., Hamner, K., & Albright, D. L. (2019). Military culture and post-military transitioning among veterans: A qualitative analysis. *Journal of Veterans Studies.* https://doi.org/10.21061/jvs.v4i2.121

McGuire, M. (2025). Impact of competition-based learning on student engagement and performance. *International Journal of Construction Education and Research*, 1–30. https://doi.org/10.1080/15578771.2025.2512348

Merriam, S. B., & Bierema, L. L. (2013). Adult Learning: Linking Theory and Practice. John Wiley & Sons.

Mezirow, J. (1997). Transformation theory out of context. *Adult Education Quarterly, 48*(1), 60–62. https://doi.org/10.1177/074171369704800105

Morland, L. A., Greene, C. J., Rosen, C. S., Kuhn, E., Hoffman, J., & Sloan, D. M. (2017). Telehealth and eHealth interventions for posttraumatic stress disorder. *Current Opinion in Psychology, 14*, 102–108. https://doi.org/10.1016/j.copsyc.2016.12.003

Newman, A., Obschonka, M., Schwarz, S., Cohen, M., & Nielsen, I. (2019). Entrepreneurial self-efficacy: A systematic review of the literature on its theoretical foundations, measurement, antecedents, and outcomes, and an agenda for future research. *Journal of Vocational Behavior, 110*, 403–419. https://doi.org/10.1016/j.jvb.2018.05.012

Nindl, B. C., Jones, B. H., Van Arsdale, S. J., Kelly, K., & Kraemer, W. J. (2016). Operational physical performance and fitness in military women: Physiological, musculoskeletal injury, and optimized physical training considerations for successfully integrating women into combat-centric military occupations. *Military Medicine, 181*(Suppl_1), 50–62. https://doi.org/10.7205/MILMED-D-15-00382

Polusny, M. A., Erbes, C. R., Thuras, P., Moran, A., Lamberty, G. J., Collins, R. C., Rodman, J. L., & Lim, K. O. (2015). Mindfulness-based stress reduction for posttraumatic stress disorder among veterans: A randomized clinical trial. *JAMA, 314*(5), 456–465. https://doi.org/10.1001/jama.2015.8361

Putnam, R. D. (2000). Bowling alone: America's declining social capital. In L. Crothers & C. Lockhart (Eds.), *Culture and politics: A reader* (pp. 223–234). Palgrave Macmillan. https://doi.org/10.1007/978-1-349-62397-6_12

Resnick, S. G., & Rosenheck, R. A. (2008). Integrating peer-provided services: A quasi-experimental study of recovery orientation, confidence, and empowerment. *Psychiatric Services, 59*(11), 1307–1314. https://doi.org/10.1176/ps.2008.59.11.1307

Rumann, C. B., & Hamrick, F. A. (2010). Student veterans in transition: Re-enrolling after war zone deployments. *The Journal of Higher Education, 81*(4), 431–458. https://doi.org/10.1080/00221546.2010.11779060

Ryan, R. M., & Deci, E. L. (2000). Intrinsic and extrinsic motivations: Classic definitions and new directions. *Contemporary Educational Psychology, 25*(1), 54–67. https://doi.org/10.1006/ceps.1999.1020

Ryff, C. D. (2014). Self-realisation and meaning making in the face of adversity: A eudaimonic approach to human resilience. *Journal of Psychology in Africa, 24*(1), 1–12. https://doi.org/10.1080/14330237.2014.904098

Salamon, L. M. (2015). *The resilient sector revisited: The new challenge to nonprofit America.* Brookings Institution Press.

Savickas, M. L. (2005). Toward a comprehensive theory of career development: Dispositions, concerns, and narratives. In *Contemporary models in vocational psychology* (pp. 303–328). Routledge.

Sayer, N. A., Spoont, M., Murdoch, M., Parker, L. E., Hintz, S., & Rosenheck, R. (2011). A qualitative study of U.S. veterans' reasons for seeking Department of Veterans Affairs disability benefits for posttraumatic stress disorder. *Journal of Traumatic Stress, 24*(6), 699–707. https://doi.org/10.1002/jts.20693

Shonin, E., Van Gordon, W., & Griffiths, M. D. (2014). Meditation awareness training (MAT) for improved psychological well-being: A qualitative examination of participant experiences. *Journal of Religion and Health, 53*(3), 849–863. https://doi.org/10.1007/s10943-013-9679-0

Smith, C. A., Beltman, S., Dinham, J., Dobinson, T. J., & Jay, J. (2020). Supporting undergraduate university students through instrumental mentoring. *Australian Journal of Teacher Education, 45*(1), 82–98. https://search.informit.org/doi/https://doi.org/10.3316/ielapa.190689846482871

Smith, R. T., & True, G. (2014). Warring identities: Identity conflict and the mental distress of American veterans of the wars in Iraq and Afghanistan. *Society and Mental Health, 4*(2), 147–161. https://doi.org/10.1177/2156869313512212

Southwick, S. M., & Charney, D. S. (2018). *Resilience: The science of mastering life's greatest challenges* (2nd ed.). Cambridge University Press.
Stanley, E. A., Schaldach, J. M., Kiyonaga, A., & Jha, A. P. (2011). Mindfulness-based Mind Fitness Training: A case study of a high-stress predeployment military cohort. *Cognitive and Behavioral Practice, 18*(4), 566–576. https://doi.org/10.1016/j.cbpra.2010.08.002
Stone, M. M., & Ostrower, F. (2007). Acting in the public interest? Another look at research on nonprofit governance. *Nonprofit and Voluntary Sector Quarterly, 36*(3), 416–438. https://doi.org/10.1177/0899764006296049
Taylor, D., & Miflin, B. (2008). Problem-based learning: Where are we now? *Medical Teacher, 30*(8), 742–763. https://doi.org/10.1080/01421590802217199
Tedeschi, R. G., & Calhoun, L. G. (2004). Posttraumatic growth: Conceptual foundations and empirical evidence. *Psychological Inquiry, 15*(1), 1–18. https://doi.org/10.1207/s15327965pli1501_01
Tedeschi, R. G., Shakespeare-Finch, J., & Taku, K. (2018). *Posttraumatic growth: Theory, research, and applications*. Routledge.
Vacchi, D. T., & Berger, J. B. (2013). Student veterans in higher education. In *Higher education: Handbook of theory and research* (Vol. 29, pp. 93–151). Springer.
van Kessel, G. (2013). The ability of older people to overcome adversity: A review of the resilience concept. *Geriatric Nursing, 34*(2), 122–127. https://doi.org/10.1016/j.gerinurse.2012.12.011
Wallerstein, N., Duran, B., Oetzel, J. G., & Minkler, M. (2017). *Community-based participatory research for health: Advancing social and health equity* (3rd ed.). John Wiley & Sons.
Weerawardena, J., McDonald, R. E., & Mort, G. S. (2010). Sustainability of nonprofit organizations: An empirical investigation. *Journal of World Business, 45*(4), 346–356. https://doi.org/10.1016/j.jwb.2009.08.004
Wenger, E. (1998). Communities of practice: Learning as a social system. *The Systems Thinker, 9*(5), 2–3.

Chapter 8
Conclusions—Brave Is a Verb

This chapter ties together theory, evidence, and lived experience. It redefines BRAVE as a verb, a continuous process of becoming rather than a fixed identity or framework. The chapter explores how resilience works dynamically across psychological, physical, social, and economic areas, demonstrating that reintegration is not a one-time event but an ongoing practice of adaptation and agency. It encourages readers to see how institutions like universities, healthcare systems, and justice networks can embody BRAVE through trauma-informed, equity-focused design. Drawing from Social Identity Theory and Transformative Learning Theory, the chapter presents identity reconstruction as an ongoing process that goes beyond the individual to include community and policy. After reading, you'll be able to: (1) explain how BRAVE operates as an enacted process rather than a static trait; (2) analyze the interdependence of the four BRAVE dimensions in shaping reintegration outcomes; (3) evaluate the institutional role in translating BRAVE principles into practice; (4) apply theoretical frameworks to understand identity reconstruction as ongoing transformation; and (5) critically assess the implications of BRAVE praxis for future research, policy, and longitudinal intervention design.

8.1 Synthesis of BRAVE Theory Across Dimensions

The BRAVE Theory has been developed as a multidimensional model that describes reintegration through four interconnected domains: psychological, physical, social, and economic. While these domains have been discussed separately in previous

T. Carlton, *BRAVE Theory*, https://doi.org/10.1007/978-3-032-13695-4_8

chapters, combining them highlights the systemic nature of resilience. Reintegration cannot be simplified to a single outcome or intervention because the dynamic interactions among capacities across these domains shape post-service life.

8.1.1 Psychological Resilience

The psychological aspect remains central in veteran and trauma research. Studies consistently show that PTSD, depression, and moral injury are not isolated clinical issues but signs of disrupted identity and meaning-making processes (Kearney et al., 2021; Saban et al., 2022). Interventions like mindfulness-based stress reduction prove effective in reducing symptoms and recalibrating psychophysiological systems, lowering inflammatory markers, and enhancing emotional regulation (Domschke et al., 2025). In BRAVE, psychological resilience is viewed as restoring regulation and coherence after disruption. My personal experiences with psychological fragmentation after combat demonstrate how this aspect goes beyond pathology. The challenge was to reduce symptoms and rebuild a coherent self-capable of functioning outside the military environment. This aligns with transformative learning theory (Mezirow, 1997), which views recovery as a critical reflection and identity reconstruction process.

8.1.2 Physical Resilience

Physical health reflects both an outcome of trauma and a key factor in successful reintegration. Veterans show high rates of musculoskeletal injuries, traumatic brain injuries (TBI), and sleep issues (Teplova et al., 2021). Research in epigenetics highlights that adverse environments can alter stress-regulation pathways, but targeted interventions can improve these effects (van Assche et al., 2023). Strength and conditioning methods were central to research and practice in my doctoral work. Physical training, nutrition, and sleep regulation served as health behaviors and interventions signaling to the body that recovery and adaptation are achievable. This emphasizes the BRAVE premise that physical resilience is about sustainable embodiment, not peak performance, capable of supporting long-term reintegration.

8.1.3 Social Resilience

The social domain highlights the importance of belonging, trust, and community involvement. Social identity theory (Turner et al., 1979) and the Social Identity Model of Identity Change (Trepte & Loy, 2017) demonstrate that reintegration involves re-negotiating one's role within social structures. Disrupted social connections are strongly associated with declines in mental health, homelessness, and recidivism among veteran populations (Bond et al., 2022; Geraci et al., 2023). My own transition showed how delicate social continuity can be. The sudden loss of the military community increased disconnection, while creating the MTF and later the WELL Program were deliberate efforts to restore belonging through structured peer and community networks. These initiatives reflect the BRAVE emphasis that social resilience is vital to rebuilding identity stability.

8.1.4 Economic Resilience

Economic stability is a key component of resilience and supports the other three areas. Elbogen et al. (2022) identified financial stress as one of the strongest predictors of poor mental health outcomes in veterans. The Individual Placement and Support (IPS) and the National Career Coach Program (Bond et al., 2022) demonstrate that structured vocational assistance significantly enhances long-term reintegration success. Economic resilience involves securing employment, housing stability, financial literacy, and planning skills. In practice, assisting veterans with navigating GI Bill or VR&E benefits alongside financial planning exemplifies an economic strategy that directly supports reintegration.

8.1.5 Interdependent Mechanisms

The key feature of BRAVE is focusing on domains alone and understanding how they depend on and influence each other. Improvements in psychological health support physical recovery; social belonging enhances economic opportunities; economic stability reduces stress and promotes social participation. These feedback loops operate in multiple directions and align with the biopsychosocial model (Engel, 1977) and the Multi-System Model of Resilience (Liu et al., 2019), both view resilience as an emergent property of interacting systems, not merely a trait. From both academic and personal perspectives, progress in one area can help protect against vulnerabilities in another, but genuine reintegration requires addressing all four areas simultaneously. Therefore, BRAVE provides a multidimensional support system that integrates individual, relational, and systemic processes, creating a framework that is both scientifically sound and practically useful.

8.2 From Noun to Verb: BRAVE as Dynamic Praxis

The BRAVE Theory was never meant to be a fixed model. Its development during doctoral studies made it clear that a framework's value lies in its ability to guide real-world practice. Resilience isn't something a person has or lacks; it must be understood as a process that develops through repeated actions across psychological, physical, social, and economic domains. Seeing BRAVE as a noun risks turning it into an abstraction; viewing it as a verb recognizes resilience as a behavior continuously enacted and shaped by context, identity, and systemic factors.

8.2.1 BRAVE as Action

Resilience research has long grappled with the tension between trait-based and process-based perspectives. Early ideas often described resilience as an individual trait, a fixed quality that allowed some people to withstand stress while others struggled (Connor & Davidson, 2003). More recent work has shifted toward viewing resilience as dynamic, emphasizing ecological and systemic interactions (Liu et al., 2019). BRAVE aligns with this latter view. Each of its four dimensions represents a site of action, where daily behaviors build into long-term reintegration pathways. Psychological resilience is shown through mindfulness practice, cognitive reframing, and intentional identity work. Physical resilience develops through training, nutritional choices, and recovery routines. Social resilience happens when individuals join peer networks, rebuild trust, and foster a sense of belonging. Economic resilience occurs when veterans access benefits, find employment, and manage finances. These are symbolic acts that embody resilience itself. The BRAVE framework highlights that reintegration outcomes are deeply connected to these ongoing practices and that measurement must be combined with active engagement.

8.2.2 Praxis in Academic Development

The doctoral program itself became a testing ground for BRAVE as praxis. Assignments, literature reviews, and research projects were opportunities to put theory into action. The WELL Program was developed as an intervention that combined mindfulness with structured health and performance strategies, directly targeting the psychological and physical domains. The V.E.T.S. Toolkit was designed to support educational navigation and financial literacy, anchoring the economic domain while promoting social connectedness through advisor engagement.

Each of these initiatives demonstrates the shift from theory to practice. The WELL Program was guided by research showing that mindfulness-based stress reduction effectively reduces PTSD symptoms and enhances emotional regulation (Kearney et al., 2021; Saban et al., 2022). It transformed these insights into a structured curriculum accessible to higher education veterans. The V.E.T.S. Toolkit, in turn, drew on vocational intervention literature, such as Bond et al. (2022), which indicated that targeted employment programs significantly increase income and stability for veterans. By integrating financial literacy training and navigation strategies, the toolkit embodies resilience rather than just describing it. In this way, the doctoral journey validated BRAVE as a verb. The framework was conceptualized and put into practice, creating tangible resources beyond academic requirements. The act of scholarship became an intervention, combining reflection, research, and application.

8.2.3 Institutional Translation

Reframing BRAVE as a praxis also has implications for institutional adoption. Universities, community organizations, and veteran service systems often rely on assessment models that identify deficits but lack mechanisms for action. A university might measure financial stress through surveys but fail to provide structured financial coaching. A veteran transition program might recognize social disconnection but offer no peer network capable of sustaining a sense of belonging. BRAVE emphasizes that institutions must move beyond diagnostic approaches to active engagement implementation. Operationalizing BRAVE at the institutional level involves integrating each dimension into service delivery. Psychological resilience can be supported through access to mindfulness programs, counseling, and trauma-informed teaching. Physical resilience can be strengthened through integrated health services, adaptive sports programs, and sleep-hygiene education. Social resilience can be built by establishing mentorship pipelines, veteran affinity groups, and community engagement initiatives. Economic resilience can be improved through financial coaching, benefits navigation, and structured career pathways.

The literature on implementation science highlights that successful institutional adoption depends on fidelity, adaptability, and sustainability (Fixsen, 2005). BRAVE as praxis provides a framework for aligning these principles. Fidelity ensures that interventions address all four dimensions. Adaptability allows customization for populations beyond veterans, such as foster youth or justice-involved individuals. Sustainability occurs when institutions incorporate BRAVE practices into core operations rather than treating them as peripheral programming.

8.2.4 Identity as Ongoing Construction

Identity reconstruction is key to reintegration, and BRAVE as a verb highlights that identity is enacted, not inherited. Social Identity Theory (Turner et al., 1979) and the Social Identity Model of Identity Change (Trepte & Loy, 2017) emphasize that belonging and self-concept are shaped through group membership and social categorization. Transformative Learning Theory (Mezirow, 1997) views identity as reconstructed through critical reflection and meaning-making. Together, these theories support BRAVE's view that reintegration is not a one-time event but a continuous process of identity work.

Veterans, foster youth, and justice-involved individuals often describe a break in their identity after leaving the systems that structured their lives. The uniform, foster system, or correctional environment provided coherence, even if it was limiting or harmful. Reintegration involves rebuilding identity outside of these systems, a task that can't be achieved through reflection alone. It occurs each time individuals engage in BRAVE practices: managing psychological stress, maintaining physical health, fostering social belonging, and achieving economic stability. These actions create a reconstructed identity that is both coherent and adaptable. The narrative aspect of BRAVE supports this idea. Personal reintegration didn't happen through abstract theorizing but through daily work with these practices. Reconstruction acts included writing research papers, leading peer programs, mentoring veterans, and navigating benefits. Every action embedded the BRAVE framework into daily life, reinforcing that resilience must be treated as praxis.

8.2.5 Precision-Based Reintegration

Operationalizing BRAVE as a verb aligns with emerging movements toward precision health and individualized intervention. Epigenetic studies demonstrate that trauma alters biological systems but also that these systems are modifiable through targeted interventions (Domschke et al., 2025; van Assche et al., 2023). Behavioral trials confirm that multimodal interventions combining psychological, physical, and social supports produce stronger outcomes than fragmented approaches (Fortier et al., 2024; Joyce et al., 2019). BRAVE as praxis provides the framework for precision reintegration. Instead of applying one-size-fits-all programs, institutions can customize engagement based on the specific needs of each individual. A veteran with a severe musculoskeletal injury but stable social support might need a focus on physical and economic domains. A foster youth entering higher education could require primary emphasis on social and psychological aspects. The verb-focused approach of BRAVE ensures that resilience is delivered through practices that are enacted and aligned with these individual needs' profiles.

8.2.6 Narrative Illustration

The difference between BRAVE as a noun and BRAVE as a verb is best demonstrated through real-life application. Resilience was shown each time a training session concluded, a research project advanced, or a student veteran received guidance through a complex benefits system. These activities represented reintegration. The doctoral journey, the development of the WELL Program, and the V.E.T.S. Toolkit illustrate that resilience was conceptualized from afar and actively practiced in real time. This narrative evidence supports the broader idea: resilience must be performed, measured, and supported as a form of action.

8.3 Systemic Adoption and Institutional Implications

The BRAVE Theory, when seen as praxis, requires individual effort and systemic implementation. Reintegration is influenced by the policies, institutions, and cultural frameworks that create opportunities for recovery. Without institutional commitment, individual resilience is limited by systemic obstacles that hinder progress. Integrating BRAVE into organizational and policy settings ensures that resilience becomes a part of service delivery systems rather than being solely the individual's responsibility.

8.3.1 Higher Education as a Site of Reintegration

Colleges and universities are key environments for post-service reintegration. Since 2009, over one million veterans have used the GI Bill to pursue higher education (Pedersen & Wieser, 2024). However, research shows that veterans often face fragmented support, bureaucratic hurdles, and limited recognition of the psychological and social challenges of transitioning (Vacchi & Berger, 2013). Integrating BRAVE into higher education involves incorporating each of its four dimensions into the academic setting. Psychological resilience can be fostered through mindfulness programs, trauma-informed teaching, and accessible counseling. Physical resilience can be enhanced through adaptive recreation, structured fitness activities, and health education. Social resilience develops through veteran student organizations, peer mentorship programs, and faculty training that recognizes military culture. Economic resilience requires effective benefits navigation, financial literacy education, and partnerships with career services.

The WELL Program piloted at Pennsylvania Western University exemplifies this integration. By combining mindfulness with structured performance and lifestyle strategies, the program applied BRAVE across multiple areas. Veterans reported improvements in stress management, physical preparedness, and social connection through group sessions. At the same time, the V.E.T.S. Toolkit gave institutional advisors a structured guide for helping veterans navigate financial aid and educational benefits, directly supporting economic resilience. These examples show that when universities implement BRAVE, they turn educational settings into comprehensive reintegration ecosystems instead of just credentialing institutions sites.

8.3.2 Health Systems and the VA Context

Healthcare continues to be a vital factor in reintegration. Veterans Affairs Medical Centers (VAMCs) and community health providers can either strengthen resilience or contribute to fragmentation. Current approaches often target isolated symptoms, such as treating PTSD separately from chronic pain or addressing financial stress independently from mental health. BRAVE offers a framework for integrated service delivery.

Psychological and physical issues can be managed through multimodal interventions that combine mindfulness, physical therapy, and peer support. Social resilience can be improved by incorporating community reintegration metrics into treatment plans. Economic resilience can be bolstered by including vocational counseling and benefits navigation during healthcare visits. Studies like Fortier et al. (2024) confirm the effectiveness of transdiagnostic interventions in veteran populations, while Domschke et al. (2025) emphasize the biological responsiveness of trauma survivors to psychosocial engagement. These findings together highlight that resilience cannot be built through isolated care.

Personal experience with VA systems showed how bureaucratic fragmentation can hinder recovery. Navigating GI Bill and VR&E benefits alongside managing psychological and physical injuries revealed the need for a comprehensive systemic approach. Implementing BRAVE within health systems provides a model that recognizes the interconnectedness of care across domains and promotes identity reconstruction as a key outcome of health.

8.3.3 Foster Care and Justice System Applications

Although BRAVE originated from military reintegration, its framework is directly applicable to other populations affected by systems. Foster youth aging out of care and justice-involved individuals reentering society face similar challenges: fractured identities, limited social networks, chronic health issues, and economic instability. Research indicates that nearly 20% of foster youth experience homelessness within a year of leaving care (Courtney et al., 2025), while recidivism rates for justice-involved individuals exceed 60% within three years of release (Durose et al., 2014). These outcomes point to systemic issues across all four BRAVE dimensions.

Adopting BRAVE in these settings requires a redesign of institutions. Foster care systems can incorporate psychological resilience through trauma-informed counseling, physical resilience through health promotion and nutrition support, social resilience via mentorship programs, and economic resilience through financial literacy and job placement initiatives. Justice reentry programs can adopt the same approach, emphasizing ongoing identity work, structured peer networks, and vocational opportunities that help reduce recidivism.

The Transitional Resilience Index (TRI), developed with Dr. Tyton Brunner, builds on this idea. By measuring resilience across psychological, physical, social, and economic areas, the TRI offers a way to evaluate system outcomes and customize interventions. This shows that BRAVE, when implemented across institutions, is not limited to veterans but serves as a universal reintegration model for all system-impacted populations.

8.3.4 Policy Implications and Systemic Barriers

The widespread adoption of BRAVE also needs policy support. Reintegration faces structural challenges like disjointed funding, inconsistent benefit access, and deep-seated stigma. Policies that separate mental health from employment or physical rehab from education reinforce the fragmentation BRAVE aims to fix. Integrating BRAVE into policy requires coordinated funding, partnerships across sectors, and outcome measures that reflect multiple aspects of reintegration. For instance, veteran success should be measured not only by employment but also by indicators of mental health, social connection, and financial security. Likewise, foster care results should be assessed not just by graduation rates but by resilience across all four domains.

Personal experiences navigating these systemic barriers show how easily individuals can fall through service gaps. Issues like missed paperwork, benefit recognition problems, and uncoordinated care often threaten reintegration. Adopting BRAVE policies would guarantee that resilience is seen as a collective responsibility, not just an individual effort burden.

8.3.5 Toward Institutional Cultures of Resilience

The core implication of systemic adoption is cultural change within organizations. BRAVE promotes a shift from deficit-based approaches to resilience-oriented practices. Organizations must see veterans, foster youth, and justice-involved individuals not as liabilities but as groups with inherent strengths that can be nurtured through structured engagement. Creating cultures of resilience requires leadership commitment, staff training, and ongoing evaluation. Implementation science highlights that organizational culture influences whether interventions are maintained (Fixsen, 2005). Incorporating BRAVE into mission statements, curricula, and policies becomes part of the organization's identity. Organizations then function not only as service providers but also as environments that support reintegration.

8.4 Identity Reconstruction as Ongoing Work

Reintegration requires more than managing symptoms or securing stability. At its core, it is the reconstruction of identity in the aftermath of systemic disruption. BRAVE positions identity not as a fixed entity but as an active process continually shaped by psychological regulation, physical embodiment, social belonging, and economic participation. Recognizing identity as ongoing work challenges the notion of reintegration as a linear event and reframes it as a lifelong practice.

8.4.1 *Theoretical Foundations of Identity Reconstruction*

Social Identity Theory highlights that belonging to groups gives individuals coherence, purpose, and meaning (Turner, 1979). The main identity foundation is removed when military service, foster care, or incarceration ends. Transformative Learning Theory (Mezirow, 1997) adds that disruptive experiences trigger critical reflection, which can either destabilize or rebuild identity. BRAVE combines these ideas by viewing identity reconstruction as an ongoing process involving four domains. Research on veteran transitions shows that identity disruption increases the risk of depression, substance use, and suicide (Demers, 2011; Joseph et al., 2023). Similar patterns are seen in foster youth aging out of care (Courtney et al., 2025) and justice-involved individuals reentering society (Maruna, 2001). These findings confirm that identity reconstruction is not a minor aspect but a key part of successful reintegration outcomes.

8.4.2 *Psychological Reconstruction*

Psychological identity is reshaped through practices that foster coherence and agency. Mindfulness-based interventions have demonstrated that trauma survivors can re-establish regulation and self-compassion, which serve as foundational elements for identity continuity (Kearney et al., 2021; Saban et al., 2022). In practice, doctoral research projects created structured spaces for veterans to engage in identity work. The WELL Program integrated mindfulness with physical performance strategies, allowing participants to see themselves not only as patients or students but as resilient actors engaged in growth. Each exercise or reflective activity was not merely therapeutic; it was an act of self-definition.

8.4.3 Physical Embodiment of Identity

Identity is also embedded in the body. Physical injuries, chronic pain, and disrupted sleep patterns can reinforce fractured self-concepts. Strength and conditioning programs, yoga, and adaptive sports demonstrate that physical practices are not only rehabilitative but also reconstructive (Groessl et al., 2017). When individuals regain function, they also rebuild their identity around capability rather than limitation. Personal engagement in training, nutrition, and recovery shows that embodiment is key to reconstruction. The transition from seeing the body as broken to viewing it as adaptable strengthens a sense of identity as capable, resilient, and forward-looking.

8.4.4 Social Identity and Belonging

Social belonging is arguably the most visible sign of identity reconstruction. Veterans often feel disconnected once they are no longer wearing the uniform. Similarly, foster youth and justice-involved individuals experience breaks in their sense of identity when leaving care or prison. Peer mentorship, group interventions, and community engagement programs have consistently shown positive impacts on reintegration outcomes (Bond et al., 2022; Geraci et al., 2023). Building the Mindfully Tactical Foundation aimed to promote social identity reconstruction on a larger scale. The foundation realized BRAVE's focus on belonging by creating spaces where veterans can connect through shared practices and mutual accountability. The outcome is a redefinition of identity centered around community participation.

8.4.5 Economic Participation as Identity Work

Economic activity provides more than just financial stability; it roots identity in purpose and contribution. Employment programs like Individual Placement and Support (IPS) and the National Career Coach Program (Bond et al., 2022) show that vocational success boosts self-efficacy and decreases stigma. Economic resilience functions both as a resource and as a way to rebuild identity. The V.E.T.S. Toolkit demonstrates this idea. By giving veterans navigation strategies for GI Bill and VR&E benefits, it helped participants see themselves as capable students and professionals instead of dependents of a broken system. This redefinition shows that economic involvement is not secondary to identity but essential to it.

8.4.6 *Identity as Lifelong Praxis*

Identity reconstruction is not finalized at discharge, graduation, or release. It is a lifelong journey that requires ongoing effort across the BRAVE dimensions. Epigenetic evidence shows that biological systems themselves adapt and readjust through sustained interventions (Domschke et al., 2025; van IJzendoorn & Bakermans-Kranenburg, 2015). This highlights that identity, like biology, remains flexible throughout life. From both academic and personal viewpoints, reintegration cannot be seen as a single transition. The doctoral journey itself was a demonstration of identity reconstruction, with each project, program, and publication reinforcing a shift from combat medic to scholar-practitioner. The process did not end with earning a degree, nor will it conclude with professional milestones. Identity reconstruction continues as long as engagement with the BRAVE dimensions does continues.

8.4.7 *Implications for Research and Practice*

Recognizing identity as an ongoing process challenges institutions to create interventions that go beyond immediate results. Programs should not only assess symptom reduction or employment rates but also monitor indicators of identity continuity and development. Long-term studies are crucial to understanding the repetitive nature of identity reconstruction, while policies must provide ongoing support instead of short-term interventions. Future research can utilize tools like the Transitional Resilience Index (TRI) to measure identity rebuilding across different areas. By defining resilience as practice, scholars and practitioners can move past deficit models and design interventions that promote identity as adaptable, continuous, and multidimensional.

Academic Synthesis

This chapter has repositioned BRAVE from a conceptual framework to a dynamic praxis model, describing resilience as a verb enacted through psychological, physical, social, and economic aspects. The synthesis combines the chapter's main points and places them within the broader scholarly discussion on resilience, reintegration, and identity reconstruction. BRAVE aligns with modern resilience theories highlighting multidimensional and systemic processes instead of fixed traits (Liu et al., 2019). The model incorporates insights from the biopsychosocial approach (Engel, 1977), trauma exposure theory, and identity theories like Social Identity Theory (Turner et al., 1979) and Transformative Learning Theory (Mezirow, 1997). Together, these theories show that reintegration needs both personal adaptation and structural support. BRAVE's focus on praxis connects these ideas by operationalizing resilience as ongoing, enacted active engagement.

Evidence from mindfulness programs, strength and conditioning studies, peer mentoring, and job training supports BRAVE's multidimensional approach (Bond et al., 2022; Fortier et al., 2024; Kearney et al., 2021). Findings from epigenetic studies (Domschke et al., 2025; van Assche et al., 2023) further confirm that resilience can be biologically changed, reinforcing the need for interventions to be actively implemented rather than assumed. Pilot programs like the WELL Program and the V.E.T.S. Toolkit demonstrated the practical ability to embed BRAVE in institutional settings, proving systemic adoption is possible.

The chapter stresses that reintegration cannot be achieved by individuals alone. Universities, healthcare systems, foster care programs, and justice reform initiatives must incorporate BRAVE practices into their service delivery. Policies should shift from deficit-based models toward integrated resilience frameworks that measure outcomes across psychological, physical, social, and economic domains. Without systemic implementation, individual efforts are limited by structural fragmentation. Identity is identified as the key reintegration process, with BRAVE framing reconstruction as a continuous act rather than a one-time achievement. Reintegration is experienced each time individuals manage stress, maintain health, foster a sense of belonging, or achieve economic stability. Identity is not a fixed endpoint but a story constantly revised through praxis. This insight aligns with transformative learning and social identity theories and emphasizes the need for long-term, dynamic approaches to reintegration research.

This synthesis presents BRAVE as both a theoretical model and a practical approach. Future research should test the effectiveness of BRAVE-based interventions through long-term, multimodal trials across diverse groups, such as veterans, foster youth, and justice-involved individuals. The Transitional Resilience Index (TRI) offers one way to measure BRAVE outcomes, allowing empirical assessment of reintegration as praxis. Ongoing research should refine how resilience is enacted, measured, and maintained over lifetimes and within systems.

This chapter confirms that BRAVE is a verb. Resilience is something you do, not something you have. Reintegration is maintained through ongoing engagement with the psychological, physical, social, and economic elements, supported by systemic adoption and institutional responsibility. Identity reconstruction is the process through which praxis becomes lived experience. This synthesis places BRAVE within resilience research while advancing it as an actionable, multidimensional model capable of guiding both research and practice.

Key Takeaways

- **Resilience is enacted, not owned**—BRAVE reframes resilience as ongoing practice across contexts rather than a fixed trait, aligning with biopsychosocial and systems views (Engel, 1977; Liu et al., 2019).
- **Interdependence drives outcomes**—Psychological, physical, social, and economic domains co-regulate one another; progress or strain in one domain propagates through the system (Elbogen et al., 2022; Liu et al., 2019).
- **Identity reconstruction is core work**—Reintegration hinges on continuous identity building supported by social belonging and reflective learning, not single milestones (Mezirow, 1997; Trepte & Loy, 2017; Turner et al., 1979).

- **Praxis beats paperwork**—Institutions must move beyond assessment to embedded action that delivers skills, relationships, and resources in all four domains (Fixsen, 2005; Pedersen & Wieser, 2024; Vacchi & Berger, 2013).
- **Precision reintegration is feasible**—Epigenetic and behavioral evidence supports tailored, multimodal interventions calibrated to individual need profiles (Domschke et al., 2025; Joyce et al., 2019; Van Assche et al., 2023).
- **Multimodal programs outperform silos**—Transdiagnostic and integrated approaches (mindfulness, S&C, peer networks, vocational supports) show superior reach and durability (Bond et al., 2022; Fortier et al., 2024; Kearney et al., 2021).
- **Economic stability is a health intervention**—Financial coaching, benefits navigation, and supported employment are protective factors for mental and social outcomes (Bond et al., 2022; Elbogen et al., 2022).
- **BRAVE scales beyond veterans**—The same praxis maps onto foster-care exit and justice reentry, where identity breaks, social capital gaps, and economic instability mirror veteran risk patterns (Courtney et al., 2025; Geraci et al., 2023; Maruna, 2001).
- **Measure what matters over time**—Tools like the TRI and multidomain metrics enable longitudinal evaluation of identity, regulation, belonging, and economic participation, moving the field past symptom-only endpoints (Fixsen, 2005; Liu et al., 2019).
- **Culture change is the lever**—When organizations adopt resilience-oriented norms and routines, BRAVE becomes everyday practice rather than a program on the side (Fixsen, 2005; Vacchi & Berger, 2013).

Applied Learning Prompts

1. Consider a veteran navigating higher education after service. Using the BRAVE framework, identify how each dimension (psychological, physical, social, and economic) would need to be addressed to support reintegration.
2. Foster youth aging out of care face many of the same disruptions as veterans. Compare the reintegration challenges of these two groups and explain how BRAVE praxis can be applied to both populations.
3. Select an existing veteran or reentry support program. Analyze the extent to which it addresses the four BRAVE dimensions. Where does it succeed, and where does it fall short?
4. Reflect on an identity transition you have experienced (e.g., entering higher education, changing careers, or moving to a new community). Map how psychological, physical, social, and economic factors shaped your adaptation and connect these to BRAVE praxis.
5. Imagine you are tasked with developing a campus-wide program for student veterans. Using BRAVE as a guide, design one initiative for each dimension and explain how they interact to create a holistic reintegration environment.

References

Bond, G. R., Al-Abdulmunem, M., Ressler, D. R., Gade, D. M., & Drake, R. E. (2022). A randomized controlled trial of an employment program for veterans transitioning from the military: Two-year outcomes. *Administration and Policy in Mental Health and Mental Health Services Research, 49*(6), 1072–1083. https://doi.org/10.1007/s10488-022-01208-z

Connor, K. M., & Davidson, J. R. T. (2003). Development of a new resilience scale: The Connor-Davidson Resilience Scale (CD-RISC). *Depression and Anxiety, 18*(2), 76–82. https://doi.org/10.1002/da.10113

Courtney, M. E., Park, S., & Harty, J. S. (2025). Foster care policy and homelessness among youth transitioning to adulthood from foster care. *Child Abuse & Neglect, 169*, 107638. https://doi.org/10.1016/j.chiabu.2025.107638

Demers, A. (2011). When veterans return: The role of community in reintegration. *Journal of Loss and Trauma, 16*(2), 160–179. https://doi.org/10.1080/15325024.2010.519281

Domschke, K., Schiele, M. A., Crespo Salvador, Ó., Zillich, L., Lipovsek, J., Pittig, A., Heinig, I., Ridderbusch, I. C., Straube, B., Richter, J., Hollandt, M., Plag, J., Fydrich, T., Koelkebeck, K., Weber, H., Lueken, U., Dannlowski, U., Margraf, J., Schneider, S., … Deckert, J. (2025). Epigenetic markers of disease risk and psychotherapy response in anxiety disorders—A longitudinal analysis of the DNA methylome. *Molecular Psychiatry*. https://doi.org/10.1038/s41380-025-03038-5

Durose, M. R., Cooper, A. D., & Snyder, H. N. (2014). *Recidivism of prisoners released in 30 states in 2005: Patterns from 2005 to 2010*. U.S. Department of Justice, Office of Justice Programs, Bureau of Justice Statistics.

Elbogen, E. B., Zeber, J. E., Vogt, D., Perkins, D. F., Finley, E. P., & Copeland, L. A. (2022). Financial status and well-being in recently separated military veterans. *Military Medicine, 188*(7–8), e2181–e2188. https://doi.org/10.1093/milmed/usac030

Engel, G. L. (1977). The need for a new medical model: A challenge for biomedicine. *Science, 196*(4286), 129–136. https://doi.org/10.1126/science.847460

Fixsen, D. (2005). *Implementation research: A synthesis of the literature*. The National Implementation Research Network, Louis de la Parte Florida Mental Health Institute, University of South Florida.

Fortier, C. B., Kenna, A., Katz, D., Kim, S., Hursh, C., Beck, B., Sablone, C. A., Currao, A., Lebas, A., Jorge, R. E., & Fonda, J. R. (2024). STEP-HOME transdiagnostic group reintegration workshop to improve mental health outcomes for post-9/11 veterans: Design, methods, and rationale for a randomized controlled behavioral trial. *Contemporary Clinical Trials, 141*, 107536. https://doi.org/10.1016/j.cct.2024.107536

Geraci, J. C., Dichiara, A., Greene, A., Gromatsky, M., Finley, E. P., Kilby, D., Frankfurt, S., Edwards, E. R., Kurz, A. S., Sokol, Y., Sullivan, S. R., Mobbs, M., Seim, R. W., & Goodman, M. (2023). Supporting servicemembers and veterans during their transition to civilian life using certified sponsors: A three-arm randomized controlled trial. *Psychological Services*. Advance online publication. https://doi.org/10.1037/ser0000764

Groessl, E. J., Liu, L., Chang, D. G., Wetherell, J. L., Bormann, J. E., Atkinson, J. H., Baxi, S., & Schmalzl, L. (2017). Yoga for military veterans with chronic low back pain: A randomized clinical trial. *American Journal of Preventive Medicine, 53*(5), 599–608. https://doi.org/10.1016/j.amepre.2017.05.019

Joseph, J. S., Smith-MacDonald, L., Filice, M. C., & Smith, M. S. (2023). Reculturation: A new perspective on military-civilian transition stress. *Military Psychology, 35*(3), 193–203. https://doi.org/10.1080/08995605.2022.2094175

Joyce, S., Shand, F., Lal, T. J., Mott, B., Bryant, R. A., & Harvey, S. B. (2019). Resilience@Work mindfulness program: Results from a cluster randomized controlled trial with first responders. *Journal of Medical Internet Research, 21*(2), e12894. https://doi.org/10.2196/12894

Kearney, D. J., Malte, C. A., Storms, M., & Simpson, T. L. (2021). Loving-kindness meditation vs cognitive processing therapy for posttraumatic stress disorder among veterans: A randomized clinical trial. *JAMA Network Open, 4*(4), e216604. https://doi.org/10.1001/jamanetworkopen.2021.6604

Liu, Y., Collins, C., Wang, K., Xie, X., & Bie, R. (2019). The prevalence and trend of depression among veterans in the United States. *Journal of Affective Disorders, 245*, 724–727. https://doi.org/10.1016/j.jad.2018.11.031

Maruna, S. (2001). *Making good*. American Psychological Association.

Mezirow, J. (1997). Transformation theory out of context. *Adult Education Quarterly, 48*(1), 60–62. https://doi.org/10.1177/074171369704800105

Pedersen, C. L., & Wieser, C. (2024). Student veterans' transition and reintegration into education: A transnational scoping review. *International Journal of Lifelong Education, 43*(6), 603–624. https://doi.org/10.1080/02601370.2024.2374749

Saban, K. L., Collins, E. G., Mathews, H. L., Bryant, F. B., Tell, D., Gonzalez, B., Bhoopalam, S., Chroniak, C. P., & Janusek, L. W. (2022). Impact of a mindfulness-based stress reduction program on psychological well-being, cortisol, and inflammation in women veterans. *Journal of General Internal Medicine, 37*(3), 751–761. https://doi.org/10.1007/s11606-022-07584-4

Teplova, A. E., Bakker, H. A. H. M., Perry, S. I. B., van Etten-Jamaludin, F. S., Plat, M.-C.J., & Bekkers, M. B. M. (2021). The impact of deployment and combat exposure on physical health among military personnel: A systematic review of incidence, prevalence, and risks. *Military Medicine, 187*(9–10), e1074–e1085. https://doi.org/10.1093/milmed/usab302

Trepte, S., & Loy, L. S. (2017). Social identity theory and self-categorization theory. In *The international encyclopedia of media effects* (pp. 1–13). Wiley Blackwell.

Turner, J. C., Brown, R. J., & Tajfel, H. (1979). Social comparison and group interest in ingroup favouritism. *European Journal of Social Psychology, 9*(2), 187–204. https://doi.org/10.1002/ejsp.2420090207

Vacchi, D. T., & Berger, J. B. (2013). Student veterans in higher education. In *Higher education: Handbook of theory and research* (Vol. 29, pp. 93–151). Springer.

Van Assche, E., Hohoff, C., Zang, J., Knight, M. J., & Baune, B. T. (2023). Epigenetic modification related to cognitive changes during a cognitive training intervention in depression. *Progress in Neuro-Psychopharmacology and Biological Psychiatry, 127*, 110835. https://doi.org/10.1016/j.pnpbp.2023.110835

van IJzendoorn, M. H., & Bakermans-Kranenburg, M. J. (2015). Genetic differential susceptibility on trial: Meta-analytic support from randomized controlled experiments. *Development and Psychopathology, 27*(1), 151–162. https://doi.org/10.1017/S0954579414001369

Chapter 9
From Theory to Practice—Case Studies and Field Applications

This chapter shifts from theory and synthesis to applied evidence. It uses the WELL Program and the V.E.T.S. Toolkit as main examples to explore how BRAVE-informed pilots turn resilience into daily practice across psychological, physical, social, and economic areas. The chapter features the Patient Zero case to demonstrate BRAVE as praxis, illustrating identity reconstruction through mentorship, system navigation, and measurable multidomain improvements. It also compares professional use in tactical athlete performance, veteran liaison work in higher education, and nonprofit program delivery to highlight shared principles and context-specific tactics. Readers will learn to identify barriers that hinder the adoption of veteran-led initiatives and to plan for scalability and sustainability through fidelity, adaptation, and ongoing evaluation. After reading, you will be able to analyze how the pilot programs operationalize resilience, evaluate the Patient Zero case as evidence of identity work in action, compare BRAVE applications across professional contexts, critically assess adoption barriers with strategies to overcome them, and apply BRAVE praxis to design or evaluate reintegration programs for diverse system-impacted populations.

9.1 Introduction: From Framework to Fieldwork

The BRAVE Theory is presented as a multidimensional framework that redefines resilience as praxis. Chapter 8 emphasizes that resilience is a verb, enacted across psychological, physical, social, and economic dimensions. The next logical step is to demonstrate how BRAVE functions in practice. This chapter offers applied case

T. Carlton, *BRAVE Theory*, https://doi.org/10.1007/978-3-032-13695-4_9

studies drawn from initial pilot programs, individual mentorship, and professional settings, showing how theory translates into real-world application.

Moving from theory to practice requires bridging two gaps. The first is the translational gap between scholarship and implementation. Academic literature is full of evidence-based interventions for trauma, identity disruption, and reintegration, yet these interventions are often isolated within specific disciplines. BRAVE combines these findings into a unified, actionable framework. The second gap is experiential. Reintegration does not happen in controlled environments; it occurs in classrooms, clinics, locker rooms, and community organizations. The challenge is to apply theory in settings shaped by resource limits, cultural factors, and individual differences. Implementation science highlights that translating theory into practice depends on fidelity, adaptability, and sustainability (Fixsen, 2005). Fidelity ensures interventions stay true to the theoretical model. Adaptability allows for customization based on the needs of different groups. Sustainability ensures programs can continue beyond pilot phases. BRAVE-based interventions have been developed with these principles in mind. The WELL Program, the V.E.T.S. Toolkit, and mentorship case studies illustrate how BRAVE can be implemented in various settings, from higher education to professional sports to community organizations.

The doctoral program itself acted as a testing ground for these applications. Assignments, literature reviews, and evidence integration projects laid the scholarly groundwork. Pilot programs translated this knowledge into practice, demonstrating that resilience is measurable but also teachable and scalable. In this way, the academic journey and professional efforts were interconnected: theory influenced practice, and practice refined theory. The upcoming sections feature case studies demonstrating BRAVE in action. Each case highlights one or more framework dimensions, discusses challenges encountered during implementation, and shares lessons for scaling and sustainability. By situating these programs within the broader resilience literature, the chapter presents BRAVE as a theoretical model and a practical approach for program design and policy development.

9.2 Case Study I: The WELL Program

The WELL Program demonstrates how the BRAVE framework turns into real-world action. While the program's structure and parts have been described in earlier chapters, this case study looks at how it works in practice: the conditions that prompted its creation, the process of launching it, the challenges faced, and the results reached. The WELL Program started after noticing a pattern of fragmentation across veteran services. Healthcare, employment help, peer support, and financial benefits existed, but they worked separately. Veterans had to navigate multiple systems at once while dealing with trauma, financial struggles, and identity issues. This situation showed the need for a veteran-led model that could connect these areas. The program moved forward through formal proposals to Pennsylvania Western University and the North Carolina Veterans Council, aiming for both institutional support and policy adoption.

Inside the Mindfully Tactical Foundation, WELL became the main framework for outreach, mentorship, and resilience projects. My role was to turn research into clear strategies, explain their importance to stakeholders, and establish trust for veteran-led initiatives. Putting the program into action involved creating deliverables that could meet academic standards while being understandable to policymakers and practitioners. Analyzing the case reveals several hurdles. First, institutional timelines were much slower than the program's development. Getting responses from universities and councils took persistence and patience, often not matching veterans' urgency during transition. Second, systemic inertia made it hard to embed WELL into existing structures. Institutions isolated veteran support, making cross-sector programs seem unfamiliar or resource-heavy. Lastly, the program needed to translate academic evidence into language that practitioners could connect with, highlighting how vital communication is as a leadership skill.

Despite these obstacles, the WELL Program achieved several measurable outcomes. At PennWest, engagement led to a veteran liaison role that enabled remote, one-on-one support and created virtual pathways to integrate PATH and LINK into advising workflows and digital student services. At the state level, submission to the North Carolina Veterans Council increased program visibility and established the Mindfully Tactical Foundation's credibility in veteran reintegration advocacy. Professional recognition, including induction into SALUTE, further reinforced the link between leadership and scholarship in advancing the program.

9.2.1 Scholarly Reflection of WELL

This case demonstrates the validity of BRAVE as a praxis. WELL effectively operationalized the framework's psychological, physical, social, and economic dimensions in a way that institutions could evaluate and implement. It also reinforced findings from the literature: peer-led sponsorship improves veteran outcomes (Geraci et al., 2023), trust is strengthened through veteran leadership (Weir et al., 2017), and integrated programs outperform siloed interventions (Fortier et al., 2024). The case confirmed that resilience must be delivered as a system rather than a series of isolated supports.

9.2.2 Leadership Reflection of WELL

Developing and advocating for the WELL Program required moving beyond immediate urgency toward strategic patience, learning to navigate institutional processes while keeping momentum. The experience also underscored the value of veteran leadership: initiatives created and led by veterans connect more effectively with peers and foster trust with institutions. WELL served as a personal demonstration of BRAVE in action practice.

9.3 Case Study II: The V.E.T.S. Toolkit

The V.E.T.S. Toolkit (Vision, Education, Translation, Strategy) was created as a veteran-led response to education and transition planning confusion. While federal programs like the GI Bill and VR&E provide the funding architecture, V.E.T.S. is designed for college counselors and academic advisors, not VA benefit officers, to translate VR&E plans into on-the-ground academic pathways. The toolkit gives campus staff a shared workflow to prioritize decisions, align credentials and timelines with the approved plan, and coordinate office handoffs. In parallel, it equips veteran students with practical, step-by-step tools to self-navigate with greater autonomy, turning eligibility into enrollment, progress, and completion. This case explores the toolkit's development, field deployment, challenges, outcomes, and implications for BRAVE as a practical approach.

9.3.1 *Context of Development*

Field experience during doctoral work uncovered two ongoing gaps. First, veterans had difficulty translating broad post-service goals into specific plans connected to the right benefits, timelines, and institutions. Second, advisors and liaisons lacked a standardized, veteran-centered framework to guide those discussions. The toolkit's mission framing approached transition as an operation needing clarity, phased goals, and disciplined execution. It relied on the BRAVE framework and previous leadership efforts to depict reintegration as a comprehensive process involving psychological regulation (clarity reduces uncertainty), social belonging (guided advising relationships), economic stability (maximized benefits and credentialing), and identity reconstruction (translating service into new roles).

9.3.2 *Design and Architecture*

The toolkit was designed as a two-track system—Veteran and Advisor—to foster a shared workflow while maintaining role-specific tools. Its four-step process puts decision-making into action. The Vision phase defined purpose and direction through a personal mission statement and SMART goals. The Education phase identified benefits eligibility and program fit using structured checklists and comparison worksheets. The Translation phase turned military experience into civilian language, aligning MOS skills with job categories and academic pathways, while creating artifacts like resumes and narratives. The Strategy phase organized execution with a tactical plan, a stackable credential map, and a 90-day action cycle with clear deliverables. Each step produced concrete outputs, helping advisors track progress and veterans feel a sense of momentum. The documents were designed to be easy to use (fillable worksheets, brief prompts) and to integrate into institutional processes (advising schedule, documentation checkpoints).

9.3.3 Implementation and Dissemination

Implementation proceeded through the MTF with direct submission to a university veteran liaison for institutional review and field use. The materials were distributed as downloadable, session-ready worksheets, allowing advisors to include them in existing appointment lengths without adding administrative burden. On the Veteran track, users could start independently and then enter an advising session with completed artifacts, enabling more effective conversations. On the Advisor track, the same artifacts offered a structured agenda for intake, follow-up, and escalation (e.g., when to involve financial aid, VR&E counselors, or career services). The toolkit also served as a common language among veterans, liaisons, and support offices—reducing the translation costs that often hinder communication progress.

9.3.4 Challenges and Adaptations

Case analysis revealed predictable implementation challenges. Eligibility nuances for the GI Bill and VR&E created variability that required localized guidance; the toolkit responded by highlighting decision trees and links to authoritative sources while keeping worksheets broad. Advisor workload limited adoption during peak times; integration with existing advising routines and the option for veteran prework helped address this. Some veterans arrived with incomplete documentation or misconceptions; embedding documentation checklists earlier in the Vision and Education phases reduced delays later on. Digital access and literacy levels varied; printable PDFs and step-by-step prompts supported low-tech use. Finally, institutional silos sometimes complicated handoffs; aligning artifacts with existing forms and routing practices improved fit. These changes demonstrate implementation science principles: maintain fidelity to core functions while allowing local tailoring.

9.3.5 Outcomes and Early Impact

Early outcomes focused on clarity, coordination, and trajectory. Veterans using the sequence reported a clearer sense of purpose and the ability to articulate a concrete plan during advising sessions. Advisors noted improvements in efficiency and depth; time shifted from basic orientation to higher-level planning because key information was gathered beforehand. A notable case involved a veteran redirected from a stalled path into an interdisciplinary degree plan aligned with long-term goals and advanced study, demonstrating the value of the Translation and Strategy phases for identity reconstruction and credential stacking. The toolkit also encouraged institutional dialogue about standardizing veteran advising workflows and produced additional materials (e.g., a resume and career transition guide) that extended the Translation phase into labor-market readiness. While large-scale outcomes need long-term evaluation, the case shows feasibility, acceptability, and face validity in real advising situations.

9.3.6 Scholarly Reflection of the V.E.T.S. Toolkit

The case advocates BRAVE as a practical approach in several ways. The Vision step enhances psychological regulation and agency by transforming ambiguity into clear goals aligned with transformative learning. The Education step focuses on economic resilience by optimizing benefits and financial planning. The Translation step acts as identity work, turning service into civilian capital and boosting social credibility in academic and job settings. The Strategy step implements sustained action, allowing for ongoing progress and course adjustments. These functions demonstrate that multimodal, process-focused interventions outperform isolated services and that peer-informed, structured advising fosters better persistence and results. The two-track design shows how institutional players can work together without undermining veteran independence.

9.3.7 Leadership Reflection of the V.E.T.S. Toolkit

Designing and implementing the toolkit involved translating lived experiences and a broad scholarly base into practical tools that practitioners would use. Leadership work included simplifying complex ideas into clear artifacts without sacrificing rigor, building trust through veteran-led authorship, and coordinating the sequence with institutional rhythms. The most consistent observation was the change in attitude when veterans shifted from diffuse frustration to concrete plans, an identity shift visible across sessions. More than any specific deliverable, that change embodies BRAVE as a verb.

9.4 Patient Zero: The TJ Narrative

The WELL Program and the V.E.T.S. Toolkit were designed as scalable interventions. However, their primary validation came from a veteran's story: As first introduced in Chapter 6 under the pseudonym "Veteran 1," Thomas "TJ" Eldridge's journey became the foundation for the WELL Program's first applied case and the validation of the BRAVE framework in practice. TJ's experience shows how the four BRAVE dimensions interact dynamically to support identity reconstruction. This case goes beyond theory by showing how resilience is built daily, how mentorship acts as a catalyst, and how veterans can navigate often-failing systems through strategic action. TJ's journey from the gym to graduate school exemplifies how BRAVE functions as a practical application.

9.4.1 Origins: Meeting in Transition

I first met TJ at the gym. He showed both the visible effects of a severe accident, walking paraplegia, and the unseen burden of stalled reintegration. Like many veterans, he had attended school during his military service, earning credits in computer networking, but struggled to find coherence after discharge. He later pursued an Associate of Arts in Automotive Technology, focusing on paint and body work, but depleted his GI Bill funds with only three courses remaining. When we started working together during COVID-19, TJ had been denied VR&E support twice. His sense of identity was broken, his confidence limited, and his options unclear. What began as strength and conditioning sessions in my home gym, possible because I had maintained a complete commercial setup during the pandemic, soon turned into discussions about next steps. These talks were slow, deliberate, and often met with hesitation. It took years to convince TJ that education was feasible and meaningful, that pursuing degrees was about regaining a sense of purpose, structure, and life worth.

9.4.2 Physical Dimension: Training the Body, Restoring Agency

Our starting point was the physical dimension. Using strength and conditioning principles, we gradually rebuilt TJ's mobility, strength, and confidence. He began achieving personal bests in several areas despite his injury. These accomplishments mattered for functional recovery and symbolized proof that he could still set goals, train systematically, and improve measurable results. This approach aligns with research on tactical athlete rehabilitation, which demonstrates that structured physical training enhances physical health and boosts psychological resilience and commitment to recovery protocols (Abt et al., 2010). For TJ, the body became the first place where resilience was demonstrated, providing momentum that would extend into other domains.

9.4.3 Psychological Dimension: Identity Reconstruction

Progress in the gym created room for psychological reframing. TJ shifted from seeing himself as permanently limited to recognizing his ability to adapt. The change was gradual, and it took repeated reinforcement and consistent guidance, but over time, his identity started to rebuild around the idea of capability instead of deficit. This aligns with principles of transformative learning theory (Mezirow, 1997), where disorienting dilemmas like injury or systemic denial of benefits can prompt reflection and self-redefinition. BRAVE describes this as psychological resilience: the ability to regulate, reconstruct, and move forward despite trauma. In TJ's words: "*This journey has been more than just overcoming physical challenges; it has been about discovering my potential.*" That statement highlights the core mechanism of psychological resilience: restoring agency and meaning.

9.4.4 Navigating Systems: From VR&E Denial to Degree Pathways

The most significant barrier was systemic. TJ was denied VR&E benefits twice, facing the financial collapse that derails many transitions. Without intervention, he would have remained with incomplete degrees, limited job options, and diminished confidence. This is where BRAVE's economic component became crucial. I accompanied TJ to his third virtual VR&E meeting. This time, we presented a well-structured, strategic request for funding. He was already enrolled in courses with mapped out degrees, and we showed how his academic plan aligned with his career goals in exercise science and psychology. This approach resembled what would later be called the PATH initiative: clear preparation, alignment, and planning ahead. With this strategy, VR&E approval was granted.

This example shows how BRAVE's economic part connects with the others. Financial stability was a foundation and not an endpoint. By linking benefits with his vision and education, TJ was able to complete his associate degree, transfer into a Bachelor of Arts (BA) in Interdisciplinary Studies, and gain acceptance into a Master of Science (MS) in Sports Psychology. Within a year, he went from having no degree to pursuing three degrees, including sponsorship to become a Certified Mental Performance Consultant (CMPC).

9.4.5 Social Dimension: Belonging and Mentorship

Isolation had long defined TJ's post-service life. BRAVE's social focus highlights that resilience is built through relationships, not loneliness. Through one-on-one mentorship, TJ found accountability and support. Over time, he started to reflect those roles by mentoring others, especially within the Mindfully Tactical Foundation (MTF). His personal statement emphasizes this change: "*I am deeply grateful…this journey has been about discovering my potential and pursuing my passion for enhancing athletic performance.*" Gratitude shows a sense of belonging. The shift from receiving mentorship to mentoring others reflects Social Identity Theory (Turner, 1975) and the Social Identity Model of Identity Change (Trepte & Loy, 2017). He no longer saw himself as an injured veteran but part of a professional and academic community, shaping a positive identity through connection.

9.4.6 Integration Across Domains

TJ's case exemplifies the interdependence BRAVE describes. Physical training sparked psychological reframing. Psychological resilience fostered confidence to confront systemic barriers. Economic stability created pathways for academic and professional success. Social belonging strengthened persistence and transformed identity. None of these factors alone would have been enough; together, they formed a mutually reinforcing resilience cycle. The results speak for themselves. TJ progressed quickly academically, earning SALUTE honors, securing publication opportunities, and taking on a mentoring role. At the same time, he participated in part-time storm work, helping communities affected by severe weather, an activity that enhanced his sense of purpose and social value. His transformation affirms BRAVE's core idea: resilience is built across multiple areas, and progress in one area boosts growth in others.

9.4.7 Scholarly Reflection of Patient Zero

TJ's story aligns with broader resilience research. Studies confirm that financial stress predicts poor mental health and suicide risk among veterans (Elbogen et al., 2022). TJ's economic stabilization through VR&E support directly lowered these risks. Evidence also shows peer mentorship boosts engagement and a sense of belonging (Geraci et al., 2023). His shift from mentee to mentor reflects this dynamic. Epigenetic research indicates that sustained behavioral change can influence trauma's biological effects (Domschke et al., 2025). TJ's physical recovery and healthier lifestyle demonstrate how embodied resilience impacts function and long-term biological health. This case shows that BRAVE is not just a descriptive framework but a prescriptive one, offering actionable pathways to support veterans where fragmentation might otherwise hinder progress.

9.4.8 Lessons from Patient Zero

Several key lessons emerge from this case:

1. **Mentorship catalyzes resilience**. Veteran-to-veteran trust creates the conditions for engagement that systems alone cannot provide.
2. **System navigation requires strategy**. Presenting clear, structured plans transforms benefit denial into approval, validating the economic domain as central.
3. **Identity reconstruction is the outcome**. Degrees, physical milestones, and financial stability all matter, but the most significant transformation was TJ's self-concept: from isolated, injured veteran to scholar, mentor, and aspiring exercise scientist.
4. **Resilience is iterative and multidimensional**. Gains across domains reinforce one another, creating compounding progress rather than isolated wins.

9.4.9 Summary

The story of TJ shows BRAVE in action. From gym sessions during COVID-19 to graduate-level sports psychology courses, his path shows how resilience is expressed physically, mentally, socially, and economically. His story confirms that resilience isn't fixed but experienced every day, and that veteran-led, evidence-based mentorship can turn systemic fragmentation into organized reintegration. Patient Zero proves that theory works when it changes lives.

9.5 Professional Practice Cases

While the WELL Program, the V.E.T.S. Toolkit, and the TJ case demonstrate structured interventions and individual mentorship, BRAVE has also been used in various professional practice settings. These examples highlight the framework's flexibility beyond higher education or clinical support, extending into professional sports, institutional liaison roles, and nonprofit initiatives.

9.5.1 Hockey Performance and Tactical Athlete Application

As Director of Performance Science and Reconditioning for a professional hockey team, I integrated BRAVE principles into athlete support. While athletes are not transitioning from military to civilian life, they share common reintegration challenges: injury recovery, identity shifts after career disruption, and economic uncertainty tied to performance.

- **Physical domain**: Structured strength and conditioning sessions emphasized resilience-based training rather than short-term output.
- **Psychological domain**: Mindfulness techniques, visualization, and reframing strategies paralleled those used in veteran contexts.
- **Social domain**: Locker-room culture was leveraged to promote belonging, mirroring the importance of unit cohesion in the military.
- **Economic domain**: Athletes were encouraged to view their careers through a resilience lens, planning for transitions after sport to reduce stress around performance-linked income.

Research supports this crossover. Tactical athlete literature highlights the importance of resilience frameworks that cover both physical and psychological recovery (Joyce et al., 2019; Walter et al., 2023). Applying BRAVE in hockey proved its adaptability beyond traditional veteran settings.

9.5.2 *Veteran Liaison Work in Higher Education*

Serving as a volunteer veteran liaison at Pennsylvania Western University created opportunities to apply BRAVE at scale. The role centered on helping veterans navigate the GI Bill, VR&E, and academic pathways. Unlike TJ's one-on-one mentorship, this work involved multiple veterans simultaneously, each with unique constellations of needs.

- **Psychological**: Providing structured check-ins to support stress management during academic transitions.
- **Physical**: Referrals and peer support for sleep, exercise, and health routines.
- **Social**: Building community networks among student veterans who often felt disconnected from traditional peers.
- **Economic**: Assisting with benefit navigation, appeals, and degree planning to maximize financial resources.

This role reinforced BRAVE's claim that reintegration must be multidimensional. Veterans rarely presented with single-domain challenges; financial instability often overlapped with psychological stress and social disconnection. Supporting them required the integrated lens BRAVE provides.

9.5.3 *Nonprofit Programming Through the Mindfully Tactical Foundation*

The Mindfully Tactical Foundation (MTF) became the organizational platform for expanding BRAVE-informed interventions. Initiatives such as the WELL Program and the V.E.T.S. Toolkit were tested under its umbrella, but MTF also supports smaller efforts: peer mentorship groups, wellness education, and policy advocacy. For example, outreach efforts during community crises focused on building resilience across different areas. Veterans involved in-service projects (like storm recovery work) showed social and psychological resilience while strengthening community identity. These activities, in turn, reinforced BRAVE's interconnected loops: physical activity boosted mental health, social belonging improved economic agency, and community contribution restored a sense of identity continuity. MTF positions BRAVE as both a theoretical framework and a practical toolkit for veteran empowerment. It also supports research on community-based reintegration, emphasizing the importance of culturally competent, peer-led initiatives (Demers, 2011; Griffiths et al., 2020).

9.6 Lessons Learned from Pilot Programs

This chapter's pilot programs and practice cases demonstrate that BRAVE is not limited to theoretical ideas. It acts as a living framework when used in veteran-led, multidimensional interventions. Several key lessons emerged from these early applications, highlighting both the promise and the difficulties of implementing resilience in fragmented systems.

1. ***Trust and credibility are essential for engagement***. Veterans consistently responded more positively when programs were created and delivered by peers with shared lived experience. This was evident in the WELL Program, where participants recognized the authenticity of a veteran-led effort, and in TJ's mentorship case, where trust became the catalyst for change. Research confirms that peer-led sponsorship models outperform external interventions in fostering belonging and adherence (Geraci et al., 2023). The lesson is clear: veteran-led design is not optional; it is fundamental.
2. ***Programs that focused on only one dimension produced temporary improvements but risked falling apart when veterans faced barriers in other areas***. The V.E.T.S. Toolkit highlighted the importance of sequencing: vision without benefits navigation caused frustration, and education without practical application left degrees underused. BRAVE's multidimensional approach prevented fragmentation by requiring attention to psychological, physical, social, and economic domains simultaneously. This aligns with resilience literature emphasizing ecological and systems-based approaches (Liu et al., 2019).
3. ***Across all cases, mentorship proved to be the key factor in maintaining progress***. For TJ, personalized mentorship changed a stalled reintegration path into one of academic and professional growth. In professional practice settings, mentorship within teams or peer groups provided accountability and a sense of belonging. These findings reinforce Turner's Social Identity Theory (Turner, 1975) and Mezirow's Transformative Learning Theory (Mezirow, 1997), both of which stress the importance of relational interaction in shaping identity.

4. ***Bureaucratic complexity repeatedly threatened reintegration***. TJ's two VR&E denials exemplify how systemic fragmentation can derail progress. The PATH component of WELL and the structured phases of the V.E.T.S. Toolkit both emerged as responses to this challenge. They redefined navigation as a strategic activity, equipping veterans to approach reintegration like a plan with phased objectives and tactical steps. This shift from reactive problem-solving to proactive strategy proved vital in securing funding, stacking credentials, and establishing sustainable pathways.
5. ***Pilot programs were effective at small scale, but organizational adoption determined their reach***. Submissions to PennWest and the NC Veterans Council illustrated both the potential and the limits of grassroots efforts. Without systemic adoption, programs risk remaining isolated successes. This lesson reflects findings from implementation science: fidelity, adaptability, and sustainability require organizational commitment (Fixsen, 2005). For BRAVE to expand, institutions must integrate it into policies and practices rather than treat it as an add-on.
6. ***The most critical lesson is that reintegration outcomes—the degrees earned, injuries healed, and benefits obtained—are important but secondary to rebuilding identity***. Veterans who went through BRAVE-informed programs consistently described themselves differently after the process. They no longer felt isolated, uncertain, or defined by deficits. Instead, they were purposeful, connected, and focused on the future. This supports BRAVE's core idea: resilience is a verb, demonstrated through identity work across multiple domains.

Academic Synthesis

This chapter's case studies and practice applications demonstrate how BRAVE moves from a theoretical idea to real-world practice. The WELL Program and the V.E.T.S. Toolkit show how resilience can be put into action through organized efforts that cover psychological, physical, social, and economic areas. The Patient Zero case of TJ offers a personal example of BRAVE's multifaceted model, showing how mentorship, system navigation, and gradual progress across areas lead to identity rebuilding. Professional practice applications such as tactical athlete training in hockey, veteran support work, and nonprofit projects show the framework's flexibility in different settings.

Several key insights come from these cases. First, resilience must be actively practiced; programs work best when they include practical steps like tactical planning, mentorship, and reflection. Second, connecting different areas helps prevent fragmentation, supporting ideas from the biopsychosocial model (Engel, 1977) and multi-system resilience frameworks (Liu et al., 2019). Third, peer mentorship and veteran-led leadership consistently build trust and involvement, aligning with Social Identity Theory (Turner et al., 1979) and Transformative Learning Theory (Mezirow, 1997). Lastly, system navigation proves crucial for success, confirming BRAVE's core idea that economic resilience is central, not peripheral.

Overall, these pilot programs validate BRAVE as an effective applied model. They also reveal the difficulties in expanding veteran-led efforts within systems that tend to be slow and siloed. The main takeaway is that identity rebuilding, not just earning credentials or reducing symptoms, is the true goal of reintegration. BRAVE offers both the theoretical framework and practical tools to support this rebuilding process, establishing itself as a guide for research, practice, and ongoing development policy.

Key Takeaways

- **BRAVE in action across four domains**: The WELL Program and the V.E.T.S. Toolkit operationalize psychological, physical, social, and economic resilience as everyday practice (Engel, 1977; Liu et al., 2019).
- **Patient Zero as proof of praxis**: TJ's trajectory shows identity reconstruction through mentorship, system navigation, and compounding gains across domains (Elbogen et al., 2022; Geraci et al., 2023).
- **Mentorship as a force multiplier**: Peer-led guidance increases trust, persistence, and belonging in ways institutions rarely achieve (Geraci et al., 2023; Weir et al., 2017).
- **Economic stability as foundation**: Benefits navigation, supported education, and employment planning protect mental health and enable progress elsewhere (Bond et al., 2022; Elbogen et al., 2022).
- **Multimodal beats siloed care**: Integrated, transdiagnostic approaches outperform single-track services in durability and reach (Fortier et al., 2024; Joyce et al., 2019).
- **Translation turns goals into plans**: The V.E.T.S. Toolkit's sequence of Vision, Education, Translation, and Strategy converts intention into measurable action and artifacts.
- **Fidelity and adaptation together**: Programs succeed when they preserve core functions of BRAVE while tailoring delivery to local constraints and roles (Fixsen, 2005).
- **Identity work is the real outcome**: Degrees, fitness, and jobs matter, and the deeper success is the shift from deficit identity to agentic, community-anchored identity (Mezirow, 1997; Turner et al., 1979).
- **Praxis is measurable**: Case outputs and trajectories invite multidomain metrics and longitudinal evaluation rather than symptom-only endpoints (Liu et al., 2019).
- **Scalability needs culture change**: Lasting impact requires institutional commitment, cross-unit coordination, and routine use of BRAVE-aligned tools in advising, healthcare, and programming (Fixsen, 2005; Vacchi et al., 2014).

Applied Learning Prompts

1. Examine TJ's trajectory from VR&E denial to a three-degree academic pathway. Using the BRAVE framework, identify how each dimension (psychological, physical, social, and economic) contributed to his progress.
2. Compare the WELL Program and the V.E.T.S. Toolkit as BRAVE-informed initiatives. How do they address different systemic gaps, and what do they reveal about the importance of integration across domains?

3. Consider a non-veteran population (e.g., athletes, first responders, or foster youth). How might the principles applied in professional hockey or nonprofit programming be adapted to this group using the BRAVE framework?
4. Design a tactical plan for navigating education or employment benefits using the four steps of the V.E.T.S. Toolkit (Vision, Education, Translation, Strategy). How does framing transition as an "operation" influence clarity and outcomes?
5. Pilot programs often remain small-scale successes. Identify barriers to institutional adoption of veteran-led programs like WELL. What strategies would you propose to ensure sustainability and scalability within universities, healthcare systems, or state policy contexts?

References

Abt, J. P., Sell, T. C., Crawford, K., Lovalekar, M., Nagai, T., Deluzio, J., Smalley, B. W., McGrail, M. A., Rowe, R. S., Cardin, S., & Lephart, S. M. (2010). Warrior model for human performance and injury prevention: Eagle Tactical Athlete Program (ETAP) Part II. *Journal of Special Operations Medicine: A Peer Reviewed Journal for SOF Medical Professionals, 10*(4), 22–33. https://doi.org/10.55460/42ci-elhp

Bond, G. R., Al-Abdulmunem, M., Ressler, D. R., Gade, D. M., & Drake, R. E. (2022). A Randomized Controlled Trial of an Employment Program for Veterans Transitioning from the Military: Two-Year Outcomes. *Administration and Policy in Mental Health and Mental Health Services Research, 49*(6), 1072–1083. https://doi.org/10.1007/s10488-022-01208

Demers, A. (2011). When veterans return: The role of community in reintegration. *Journal of Loss and Trauma, 16*(2), 160–179. https://doi.org/10.1080/15325024.2010.519281

Elbogen, E. B., Zeber, J. E., Vogt, D., Perkins, D. F., Finley, E. P., & Copeland, L. A. (2022). Financial status and well-being in recently separated military veterans. *Military Medicine, 188*(7–8), e2181–e2188. https://doi.org/10.1093/milmed/usac030

Engel, G. L. (1977). The need for a new medical model: A challenge for biomedicine. *Science, 196*(4286), 129–136. https://doi.org/10.1126/science.847460

Fixsen, D. (2005). *Implementation research: A synthesis of the literature*. The National Implementation Research Network, Louis de la Parte Florida Mental Health Research Institute, University of South Florida.

Fortier, C. B., Kenna, A., Katz, D., Kim, S., Hursh, C., Beck, B., Sablone, C. A., Currao, A., Lebas, A., Jorge, R. E., & Fonda, J. R. (2024). STEP-HOME transdiagnostic group reintegration workshop to improve mental health outcomes for post-9/11 veterans: Design, methods, and rationale for a randomized controlled behavioral trial. *Contemporary Clinical Trials, 141*, 107536. https://doi.org/10.1016/j.cct.2024.107536

Geraci, J. C., Dichiara, A., Greene, A., Gromatsky, M., Finley, E. P., Kilby, D., Frankfurt, S., Edwards, E. R., Solomon Kurz, A., Sokol, Y., Sullivan, S. R., Mobbs, M., Seim, R. W., & Goodman, M. (2023). Supporting servicemembers and veterans during their transition to civilian life using certified sponsors: A three-arm randomized controlled trial. *Psychological Services*. https://doi.org/10.1037/ser0000764

Griffiths, H. K., Hawkins, B. L., & Crowe, B. M. (2020). Identifying contextual factors that impact community reintegration in injured female veterans. *Journal of Military, Veteran and Family Health, 6*(1), 38–47. https://doi.org/10.3138/jmvfh-2018-0043

Joyce, S., Shand, F., Lal, T. J., Mott, B., Bryant, R. A., & Harvey, S. B. (2019). Resilience@Work mindfulness program: Results from a cluster randomized controlled trial with first responders. *Journal of Medical Internet Research, 21*(2), e12894. https://doi.org/10.2196/12894

Koelkebeck, K., Weber, H., Lueken, U., Dannlowski, U., Margraf, J., Schneider, S., … Deckert, J. (2025). Epigenetic markers of disease risk and psychotherapy response in anxiety disorders—A longitudinal analysis of the DNA methylome. *Molecular Psychiatry*. https://doi.org/10.1038/s41380-025-03038-5

Liu, Y., Collins, C., Wang, K., Xie, X., & Bie, R. (2019). The prevalence and trend of depression among veterans in the United States. *Journal of Affective Disorders, 245*, 724–727. https://doi.org/10.1016/j.jad.2018.11.031

Mezirow, J. (1997). Transformation theory out of context. *Adult Education Quarterly, 48*(1), 60–62. https://doi.org/10.1177/074171369704800105

Trepte, S., & Loy, L. S. (2017). Social Identity Theory and Self-Categorization Theory. *The international encyclopedia of media effects, 63,* 1–13.

Turner, J. C., Brown, R. J., & Tajfel, H. (1979). Social comparison and group interest in ingroup favouritism. *European Journal of Social Psychology, 9*(2), 187–204. https://doi.org/10.1002/ejsp.2420090207

Vacchi, D., Berger, J., & Paulsen, M. (2014). Higher Education: Handbook of Theory and Research.

Weir, B., Cunningham, M., Abraham, L., & Allanson-Oddy, C. (2017). Military veteran engagement with mental health and well-being services: A qualitative study of the role of the peer support worker. *Journal of Mental Health, 28*(6), 647–653. https://doi.org/10.1080/09638237.2017.1370640

Chapter 10
Toward a Resilience Index—Future Directions for BRAVE Research

This chapter introduces the Transitional Resilience Index (TRI) as the next step in the evolution of the BRAVE framework, a unified tool designed to measure and compare resilience across populations like veterans, foster youth, and justice-involved individuals. The chapter explains the reasoning behind creating a standardized, multidimensional index that captures the psychological, physical, social, and economic aspects central to reintegration. It discusses how the foundational ideas of BRAVE and FORGE come together within TRI, linking identity reconstruction and adaptive functioning to measurable indicators. Readers will see how TRI can be used in research, clinical practice, and policy evaluation to track progress and inform precision-based interventions. The discussion also highlights how TRI advances resilience science by providing a common language for recovery, adaptation, and well-being across different populations. After reading, you can explain the purpose and necessity of TRI, analyze its theoretical integration with BRAVE and FORGE, identify its four core domains and corresponding indicators, evaluate its practical applications across multiple settings, and assess its broader implications for advancing reintegration and resilience research.

10.1 Introduction: Frameworks to Measurement

The evolution of BRAVE through the WELL Program, the V.E.T.S. Toolkit, and the Patient Zero case shows resilience as something people do, not merely possess. Across psychological, physical, social, and economic domains, these efforts turned a framework into daily habits and institutional workflows. They also revealed a limit that practice alone cannot cross: without reliable ways to measure change

T. Carlton, *BRAVE Theory*, https://doi.org/10.1007/978-3-032-13695-4_10

across different people and settings, success remains local, descriptive, and hard to compare. A campus may see progress, a mentor may watch a student turn a corner, a nonprofit may report promising trends, yet none of that readily translates into evidence that can guide programs at scale or shape policy confidently. This problem extends beyond veterans. In resilience science, definitions often drift, and measurement tools frequently focus on narrow outcomes such as symptom reduction, single-domain performance, or social participation in isolation. That narrowness breaks the very system we are trying to understand, because resilience is an interaction effect. Gains in one area echo into the others, and losses do the same. When our measures ignore those interactions, the evidence base becomes uneven. Interventions can look compelling in context but remain difficult to compare across sites, populations, and time.

The Transitional Resilience Index was created to close that gap. It joins BRAVE's four working domains with the FORGE model's attention to identity, stability, and adaptive functioning so that the qualities described in narrative and program design can be captured as indicators that hold up in research and practice. The index gives researchers a coherent structure for analysis, allows practitioners to track multidomain progress without losing the person in the process, and gives policymakers a common language for accountability that reaches beyond a single metric like employment or symptom scores. Introducing the TRI is the next step in the book's logic. BRAVE established a theoretical architecture. WELL and V.E.T.S. showed how that architecture operates in the real world through peer leadership, advising workflows, and mentorship. The TRI supplies the instrument that allows us to move from asking what resilience looks like to determining how it can be scored, compared, and monitored over time. That shift matters because it converts scattered successes into a cumulative evidence base that can inform program design, resource allocation, and long-term policy commitments.

Throughout the manuscript, resilience has been treated as practice, with identity reconstruction as the mechanism that ties the domains together. The TRI carries that position into study design. By capturing change across interconnected domains, it lets us trace how a gain in economic stability can reduce psychological strain, open social participation, and support physical routines, or how a setback in health can threaten finances and belonging unless countered by targeted support. In other words, it does not simply total scores. It reveals pathways and sequences that practitioners and participants experience on the ground. The need for a tool like this is not theoretical. Veterans, foster youth, and justice-involved individuals move through very different institutions. Yet, they face a striking set of shared problems: fragmented services, histories of trauma, disrupted identity, and financial precarity. A standard index that remains sensitive to context allows comparison without erasing differences. It also makes precision possible, since the same instrument can highlight distinct weak points for each population and person.

The move from frameworks to measurement is therefore necessary rather than optional. BRAVE established the case for multidomain resilience and showed it can be enacted. The pilots demonstrated feasibility and produced early signals of impact. The TRI provides a standardized, psychometrically planned method for tracking resilience over time so that theory, practice, and policy are no longer separate conversations but parts of the same evidence-driven story.

10.2 Theoretical Foundations of TRI

The Transitional Resilience Index (TRI) is based on a combination of conceptual models developed across various disciplines. The need for this integration comes from the long-standing fragmentation of resilience research: although psychology, medicine, education, and social work have created valuable frameworks, few tools combine these perspectives into a multidimensional, measurable construct. The TRI aims to unify theory into a practical instrument that can guide research, practice, and policy across diverse system-impacted fields and populations.

10.2.1 BRAVE Theory: Veteran Reintegration as Multidimensional Praxis

The first foundation of the TRI is the BRAVE Theory, developed through veterans' lived experiences and supported by over 600 studies during a three-year doctoral program. BRAVE (Building Resilience and Advancing Veteran Empowerment) views reintegration as a dynamic process involving four domains: psychological, physical, social, and economic. Each domain interacts with the others, creating resilience as an emergent property rather than a fixed state trait.

- Psychological resilience encompasses emotional regulation, identity reconstruction, and agency following trauma (Kearney et al., 2021; Mezirow, 1997).
- Physical resilience refers to recovery from injury, maintenance of health, and sustainable embodiment (Walter et al., 2023).
- Social resilience emphasizes belonging, peer support, and institutional trust (Geraci et al., 2023).
- Economic resilience includes financial stability, benefits navigation, and career alignment (Elbogen et al., 2022).

BRAVE showed that veteran transition is more than changing careers; it's a comprehensive reintegration that requires balancing multiple areas. These concepts laid the foundation for TRI, outlining the main categories to be measured.

10.2.2 FORGE Model: Identity, Stability, and Adaptation in Foster Youth

The second foundation is the FORGE Model, developed through research with foster youth aging out of care. FORGE highlights the challenges of stability, identity development, and adaptive functioning in populations affected by systemic disruption. Like veterans, foster youth experience sudden separation from a structured environment, often without sufficient preparation for independence.

Key constructs from FORGE include:

- **Identity**: the challenge of constructing a coherent self outside of institutional definitions.
- **Stability:** Housing, education, and financial continuity are prerequisites for resilience.
- **Adaptive functioning**: regulating stress, navigating systems, and engaging in future-oriented planning.

Integrating FORGE with BRAVE expands the TRI beyond veterans to address resilience as a shared need across system-impacted populations.

10.2.3 Biopsychosocial and Ecological Systems Models

Beyond BRAVE and FORGE, the TRI draws on broader theoretical frameworks. Engel's (1977) biopsychosocial model demonstrated that health outcomes result from the interaction of biological, psychological, and social systems. Bronfenbrenner's (1979) ecological systems theory highlighted the layered contexts of family, community, institutions, and policy that influence human development. Both frameworks support the idea that resilience should not be studied in isolation but as a systemic and relational phenomenon.

10.2.4 Multi-System Models of Resilience

Recent scholarship advances these systems thinking further. Liu et al. (2017) propose a multi-system model of resilience, emphasizing interactions between biological, psychological, social, and environmental systems. Domschke et al. (2025) demonstrate that trauma-related biological vulnerabilities can be modified through psychosocial interventions, underscoring the dynamic nature of resilience. These findings validate the TRI's emphasis on measuring domains as interdependent capacities that change over time.

10.2.5 Toward an Integrated Measurement Framework

The TRI combines these foundations into a single measurement tool. It uses the four resilience domains from BRAVE. It includes identity, stability, and adaptive functioning from FORGE. It also adopts the idea from biopsychosocial, ecological, and multi-system models that resilience is systemic, dynamic, and depends on the context. This integration lets the TRI work as a standard index and a flexible tool for veterans, foster youth, and other groups experiencing systemic transitions.

10.3 Core Domains of the TRI

The TRI measures resilience across four main areas: psychological, physical, social, and economic. These areas were developed by combining BRAVE Theory and the FORGE Model, reflecting real-life experiences and academic research. Each area includes specific indicators that can be measured reliably while remaining flexible for different groups, such as veterans and foster youth.

10.3.1 Psychological Resilience

The psychological domain includes cognitive, emotional, and identity-related abilities that help people adapt to trauma, stress, and systemic disruption. Indicators include emotional regulation, agency, meaning-making, and self-coherence.

- **For veterans**: Psychological resilience involves recovering from combat trauma, moral injury, or identity fracture after discharge. It includes the ability to integrate military experience into a new civilian identity and manage conditions such as PTSD or depression (Kearney et al., 2021; Saban et al., 2022).
- **For foster youth**: It involves constructing identity outside of state systems, managing the emotional challenges of instability, and building self-efficacy in environments where adult support may be limited (Courtney et al., 2011).

The TRI positions psychological resilience as outcome and process, recognizing identity reconstruction as the central reintegration mechanism.

10.3.2 Physical Resilience

Physical resilience refers to the ability to maintain and recover physical health. It includes injury healing, managing chronic conditions, regulating sleep, and having energy for daily activities.

- **For veterans**: Common challenges include musculoskeletal injuries, traumatic brain injuries, chronic pain, and disrupted sleep cycles (Teplova et al., 2022). Physical resilience is enacted through rehabilitation, exercise, nutrition, and health-promoting behaviors.
- **For foster youth**: Many enter adulthood with untreated health conditions, inconsistent access to care, and increased vulnerability to chronic illness due to early life instability (Bruskas & Tessin, 2013). Physical resilience includes securing regular healthcare, developing self-care routines, and engaging in health literacy.

By embedding physical indicators into the TRI, resilience is understood as mental or social strength and embodied capacity.

10.3.3 Social Resilience

The social domain captures belonging, trust, and supportive relationships. Indicators include perceived social support, quality of mentorship, institutional trust, and community participation.

- **For veterans**: Social resilience involves rebuilding networks outside the military. Research shows that a lack of belonging is linked to higher risks of suicide and difficulties in reintegration (Geraci et al., 2023; Sayer et al., 2011). Programs that promote peer mentorship and structured group activities, like LINK, directly support this area.
- **For foster youth**: The sudden loss of structured networks at age 18 or 21 increases vulnerability to isolation and homelessness. Social resilience here means developing reciprocal peer and adult relationships, often outside biological family systems (Greeson et al., 2015).

Social resilience reinforces other domains: belonging provides the support necessary to pursue education, maintain health, and plan economically.

10.3.4 Economic Resilience

Economic resilience refers to stability in employment, education, housing, and financial literacy. Indicators include consistent income, housing security, benefit utilization, and long-term planning.

- **For veterans:** Economic stress is one of the strongest predictors of poor mental health (Elbogen et al., 2022). Core elements include navigating GI Bill or VR&E benefits, securing employment aligned with skills, and planning for long-term financial stability.
- **For foster youth:** Economic resilience often begins from a place of precarity, with many facing housing insecurity and limited access to financial literacy education.

Structured support in employment readiness, budgeting, and stable housing is critical (Courtney et al., 2011).

The TRI frames economic resilience as survival and empowerment, the ability to envision and pursue a sustainable future.

10.4 Scoring and Measurement Design

The TRI is proposed as a conceptual measurement framework; psychometric validation is planned for future studies. Its design highlights three main priorities: (1) clarity and ease of use for both researchers and practitioners, (2) a multidimensional scoring system that recognizes the interdependence of various domains, and (3) flexibility for application across different population contexts. A worked example appears in Table 10.1, which shows sample indicators, items, and scoring snapshots for each TRI domain.

Table 10.1 Transitional resilience index (TRI): domain indicators, example items, and pre/post scoring snapshot

Domain	Indicator examples	Sample item (1–5 Likert)	Scoring notes	Pre	Post
Psychological	Emotion regulation; identity coherence; agency	"I can manage stress without feeling overwhelmed."	Mean of items in domain; higher = greater capacity	2.8	4.1
Physical	Sleep regularity; Transitional pain/ function; activity & recovery	"I keep a consistent sleep and recovery routine."	Combine behavior + function items	2.6	3.9
Social	Belonging; mentorship; institutional trust; participation	"I feel connected to a community that supports me."	Include peer and institutional ties	2.9	4.0
Economic	Income stability; housing; benefit use; planning	"I have a plan to manage financial stress."	Weighting optional by population needs	2.4	3.8
Composite (mean of domains)	–	–	Equal or weighted mean	2.7	4.0

Note Scores are illustrative placeholders. Replace with validated items and domain means. Response scale = 1–5 (higher scores indicate greater capacity). The composite score may be calculated as an equal or population-weighted mean of domain scores. Abbreviations: TRI = Transitional Resilience Index

10.4.1 Item Structure

The TRI uses a modular structure comprising core items relevant across different populations and optional items customized for specific groups (e.g., veterans, foster youth, justice-involved individuals). Items are written in clear, accessible language, with response formats designed to reduce cognitive load while capturing subtle differences. Each item is scored on a five-point Likert scale from 1 ("strongly disagree") to 5 ("strongly agree"), maintaining consistency with other validated resilience and well-being measures. Domains are represented through items that focus on both behaviors (e.g., "I have a plan to manage financial stress") and perceptions (e.g., "I feel connected to a community that supports me").

10.4.2 Domain Scoring

The four psychological, physical, social, and economic domains are scored individually. Domain scores are calculated as the mean of item responses, allowing researchers to identify specific strengths and vulnerabilities. In addition to domain-level scores, the TRI produces a composite resilience score, representing an individual's overall capacity for reintegration.

- **Psychological score**: reflects agency, emotional regulation, and identity coherence.
- **Physical score**: reflects health behaviors, rehabilitation, and functional capacity.
- **Social score**: reflects belonging, trust, and mentorship.
- **Economic score**: reflects stability, benefit navigation, and financial literacy.

10.4.3 Weighting and Composite Index

The TRI is designed to allow either equal weighting of domains or population-specific weighting based on empirical data. For example, among foster youth, social and economic resilience may be stronger predictors of long-term outcomes, whereas for veterans, psychological resilience might have more predictive power. Flexibility in weighting enables cross-population comparison without losing contextual relevance and specificity.

10.4.4 Psychometric Validation

Validation of the TRI will proceed through standard psychometric procedures:

- **Construct validity**: Confirmatory factor analysis (CFA) will be used to test whether items align with the hypothesized four-domain structure.
- **Reliability**: Internal consistency will be assessed using Cronbach's alpha for each domain, with test–retest reliability evaluated over time.
- **Measurement invariance**: Multi-group confirmatory factor analysis will test whether the TRI functions equivalently across populations (e.g., veterans vs. foster youth). This step ensures that scores can be meaningfully compared.
- **Criterion validity**: TRI scores will be correlated with existing validated measures, such as the WHO-5 Well-Being Index, Social Well-Being Scale, and financial stress measures, to confirm predictive and convergent validity.

10.4.5 Adaptability and Cultural Sensitivity

A key feature of the TRI is its flexibility. The core items remain the same; extra items can be added to address cultural or contextual needs. For example, indigenous veterans might encounter specific community reintegration challenges, and foster youth in rural versus urban settings may require different indicators of stability. The TRI's modular design allows such customization while maintaining comparability across groups.

10.5 Applications Across Systems

The Transitional Resilience Index (TRI) was developed as a versatile tool for use across different populations facing systemic disruptions. Veterans, foster youth, and justice-involved individuals each face unique transition challenges, yet all must navigate fragmented systems, fractured identities, and uncertain economic futures. By providing a standardized measure of psychological, physical, social, and economic resilience, the TRI helps practitioners, researchers, and policymakers evaluate reintegration outcomes consistently and effectively.

10.5.1 Veterans

For post-9/11 veterans, reintegration challenges extend beyond employment to include trauma recovery, health management, and identity rebuilding. Existing programs like the GI Bill and VR&E offer significant benefits, but outcomes vary greatly depending on how well veterans engage with them. By assessing multidimensional resilience, the TRI offers a common language for clinicians and policymakers, connecting small-scale interventions with broader accountability.

The TRI can be used in several ways:

- **Program evaluation**: Universities and veteran service organizations can administer the TRI before and after participation in interventions such as the WELL Program or the V.E.T.S. Toolkit to measure effectiveness across different areas.
- **Individual planning**: Counselors can utilize TRI profiles to identify specific vulnerabilities—for example, a veteran with strong physical and social resilience but low economic resilience might need financial literacy training and career guidance.
- **Policy monitoring**: Combined TRI data can help state and federal policymakers identify systemic gaps in veteran services and direct resources toward under-supported areas.

10.5.2 Foster Youth

Foster youth aging out of care face sudden transitions into independence, often lacking stable housing, financial literacy, or long-term social networks. Research shows that nearly one in five foster youth experience homelessness within a year of leaving care (Courtney et al., 2011). The TRI offers a way to measure survival outcomes and developmental progress, shifting foster youth from passive recipients of services to active agents of resilience-building.

The TRI can assist this population in several key areas:

- **Independent living programs**: Agencies can administer the TRI at start and end to assess whether housing support, job training, and counseling services enhance resilience across different areas.
- **Educational advising**: Counselors can use TRI indicators to align educational decisions with psychological readiness and financial stability, helping to prevent dropouts related to instability.
- **Community partnerships**: Nonprofits can compile TRI data to demonstrate outcomes to funders, strengthening the case for ongoing support of foster care alumni.

10.5.3 Justice-Involved Populations

Justice-involved individuals face some of the highest barriers to reintegration, including stigma, limited employment opportunities, and disrupted social identities. Recidivism rates remain above 60% within three years of release in the United States (Durose et al., 2014).

The TRI can provide both diagnostic and evaluative functions:

- **Risk assessment**: By identifying vulnerabilities across TRI domains, reentry programs can more effectively target interventions—for example, addressing social isolation and economic instability that often drive recidivism.

- **Program comparison**: TRI scores can be used to compare reentry programs across jurisdictions, highlighting which approaches most effectively foster resilience and reduce recidivism.
- **Policy advocacy**: Aggregated TRI data can demonstrate the systemic barriers justice-involved individuals face, providing evidence for reforms in housing policy, workforce development, and stigma reduction initiatives.

10.5.4 Cross-System Applications

Each population faces unique challenges, and the TRI emphasizes their common vulnerabilities: systemic fragmentation, disrupted identity, trauma exposure, and economic instability. This shared framework enables cross-population research and policy comparisons. For example, policymakers can investigate whether interventions that enhance social resilience among foster youth also improve outcomes for veterans, or if economic supports for justice-involved individuals lead to similar benefits in identity reconstruction as they do for veterans. Cross-system application highlights the greater value of the TRI: it offers a unifying framework for measuring resilience across populations that have traditionally been studied separately. It fosters comparative research, supports integrated policy efforts, and advances resilience science overall. To illustrate how the Transitional Resilience Index (TRI) can be operationalized in practice, Table 10.1 provides example domains, indicators, sample items, and a pre/post scoring snapshot.

10.6 Implications for Research and Policy

The Transitional Resilience Index (TRI) development has implications that extend well beyond academic interest. By operationalizing resilience as a multidimensional construct, the TRI enables new avenues for research, enhances accountability in-service delivery, and informs policy reform across sectors. Its design reflects the need to bridge individual outcomes with systemic evaluation, allowing resilience to be studied not only as a personal trait but as a reflection of institutional effectiveness.

10.6.1 Advancing Resilience Research

Resilience research has historically been hindered by fragmented definitions and inconsistent measurement tools. As summarized in Table 10.1, domain-level and composite scores enable longitudinal tracking and comparison across settings. The TRI offers a standardized framework for longitudinal tracking of resilience trajectories. By administering the index at multiple points during reintegration, researchers can evaluate how psychological, physical, social, and economic domains interact over time. For example, does improvement in economic resilience predict long-term gains in psychological health? Does social belonging buffer against setbacks in physical recovery? These questions can only be answered through instruments capable of capturing multidimensional change.

Furthermore, the TRI supports comparative research across populations. Veterans, foster youth, and justice-involved individuals share structural barriers but differ in lived contexts. Using a common measurement tool allows scholars to identify both unique challenges and generalizable resilience mechanisms. This comparative perspective advances the science of resilience by clarifying which interventions are population-specific and which can be adapted across systems.

10.6.2 Enhancing Program Accountability

The TRI also functions as a program evaluation tool. Service providers often rely on narrow metrics such as job placement rates, housing stability, or symptom reduction. While valuable, these indicators provide only partial pictures of reintegration. TRI scores offer a comprehensive measure of resilience across domains, enabling organizations to demonstrate multidimensional outcomes. This accountability function strengthens funding cases for nonprofits and universities while ensuring that interventions are not evaluated solely on economic productivity. A program that raises psychological resilience and social belonging but does not immediately improve employment rates can still demonstrate value through TRI data. This shifts the evaluation landscape toward holistic well-being, aligning with trauma-informed and biopsychosocial approaches to care.

10.6.3 Informing Policy Reform

At the policy level, the TRI provides evidence to guide systemic change. Aggregated data can highlight structural deficits in resilience support. For example, if TRI assessments consistently show low economic resilience among veterans despite adequate educational access, policymakers can prioritize financial literacy and benefit navigation programs. Similarly, if foster youth consistently demonstrate low social resilience, funding can be directed toward mentorship and community integration initiatives. By identifying systemic weaknesses, the TRI positions resilience not as an individual responsibility but as a shared societal obligation. This reframing challenges deficit-based policies that blame individuals for poor outcomes and instead highlights institutional accountability. In doing so, the TRI contributes to the broader shift toward equity-focused, trauma-informed systems design.

10.6.4 Building a Bridge Between Micro and Macro Systems

The TRI's greatest contribution may be its ability to connect micro-level interventions with macro-level reforms. At the individual level, it helps veterans, foster youth, and justice-involved individuals map their strengths and vulnerabilities. At the institutional level, it allows service providers to evaluate program effectiveness. At the policy level, it generates evidence for structural change. This multilevel functionality ensures that resilience measurement does not remain confined to academic theory but becomes a tool for systemic improvement.

10.7 Future Directions

The Transitional Resilience Index (TRI) represents a critical step in moving resilience from a theoretical construct to a measurable outcome. Yet as with any new instrument, its value will be realized through continued testing, refinement, and expansion. Future directions for the TRI include empirical validation, population expansion, technological integration, and contributions to global resilience discourse.

10.7.1 Empirical Validation

The first priority is rigorous validation of the TRI through empirical research. Initial pilot studies with veterans and foster youth will test reliability, construct validity, and measurement invariance across groups. Confirmatory factor analysis will confirm whether the hypothesized four-domain structure holds consistently. Longitudinal studies will be critical, tracking resilience trajectories over months and years to determine how domain scores predict long-term outcomes such as degree completion, stable employment, or sustained health. Validation will also require comparison with established measures such as the WHO-5 Well-Being Index, the Connor-Davidson Resilience Scale (CD-RISC), and the Social Well-Being Scale. Demonstrating convergent validity with these tools while also showing added value through the TRI's multidimensional design will establish its legitimacy within resilience science.

10.7.2 Expansion to Additional Populations

Although initially developed for veterans and foster youth, the TRI is designed to be adaptable to other system-impacted populations. Given parallels in systemic disruption, stigma, and economic precarity, justice-involved individuals represent a logical next application. Beyond domestic contexts, refugees and asylum seekers face similar reintegration challenges and would benefit from a culturally adapted TRI. Expansion to healthcare populations such as patients recovering from chronic illness or trauma offers additional possibilities. By expanding to multiple groups, the TRI can function as a comparative tool, identifying universal resilience mechanisms while highlighting population-specific needs. This dual capacity enhances both scholarly understanding and policy design.

10.7.3 Integration into Digital Platforms

The future of resilience measurement will likely be digital. The TRI can be adapted into mobile and web-based applications, enabling real-time tracking of resilience trajectories. Such platforms could provide veterans or foster youth with immediate feedback on strengths and vulnerabilities and tailored resources linked to their scores. For practitioners, digital dashboards could aggregate anonymized data, supporting program evaluation and institutional decision-making. Digital integration also enables adaptive measurement. Instead of static surveys, the TRI could employ branching logic, tailoring items to an individual's context while still preserving comparability. Integration with wearable technologies could further enhance physical domain assessment, linking biometric data with self-reported resilience indicators.

10.7.4 Global and Intergenerational Applications

The TRI also holds promise for contributing to global resilience discourse. Communities worldwide grapple with displacement, systemic disruption, and identity reconstruction. A standardized yet adaptable resilience index could support comparative research across cultural contexts, advancing resilience science as a truly global field. Additionally, the TRI can be applied intergenerationally. The effects of trauma often ripple across generations, influencing not only veterans and foster youth but also their families and communities. Longitudinal TRI studies could illuminate how resilience is transmitted—or disrupted—across generations, offering insights into prevention and early intervention strategies.

10.7.5 Refinement Through Practice

Finally, the TRI must remain responsive to practitioner feedback. As it is implemented in real-world contexts, item wording, domain weighting, and scoring structures may require refinement. Continuous feedback loops between researchers, practitioners, and participants will ensure that the tool remains both rigorous and usable.

10.8 Conclusion

The development of the Transitional Resilience Index (TRI) represents the culmination of a scholarly and practical journey that began with the BRAVE framework. BRAVE established that reintegration is a multidimensional process enacted across psychological, physical, social, and economic domains. Through the WELL Program, the V.E.T.S. Toolkit, and individual mentorship cases such as TJ's narrative, BRAVE demonstrated its utility as praxis—a framework not confined to theory but lived out in daily practices and systemic interventions. Yet the limitations of existing resilience science made clear that conceptual frameworks and pilot programs, while powerful, were not enough. Without standardized tools for measurement, resilience remained inconsistently defined and unevenly assessed. The TRI addresses this gap by transforming resilience into a quantifiable construct. It integrates the conceptual foundations of BRAVE and FORGE, builds upon biopsychosocial and ecological models, and offers a psychometrically rigorous approach to evaluating resilience trajectories across system-impacted populations.

The TRI is an assessment tool, yet it represents the next stage in resilience scholarship: the bridge between theory, practice, and policy. By enabling longitudinal research, comparative studies, and systemic evaluation, the TRI ensures that resilience can be studied scientifically, implemented pragmatically, and embedded institutionally. Its adaptability across veterans, foster youth, and justice-involved populations positions it as a unifying framework for resilience science, capable of informing both individual support strategies and large-scale policy reforms. As this book has argued, resilience is not a static trait but a verb—something enacted, practiced, and sustained across time and domains. The TRI extends this insight by allowing resilience to be measured in a way that honors its complexity without sacrificing clarity. In doing so, it provides researchers, practitioners, and policymakers with a shared language and a standard tool for advancing reintegration.

The work ahead is substantial: validation studies, population expansions, digital integration, and global applications will all be required. But the foundations are in place. The trajectory has been clear from lived experience to doctoral research, frameworks to fieldwork, and practice to measurement. BRAVE established the multidimensional nature of resilience; the WELL and V.E.T.S. programs demonstrated its applicability; and the TRI ensures its measurability. Together, these contributions reaffirm a simple but powerful truth: resilience cannot be described from a distance. It is to be enacted, supported, and measured as an ongoing reconstruction process. The TRI marks the transition of BRAVE from narrative to framework, from framework to praxis, and from praxis to science. It represents not an endpoint, but a beginning—the opening of a new chapter in resilience research and application, where theory and practice are united by measurement and action.

Academic Synthesis

The TRI extends the conceptual foundation of BRAVE and FORGE by operationalizing resilience into a measurable construct. Its multidimensional design reflects the biopsychosocial model (Engel, 1977), ecological systems theory (Bronfenbrenner, 1979), and multi-system resilience frameworks (Liu et al., 2017), while its practical application responds to systemic fragmentation observed in veteran, foster youth, and justice-involved populations. By integrating psychological, physical, social, and economic domains into a single index, the TRI provides a holistic measurement framework capable of capturing individual strengths and systemic barriers. Validation plans, including confirmatory factor analysis, reliability testing, and measurement invariance, ensure psychometric rigor, while modular design allows cultural and contextual adaptability.

The TRI's significance lies in its ability to bridge micro- and macro-levels of resilience. At the individual level, it supports self-assessment and tailored planning. At the programmatic level, it provides tools for evaluating multidimensional outcomes. At the policy level, it generates data to identify structural deficits and guide resource allocation. By functioning across these layers, the TRI advances resilience science from descriptive models toward evidence-based systems reform. Ultimately, the TRI reflects the central claim of this book: resilience is not static but enacted, and identity reconstruction is its primary outcome. Measurement ensures that resilience can be studied, supported, and sustained as praxis. Moving from framework to field application and now to standardized measurement, BRAVE and TRI position resilience as both a lived process and a scientific construct.

Key Takeaways

- **Measurement closes the loop**—TRI converts BRAVE (and FORGE) from framework to quantifiable outcomes, enabling comparison, iteration, and accountability (Bronfenbrenner, 1979; Engel, 1977).
- **Multidomain by design**—Psychological, physical, social, and economic domains—and their indicators—capture resilience as an interacting system, not a single score (Liu et al., 2017).
- **Identity is the through line**—TRI tracks the conditions that reconstruct identity over time, aligning with praxis rather than trait views of resilience (Mezirow, 1997).
- **Cross-population language**—A shared index supports comparative work across veterans, foster youth, and justice-involved groups while preserving contextual nuance (Courtney et al., 2011; Durose et al., 2014).
- **Precision ready**—Flexible weighting and modular items allow tailoring by population and use case without losing comparability.

- **Validity is planned, not presumed**—CFA, reliability, and measurement invariance anchor psychometric rigor; linkage to established scales enables convergent validity.
- **Beyond symptom checklists**—TRI supports program and policy evaluation on outcomes that matter: regulation, embodiment, belonging, and economic stability (Engel, 1977).
- **A policy lever, not just a dashboard**—Aggregated TRI data identify structural gaps and guide resource allocation toward the weakest domains.
- **Digital and longitudinal**—App-based delivery, adaptive items, and time-series use make TRI suitable for real-time support and long-horizon tracking.
- **Equity and cultural fit**—Core items stay constant; optional modules adapt to culture, community, and context without sacrificing rigor.
- **Science agenda built-in**—TRI invites tests of cross-domain effects (e.g., economic → psychological), population differences, and biologically plausible change pathways (Domschke et al., 2025; Liu et al., 2017).
- **From framework to science**—TRI positions resilience as enacted, measurable, and system-responsive, tying individual progress to institutional responsibility.

Applied Learning Prompts

1. **Case Analysis**: Imagine administering the TRI to a cohort of student veterans. How would domain-specific scores (e.g., high psychological but low economic resilience) guide tailored interventions?
2. **Comparative Application**: Consider foster youth and justice-involved populations. How might TRI indicators differ between these groups, and what does that reveal about population-specific resilience needs?
3. **Program Evaluation Exercise**: Design a small pilot program for veterans using the WELL or V.E.T.S. models. How would you use TRI scores pre- and post-program to evaluate effectiveness across all four domains?
4. **Policy Critique**: If TRI data revealed consistently low economic resilience scores among veterans nationwide, what policy reforms would you recommend? How could TRI evidence strengthen your case?
5. **Innovation Challenge**: Propose a digital or technological adaptation of the TRI (e.g., a mobile app or wearable integration). How might real-time measurement change resilience support for system-impacted populations?

References

Bronfenbrenner, U. (1979). *The ecology of human development: Experiments by nature and design.* Harvard University Press.

Bruskas, D., & Tessin, D. H. (2013). Adverse childhood experiences and psychosocial well-being of women who were in foster care as children. *The Permanente Journal, 17*(3), e131–141. https://doi.org/10.7812/TPP/12-121

Courtney, M. E., Dworsky, A., Lee, J. S., & Raap, M. (2011). *Midwest evaluation of the adult functioning of former foster youth: Outcomes at age 26*. Chapin Hall at the University of Chicago.

Domschke, K., Schiele, M. A., Crespo Salvador, Ó., Zillich, L., Lipovsek, J., Pittig, A., Heinig, I., Ridderbusch, I. C., Straube, B., Richter, J., Hollandt, M., Plag, J., Fydrich, T., Koelkebeck, K., Weber, H., Lueken, U., Dannlowski, U., Margraf, J., Schneider, S., & Deckert, J. (2025). Epigenetic markers of disease risk and psychotherapy response in anxiety disorders – A longitudinal analysis of the DNA methylome. *Molecular Psychiatry*. https://doi.org/10.1038/s41380-025-03038-5

Durose, M. R., Cooper, A. D., & Snyder, H. N. (2014). *Recidivism of prisoners released in 30 states in 2005: Patterns from 2005 to 2010* (NCJ 244205). U.S. Department of Justice, Bureau of Justice Statistics.

Elbogen, E. B., Zeber, J. E., Vogt, D., Perkins, D. F., Finley, E. P., & Copeland, L. A. (2022). Financial status and well-being in recently separated military veterans. *Military Medicine, 188*(7–8), e2181–e2188. https://doi.org/10.1093/milmed/usac030

Engel, G. L. (1977). The need for a new medical model: A challenge for biomedicine. *Science, 196*(4286), 129–136. https://doi.org/10.1126/science.847460

Geraci, J. C., Dichiara, A., Greene, A., Gromatsky, M., Finley, E. P., Kilby, D., Frankfurt, S., Edwards, E. R., Solomon Kurz, A., Sokol, Y., Sullivan, S. R., Mobbs, M., Seim, R. W., & Goodman, M. (2023). Supporting service members and veterans during their transition to civilian life using certified sponsors: A three-arm randomized controlled trial. *Psychological Services*. https://doi.org/10.1037/ser0000764

Greeson, J. K., Garcia, A. R., Kim, M., Thompson, A. E., & Courtney, M. E. (2015). Development & maintenance of social support among aged out foster youth who received independent living services: Results from the Multi-Site Evaluation of Foster Youth Programs. *Children and youth services review, 53*, 1–9, https://doi.org/10.1016/j.childyouth.2015.03.016

Kearney, D. J., Malte, C. A., Storms, M., & Simpson, T. L. (2021). Loving-kindness meditation vs cognitive processing therapy for posttraumatic stress disorder among veterans: A randomized clinical trial. *JAMA Network Open, 4*(4), Article e216604. https://doi.org/10.1001/jamanetworkopen.2021.6604

Mezirow, J. (1997). Transformation theory out of context. *Adult Education Quarterly, 48*(1), 60–62. https://doi.org/10.1177/074171369704800105

Saban, K. L., Collins, E. G., Mathews, H. L., Bryant, F. B., Tell, D., Gonzalez, B., Bhoopalam, S., Chroniak, C. P., & Janusek, L. W. (2022). Impact of a mindfulness-based stress reduction program on psychological well-being, cortisol, and inflammation in women veterans. *Journal of General Internal Medicine, 37*(3), 751–761. https://doi.org/10.1007/s11606-022-07584-4

Sayer, N. A., Spoont, M., Murdoch, M., Parker, L. E., Hintz, S., & Rosenheck, R. (2011). A qualitative study of U.S. veterans' reasons for seeking Department of Veterans Affairs disability benefits for posttraumatic stress disorder. *Journal of Traumatic Stress, 24*(6), 699–707. https://doi.org/10.1002/jts.20693

Closing Synthesis: From Battlefield to BRAVE

This book charts my personal, academic, and systemic journey. It starts with my lived experience and addresses the realities of transitioning from military to civilian life: fractured identity, untreated trauma, systemic disconnection, and the often-overlooked burden of reintegration. The initial chapters clarify that reintegration isn't just about securing a new career or adapting to civilian norms; it's about rebuilding a cohesive identity across psychological, physical, social, and economic aspects. From this foundation, the BRAVE framework was developed. Based on over 600 studies, enriched by grounded theory analysis, and validated through real-world use, BRAVE redefined resilience as praxis: something practiced daily rather than something you possess. The WELL Program, the V.E.T.S. Toolkit, and Patient Zero showed how theory can be applied in practice. Professional practice cases demonstrated that resilience is relevant for veterans, athletes, students, and community members, proving that BRAVE has broad applicability.

The Transitional Resilience Index (TRI) development expanded this work by providing a standardized, psychometrically solid way to assess resilience. While BRAVE laid out the conceptual framework and its pilot programs showed practical value, the TRI can evaluate resilience across different populations, programs, and policies. BRAVE and TRI offer a complete system: theory, practice, and measurement.

Several themes recur throughout the text. First, resilience is multidimensional. Trying to reduce it to mental toughness, financial independence, or physical strength alone always fails. The interaction of these areas creates sustainable reintegration. Second, resilience is relational. Mentorship, peer support, and community belonging are not optional extras but key parts of identity rebuilding. Third, resilience is systemic. Veterans, foster youth, and justice-involved populations do not fail on their own; broken systems often let them down. BRAVE and TRI emphasize that resilience must be developed individually and through institutions. Finally, resilience is demonstrated through daily practices, incremental progress, and ongoing efforts to reconstruct identity. This view shifts the focus away from labeling who is or isn't resilient and instead asks how resilience is built, measured, and supported across different lifespans and systems.

T. Carlton, *BRAVE Theory*, https://doi.org/10.1007/978-3-032-13695-4

The journey from battlefield to BRAVE is my story and is shared by countless veterans, foster youth, and others navigating systemic disruptions. It is a narrative of struggle and hope, of fragmentation and rebuilding. Most importantly, it illustrates resilience as an active, ongoing process. The work ahead is clear: programs must continue evolving, institutions must commit to systemic change, and research must validate and refine the tools introduced here. But the foundation remains strong. BRAVE provides the framework, WELL and V.E.T.S. exemplify the practice, and TRI establishes the measurement. Together, they outline a path forward: resilience as an integrated, measurable, and lived experience capable of transforming both individuals and systems.

Index

T. Carlton, *BRAVE Theory*, https://doi.org/10.1007/978-3-032-13695-4

MIX
Papier aus verantwortungsvollen Quellen
Paper from responsible sources
FSC® C105338

If you have any concerns about our products,
you can contact us on
ProductSafety@springernature.com

In case Publisher is established outside the EU,
the EU authorized representative is:
Springer Nature Customer Service Center GmbH
Europaplatz 3, 69115 Heidelberg, Germany

Printed by Libri Plureos GmbH
in Hamburg, Germany